Winning Chess Brilliancies

Yasser Seirawan
International Grandmaster

PUBLISHED BY
Microsoft Press
A Division of Microsoft Corporation
One Microsoft Way
Redmond, Washington 98052-6399

Library of Congress Cataloging-in-Publication Data pending.

Printed and bound in the United States of America.

1 2 3 4 5 6 7 8 9 MLML 0 9 8 7 6 5

Distributed to the book trade in Canada by Macmillan of Canada, a division of Canada Publishing
Corporation.

A CIP catalogue record for this book is available from the British Library.

Microsoft Press books are available through booksellers and distributors worldwide. For further
information about international editions, contact your local Microsoft Corporation office. Or
contact Microsoft Press International directly at fax (206) 936-7329.

The photograph in Game Three of Ljubomir Ljubojevic is courtesy of Catherine Jaeg. The photograph
in Game Four of Victor Korchnoi is courtesy of Frits Agterdenbos. The photograph in Game Seven
of Vassily Smyslov is courtesy of International Chess Enterprises, Inc. The photograph in Game Eight
of Dr. John Nunn is courtesy of Bas Beekhuizen-Fotograaf. The photograph in Game Ten of Jan
Timman is courtesy of Vrij van Rechten.

Acquisitions Editor: Casey D. Doyle
Project Editor: Brenda L. Matteson
Editing and Production: Editorial Services of New England, Inc.

Contents

Acknowledgments

It has been a long journey. In 1989, the good folks at Microsoft Press hired me to do a series of instructional chess books. This, the fourth book in that journey, represents the final step. Six years is a lot of dedication and hard work. It wasn't possible without the support of a lot of people.

The initiative for this series came from the publishers and acquisitions editors at Microsoft Press. Special thanks to Min Yee, Jim Brown, Dean Holmes, and Casey Doyle.

For this work, I'd like to thank Penny Stratton, Susanna Brougham, and Peter Whitmer at Editorial Services of New England, and Jeanne Reinelt of Reinelt Designs. At Microsoft Press, Kim Eggleston for the book's interior design; Greg Hickman for his beautiful cover; my secret in-house reviewer, Larry Powelson; and most especially, Brenda Matteson, who coordinated us all and was right there with a happy hello when needed.

For helping me with the chess side of the manuscript, I have to thank my own staff at *Inside Chess,* especially Yvette Nagel and Michael Franett, who were always on call.

The idea for this book came from my co-author in the first three works of this series, Jeremy Silman. Jeremy told me, "Yaz, more than anything else, students want a chess book that explains the reasons for each and every move of a top grandmaster game. You should write that book." I did. But I couldn't have done it without you. Thank you, one and all.

Introduction

From the time that I was bitten by the "chess bug," fantasies of entering a packed hall and playing a brilliancy have stayed with me. I'd dream of making a comeback from a half-point behind the leader, with one round to go. ". . .Yaz desperately needs a win against one of the world's most solid grandmasters. Can he pull it off and take clear first?" My fantasy would crank up as I anticipated the oohs and aahs of the audience, amazed by my brilliant, decisive moves.

Yes indeed. Just as basketball players relish taking the final shot with seconds on the clock, chess players hunger for the opportunity to sacrifice pieces and come up with an idea of such wonder that it sets the world back on its heels and makes it take notice. While both chess and basketball place great demands on the emotions and the abilities of the players, there is one obvious difference between the games. Even the most casual sports fan can wonder at a Michael Jordan soaring above his defender, double-clutching to get an open shot, firing, and making a swish. By contrast, if a chess player sacrifices first one piece, then another, then another, and then finally mates with a lowly pawn, only the initiate will understand all the fuss.

Such circumstances give members of the chess world a special bond, almost a kinship. Understanding a game of chess played on the highest level is the reward for hard-won knowledge wrested from hours of study, strife, and plenty of losses! I can recall my own first struggles as I delved into the games of the masters. "Why did the grandmaster do that?" "Why didn't he just move over there?" These questions tortured me every time I played through the games of the leading players of the day. Answering such questions is the aim of this book.

A chess master friend of mine, James McCormick, once told me about the training techniques used for the Japanese game of Go. When beginners first enter the schools to learn Go, they are given 100 of the greatest games of Go ever played and are instructed to memorize the moves so that the patterns of play become etched into their minds. This struck me as a superb way to learn a game. I therefore made a commitment: whenever I replayed an exceptional game of chess, I'd try to memorize that game.

While I don't insist that you memorize the games in this book, you will be well rewarded if you do. I believe your play will improve by analyzing them carefully. I've tried to answer questions about these model games before they're asked, and I've dissected the moves to identify the most compelling reasons why they were chosen. My notes will continually recall the principles expounded in the three companion works to this capstone book in the Microsoft Press Winning Chess Series. The chess terminology I introduced in the previous volumes is used freely in this book, and I expect that you are already familiar with it.

In my first book, *Play Winning Chess*, I discussed chess's four elements:

- Time (deployment of pieces)

- Force (being ahead or behind in pieces and pawns)

- Pawn structure (for determining a plan)

- Space (how much of the opponent's territory a player controls)

These four elements are — or should be — the underpinnings for the principles that guide all our moves.

The second book, *Winning Chess Tactics*, explained all the traps, ambushes, and swindles that can befall a player. Pins, forks, skewers, double attacks, and discovered checks are but a few of the most common types of tactics described in this volume.

Winning Chess Strategies, the third book, explained the importance of playing with a plan, one that unfolds like magic before the eyes if the player simply applies the four elements of chess to the position and focuses on the pawn structure. A plan, once chosen, must be methodically implemented. Even when a correct plan has been chosen, the player must constantly be on the lookout for the best tactics to reinforce a given position. Nothing can ruin a plan more than an overlooked tactic.

Boy, that's a lot to think about! If a basketball team had to stop and consider collectively their every drive to the basket, full court press, pick and roll, rebound strategy, and defensive coverage, perhaps even each player's role in a given play, they might never score a point! They'd be paralyzed! But basketball players make all these moves appear to come naturally. It looks simple because the players are professionals. Years of toil and hard work, individually and as a team, have made the most difficult plays seem routine.

The same is true for today's chess grandmasters. They've analyzed the openings, tactics, various types of plans, technical endings, and attacks. These players appear to flow effortlessly from one advantage to another. They have honed their skills through thousands of hours of concentrated work. They make it look simple — the key to greatness as well as to the brilliancy. Applying the tools of the trade subtly and simply appears natural and yet is satisfying because the results are brilliant.

When two top-flight grandmasters sit down and go for the glory, who's to say who will win? Why is it that a player might be able to pound his equally skilled adversary on one day but not on the next? There are probably dozens of reasons, but the one that I'd like to focus upon is *inspiration*. A player soars to a level of unusual creativity and plucks out of the imagination a concept so beautiful that it appears to freeze time. It is a brilliant moment.

In this work I will take a look at 12 inspired games, or rather 12 brilliancies, of the past generation by putting them under my "chessic" microscope. It was, of course, enormously difficult to select such a small handful of games. Hundreds, if not thousands, of beautiful games have been played in only the last ten years. How could I choose from so many? It wasn't easy! First of all, nearly *all* the wins from *my* career sprang to mind. (How was I supposed to keep my ego at bay? I couldn't!) I humbly put forth only two of my games, so don't skip them!

I will begin each game with a short introduction describing the historical atmosphere of the chess world — and sometimes the world at large — at the time the game was played. When I begin discussing the game itself, I will wax poetic about the reasoning behind the opening moves. As play moves through its middlegame and into the concluding endgame, I will continue to examine the moves in terms of piece development and possible tactical opportunities, but my comments will grow shorter and become more robust as the game reaches its critical moments.

A few comments are necessary at this point to explain the common conventions I have used throughout these games. The chessboard below illustrates the grid upon which chess notation is based. The coordinate of each square on the board is a

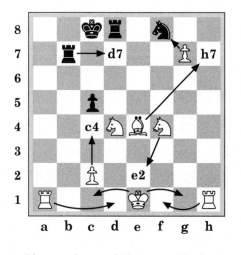

combination of a letter (a-h) and a number (1-8). For instance, in the diagram, a White Knight sits on the d4-square.

In standard (algebraic) notation, each chess piece is represented by its initial (although N is used for Knight and no letter is used for pawns). A move is represented by the given piece's initial and the coordinate of the square to which it is moved ("Bh7" is Bishop to h7; "Ne2" is Knight to e2). Other notations are as follows:

- If two pieces of the same kind can go to the same square (as shown, both Black Rooks can go to the d7-square), a coordinate of the correct piece's departure square solves the question: "R7d7" means the Rook on the seventh rank is being moved.

- Adding an "x" to the notation indicates a capture — "g7xf8" signifies that the g7-pawn was moved and captured a piece on the f8-square.

- "O-O" designates castling short (White King and h1-Rook in the diagram above); "O-O-O" connotes castling long (White King and a1-Rook).

- A move notation followed by a "+" means check; "++" means double-check.

As part of my commentary, I occasionally punctuate the moves. The following key explains these marks: ! good; !? interesting; !! very good; ? weak; ?! dubious; ?? a blunder. Parentheses around the symbol, like 20...Nc3(!), indicate that my opinion differs from other writers or that of the players themselves. (Give yourself the task of sorting out whose judgment is right!)

Finally, some of my explanations for a given move reveal deeply buried insights. In order that you don't get lost in the thicket of variations, I've employed separate and distinct analysis diagrams. These diagrams have the same border as the diagram above; regular game chessboards will have a solid border.

With that said, now back to my dilemma! Having rejected 20 games for each 1 chosen, my next task was to personalize the games. That is, I wanted to see what the players themselves had to say about them. Nearly all the players, especially the winners, were happy to share their comments. In fact, their seconds, coaches, and a stream of analysts have shared their views with me. Whenever I've incorporated commentary from the players or other authors, I've credited the source. On this point, a special thanks is due to the *Chess Informant* — a series filled with the best games of the previous four months, with commentaries by the players. I'd also like to thank the writers from my own magazine, *Inside Chess*, who have shared their elation and sorrows in its pages. Also I offer thanks to the authors of the many books that I scoured in search of information. Without them, this book wouldn't be as fun or interesting.

A final word of thanks goes to the players of these games. To the victor go the spoils, but for a game to be brilliant, the opponent has to put up a heroic defense in order to allow the winner to display creative genius. Both players of each game have my respect.

Yasser Seirawan

▀▄▀

Making History

T o begin this book, I'll start at the beginning of my own chess career. In the summer of 1972, my family relocated from Virginia Beach, Virginia, to Seattle and the Great Northwest. After settling down, days of rain-induced boredom crept into my life. It was the perfect moment for the chess bug to bite. I was looking for something to do, and when a neighbor, David Chapman, challenged me to a game of chess, I was enchanted.

I am adept at sports and physical labor, and it surprised me to discover a game that I was genuinely bad at: chess. Soon it became crucial that I beat David in a game of chess. But no matter what I did, David always won. He suggested that I go to a coffeehouse near the University of Washington to play chess with the locals.

It was during these visits that I learned that a chess World Championship match was being waged in Reykjavik, Iceland. America's own Bobby Fischer was dueling Boris Spassky from the Soviet Union. The cold war was being captured on the chessboard. The match caught the attention of the world's media. Soon everybody had a personal opinion about the match and whether Fischer could wrest the title from Spassky. Chess fever swept the United States and the world. It was a heady time to pick up the chess pieces myself. When I played through the following game for the first time, I was shocked. These guys were good. I mean *really* good!

This is game 6 of that historic match. Fischer had lost the first game by grabbing a "poisoned pawn." He forfeited the second in a dispute with the organizers. He then tried a Benoni Defense with a daring Knight maneuver to earn his first win *ever* against his rival. Game 4 was a tough Sicilian that ended in a draw. Fischer barely held that one because he had a lost position. Game 5 saw Spassky miss a simple tactic, and his position crumbled.

Suddenly the match was tied! Therefore, game 6 would be crucial. If Fischer were to win, it would be his third win without a loss. He would have the lead for the first time and most certainly would crack Spassky psychologically. If Spassky were to win, he would regain the lead and Fischer, who was the challenger, would be behind by two games. In case of a tied match, the champion, Boris Spassky, would retain his title. Tension was high around the world — particularly in the heart of a young boy in Seattle.

■ ■ ■ ■ ■ ■ ■ ■ ■ ■ ■ ■ ■ ■ ■ ■

Queen's Gambit Declined

GM Robert James Fischer
GM Boris Spassky
1972 World Championship, Reykjavik
(Game 6)

Opening

1.c4

This first move stuns the chess world. Is Fischer tired of taking the fight to Spassky? Does he want a breather? A different kind of game? Or has he found an idea to bust one of Spassky's Queen Pawn Defenses? The text sends the opening theoreticians scrambling to see if Fischer has ever played this move in his career.

In general, there are two types of openings. Those in which White plays 1.e4 are known collectively as King Pawn Openings. The second type, in which White plays 1.d4, are known as Queen Pawn Openings. King Pawn Openings tend to be much sharper: a single inaccuracy in King Pawn games can cost the player a game before it starts. In contrast, Queen Pawn Openings tend to be more tame. The battle is postponed until the opponents have developed their pieces. Only then does the siege begin. In those days Bobby was known as a superb calculator. Throughout his career, 1.e4 had *always* been Fisher's choice. He reveled in sharp tactical positions and was naturally drawn to King Pawn Openings. He described his attitude by saying, "With 1.e4! I win." Few were able to challenge this opinion!

The opening that Fischer chose to use in this game is known as the English Opening and is a bit of a fringe opening. Most often, games that start this way shift back into mainstream Queen Pawn Openings. A player might choose the English move rather than the direct Queen Pawn Opening (1.d4) in order to outfox the opponent. Fischer probably wants to play against the classical Queen's Gambit Declined, but if he plays 1.d4 at once, he might allow Spassky to vary his defenses.

Besides luring the opponent into selecting the defense that you want him to play, the English has a lot of independent merit. The c4-pawn controls the critical d5-center square. This often fits into a strategy in which White fianchettos his King's Bishop with g2-g3 and Bf1-g2, controlling d5, and complements this move with Nb1-c3, also hitting the d5-square.

Another reason for choosing the English is its flexibility. White makes no major commitments, allowing him either to play a slow, developing game or to move into a classical Queen Pawn game.

1...e6

Back to the action. After overcoming his surprise, Spassky selects his favored defense: a Queen's Gambit Declined. He intends to battle Fischer's c4-pawn for control over the d5-square. Given the opportunity, he plans to follow up this first move with ...d7-d5 and keep this central pawn firmly planted on the d5-square. In this way he assures himself of a solid game while also reminding White that he controls White's important e4-square.

Spassky is employing his favorite defense rather than exploiting the main drawback of the English Opening: it allows Black the opportunity for 1...e5,

which would have been the best response according to chess principles. Thus, the opening moves would have been those of a reversed Sicilian (1.e4 c5). After 1...e7-e5, Black could have immediately fought for the initiative through active development of his pieces, and the game would have been sharpened considerably.

2.Nf3

With this move, Fischer develops a piece while observing the center. The text looks after the e5-square and the d4-square. White still hasn't committed himself fully to a specific opening and is expecting Black to show his intended defense.

2...d5

A defining moment. Black stakes out the center with his d5-pawn in order to develop his pieces. Notice that Black's pawn structure has one drawback. The e6-pawn blocks the c8-Bishop. For Black to achieve a harmonious deployment of his pieces, he will have to solve the problem of activating the c8-Bishop.

3.d4

White now develops a pawn to take control over two more squares, c5 and e5. The c1-Bishop is unleashed so that he can be developed. This move leaves White's c4-pawn under capture — the reason that this Queen Pawn game became known as a Queen's Gambit.

The players have now moved into the Queen's Gambit, although they haven't finished refining the opening. Keep in mind that many chess openings run one dozen to two dozen moves deep, with many side branches as well. As the opening moves unfold, the players are following the games of thousands of others. Thus, some chess openings have extraordinarily unusual names. Some are real tongue twisters!

3...Nf6

Black develops his King's Knight and prepares to castle early in the game, following time-tested opening principles.

Black had two other choices that, superficially at least, could appear attractive. In White's last move, he played a gambit, offering the c4-pawn as bait. Why shouldn't Black take it? Here is how that choice would play out.

If 3...dxc4, strictly speaking, the c4-pawn isn't lost. White could use a double attack with 4.Qa4+, followed by Qa4xc4, and reclaim the pawn. Black doesn't fear this immediate recapture of the c4-pawn. He reckons, however, that after 3...dxc4,

4.e4! would create a big problem for him. His d5-pawn would no longer be preventing e2-e4, and now White would have a nice central pawn duo. Also, if White were allowed to play Bf1xc4, Black would fall far behind in development.

Therefore, a series of turbulent moves are put into action: after 3...dxc4 4.e4!, in order to justify munching White's c4-pawn, Black must try to hang on to his extra pawn: 4...b5 protects the c4-pawn. Then with 5.a4!, White prepares to destroy the c4-pawn's support. With 5...c6, Black tries to defend the b5-pawn. Note that 5...a6 would be a terrible move, because 5...a6 would be followed by 6.axb5! — White could snap off the b5-pawn, pinning the a6-pawn because the a8-Rook isn't protected.

Let's recap: Black didn't grab White's c4-pawn on move 3 because it would produce this series of moves: 3...dxc4 4.e4! b5 5.a4! c6. Then White would play 6.b3! in order to expose the b5-pawn to the f1-Bishop and to advantageously recapture his gambited pawn. Play the position with a friend: 6...cxb3 7.axb5! cxb5 8.Bxb5+. You will see that White has developed a piece and controls the center while Black has made only pawn moves.

The second possibility for Black at move 3 would have been 3...Bb4+, checking

4

the White King. In my early years, I was always eager to attack my opponent's King. This syndrome has been mocked by generations of masters: "Patzer [weak player] sees a check, patzer plays a check." That is, when a beginner sees the opportunity to check, he immediately goes for it without realizing that he has no follow-up. By checking a King without coordinating an attack, the beginner doesn't realize that he can actually *help* his opponent!

Here is the sequence that would follow such a move by Black. After 3...Bb4+, White blocks the check with 4.Bd2, thus *attacking* Black's Bishop. Seeing another check, Black thinks he's on a roll and plays 4...Bxd2+ with triumph. White responds with 5.Qxd2, recapturing the Bishop. Black now searches around for another check, but he can't find one! Instead, Black has managed to help White develop his position!

Go back to the position before 3...Bb4+. Black is on the move, and he has an opportunity to develop a piece. Black squanders his move, develops a Bishop with check, and after a subsequent exchange, all that has happened is that White has developed his Queen, or, with 5.Nbxd2, a Knight. White's game has improved.

4.Nc3

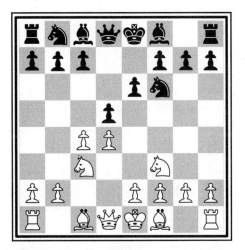

Continuing to develop his army, White blocks a possible ...Bf8-b4+. More important, he continues to fight for control over the center. The c3-Knight does a fine job of protecting the e4-square and attacking the d5-pawn.

The paramount principle of opening a chess game is to concentrate pieces and pawns in the center of the board. Beginner games are marked by a failure to control the center and to develop all pieces.

4...Be7

In this modest but consequential development, Black prepares to castle, tucking his King behind a nice shield of pawns on the kingside. Because Black has declined to capture the c4-pawn (the gambit), the opening now becomes known as a Queen's Gambit Declined (QGD). In the QGD, Black's principal aim is to watch over his d5-pawn and to keep it firmly stationed in the middle of the board. Should he fail to do this, his game will be ruined.

Note that this move defends against the possibility of Bc1-g5, which would pin the f6-Knight to the d8-Queen. For that reason, the more aggressive 4...Bd6 would actually have misplaced the Bishop. After 4...Bd6?, Black would have exposed himself to the possible attacks 5.c5 or 5.Nb5. But a bigger problem would be 5.Bg5! and White's continuing deployment of *all* his pieces — he avoids moving a piece that has already been developed. After 5.Bg5, Black's center would come under pressure as White threatened to capture the f6-Knight and to snap off the d5-pawn.

5.Bg5

This move activates the c1-Bishop and attacks the f6-Knight. By attacking the f6-Knight, White indirectly attacks Black's defensive bastion, the d5-pawn. As the d5-pawn is defended by three pieces, it isn't in fear of immediate cap-ture, but White will look for ways to crank up the pressure.

Two important points should be men-tioned regarding this move as well. First, we know that a crucial principle in the opening is to find a nice, safe place for the King. Why, then, didn't White try to activate his kingside pieces with 5.e3 so that he could move the f1-Bishop and cas-tle? In fact, that's precisely what White *wants* to do! The problem with 5.e3 at this point is that it would block in the c1-Bishop. If the c1-Bishop is developed *outside* the pawn chain, it will control more space and play an *active* role in the middlegame.

Second, if White plans to develop the c1-Bishop and then plays e2-e3, what's wrong with Bc1-f4? The answer is, abso-lutely nothing! With 5.Bf4, White acti-vates the Bishop on the h2-b8 diagonal while controlling the crucial e5-square. Therefore we have a question of taste, or rather style. (Later in the match, in game 14, Fischer would employ 5.Bf4, which ended in a draw after 40 moves.)

In the earliest phases of the opening, there aren't any absolutely *best* moves. There are, however, a great number of *good* moves. It is up to the players to choose the openings and defenses they like best.

5...O-O

Here Black completes a primary directive of the opening — make sure you have a safe King! Black's King hides behind a solid wall of pawns, and he can stop worrying — at least for now! Black's next concern will be to develop his queenside pieces with a view toward controlling the center.

Also note the number of pieces and pawns that both players have moved from their original squares. White has deployed five: two Knights, two pawns, and a Bishop. Black's last move, however, has allowed him to develop *six*. That's why strong players love to castle. It is the only move in which a player gets to move two pieces simultaneously — very useful in the time count.

6.e3

Now White prepares to develop the f1-Bishop, to be followed by castling kingside to safeguard the White King. The text is a crucial link in White's opening strategy. He reinforces the d4-pawn and protects the c4-pawn.

6...h6!

An excellent move with a long-term purpose. This type of move is known as "putting the question to the Bishop." When White developed his c1-Bishop, he brought it out not necessarily with the intention of exchanging it for the f6-Knight. Actually, he didn't want to lock it in before playing e2-e3. Now he faces the question of whether to retreat or exchange the Bishop.

Grandmasters (GMs) understand the usefulness of having two Bishops working side by side. Therefore, they avoid giving up their Bishops too early; after one of their Bishops has been *questioned*, most grandmasters retreat the Bishop.

From Black's perspective this is a fine situation. He gets the move ...h7-h6 with tempo. That is, he has played ...h7-h6 to attack the Bishop; if the Bishop retreats, the Black pawn has been developed to the h6-square. The move ...h7-h6 hasn't cost Black his move — he has played the move for free.

So what's the big deal? Black no longer has to worry about a back-rank mate, in which pawns are exchanged and files are opened up for the Rooks. Spending a tempo to prevent a back-rank mate is known as making luft. *Luft* is the German word for "air." Making luft means giving your King a square to move to, in case of a back-rank check. Now Black's King can *breathe*. In tense middlegame situations, every tempo is important. Black's King has already been given luft, making his future even more rosy.

7.Bh4

Fischer retreats the White Bishop, consonant with his career as a player who loves the two Bishops. He has attained a splendid number of victories because of this advantage.

7...b6

This defining moment in the opening shows Black's intention to fianchetto the c8-Bishop; that is, Black is planning for ...Bc8-b7. This would reinforce the d5-pawn, extending Black's objective of giving the little fellow protection. The fianchetto has a further purpose as well. The b7-Bishop will have an influence over the e4-square once it occupies the long a8-h1 diagonal.

Before leaving this move, let's raise a fair question: why didn't Black move ...g7-g5, attacking the h4-Bishop yet again? In fact, the move does appear tempting. Black could develop his g5-pawn with tempo, and after the forced 8.Bg3, Black could look for another developing move. The answer to the question lies with Black's King. The g7-pawn acts as a shield, and by thrusting the shield farther away from the body, it gives less protection. The problem with ...g7-g5 is that the pawn could never go back in case the Black King needed its protection. Although ...g7-g5 would gain a tempo, it would weaken Black's King defenses. Only some material compensation, like the win of a pawn or piece, should induce a player to make a move resulting in such long-term weakness.

The idea for the move ...b7-b6 belongs to Savielly Tartakower (1887–1956). Thus the variation from the diagram is known as the Tartakower System of the QGD. At the time game 6 was played, Spassky was known as the world's leading exponent of this variation.

Fischer knew he could count on Spassky to employ this defense. He therefore did a great deal of homework, known as "preparation." As part of his grandmaster preparation for this match, Fischer had not only played over the games of Boris Spassky — he had practically *memorized* them. From this, Bobby intended to spring a surprise, or an opening novelty, in this variation. In short, Fischer hoped to ambush his opponent with some homespun preparation.

8.cxd5

The first trade occurs. White opens up the c-file for his Rook. That is, by trading his c4-pawn, White will play Ra1-c1 in order to put pressure on the c-file.

If this was such a good idea, why didn't White do it earlier? The answer can be traced to the c8-Bishop. As long as the e6-pawn is on the board, the c8-Bishop will be blocked. Now that Black has spent a tempo playing ...b7-b6, he has all but solved the problem of how to get his c8-Bishop into play.

If White had played c4xd5 earlier in the opening, Black would have responded with ...e6xd5. The c8-Bishop could then jump out to the f5-square or the g4-square.

8...Nxd5

An important recapture. As Black's strategy has been built around having a d5-pawn, shouldn't 8...exd5 have been automatic? The answer is yes! Recapturing with the e-pawn would have been the natural thing to do in this position. But Black is employing a strategic principle: *when behind in space, trade pieces.*

Look at the position following the possible moves 8...exd5 and 9.Bd3, and count the number of squares that White's pieces control versus Black's. After 9.Bd3, the White d3-Bishop would control b5, a6, f5, g6, and h7 — that's five. The d4-pawn controls two, White's two Knights control four, and the h4-Bishop controls two, for a total of thirteen. Black would control only eight of White's squares. White would control more of Black's territory. Black should therefore seek to reduce White's control by trading pieces.

A further purpose motivated this recapture. Now that the d5-pawn has been removed, the long a8-h1 diagonal is *open*. Once Black's c8-Bishop is fianchettoed, the Bishop's power will roar down the long diagonal.

The opening phase is beginning to resolve itself, and the middlegame, with its myriad plans, is taking hold.

9.Bxe7

Exchanging of Bishops takes place — White's third move with a Bishop in his first nine moves. White could have played 9.Bg3, hitting the c7-pawn, but would have spent another tempo. After 9.Bg3 Bb7, Black could have continued his development unfettered. By exchanging

Bishops, it is Black who will have to spend a tempo to recapture.

9...Qxe7!

Black makes the correct recapture. Spassky develops his Queen, moving it from its original square and extending its influence to three squares: b4, a3, and h4. The other choice was 9...Nxe7, which would have removed the d5-Knight from the action in the center. Black is proud of the noble beast on d5, however, and leaves it on its perch, from which it eyes four White squares.

10.Nxd5

Knights are exchanged right away — another important strategy at work. If your opponent's pieces are working better than your own, trade them off! In this case, the d5-Knight is more valuable than the c3-Knight. One controls four squares, the other only two. This move also fits the strategy that White has been cultivating ever since playing 8.cxd5, which opened up the c-file. With this exchange, White removes the c3-Knight, which opens up the c-file for his Rook.

10...exd5

A forced capture, and a good one. Now, just as White has the half-open c-file, Black enjoys a half-open e-file, though an important difference exists between the two. The c7-pawn is a far more important target than the e3-pawn. The e3-pawn has a hard-working comrade on f2 to back it up. The c7-pawn has to rely upon the support of its officers, not a fellow pawn.

The strategic lines are further drawn by the pawn structure. White has a king-side majority, and Black a queenside majority. The way to put a majority to work is to *move the pawns*. In this position, White doesn't want to push his pawns because that would lead only to the weakening of his King's future position. Therefore, White has to put the plan of utilizing his majority on hold for a while. Instead, he will have to tame Black's queenside majority; that is, he will make it as difficult as possible for Black to push his majority. and will restrain and blockade Black's attempts to do so. Fixed or blockaded pawns become stationary targets.

The outcome of this opening battle will be decided on the queenside — in fact, whoever gains an advantage there will win the game. (All of this is common knowledge to top-ranked chess players.) The question is, what strategy has Fischer prepared to stop Black on the queenside?

11.Rc1

White plays a very natural developing move. Rooks crave open files, so White brings his Rook to the half-open file, putting pressure on the c7-pawn. This move's one drawback concerns White's King. He is still stuck in the center, not having castled. Fortunately for White's King, the Black army on the queenside hasn't yet been developed. If Black's pieces had been developed, you can bet that White's King would be making a speedy exit to the kingside.

11...Be6!

By this solid move, Black moves toward developing his pieces as quickly as possible. Black faces a question concerning the c8-Bishop — should he fianchetto it or bring it out in the center? Considerations of space provide the answer. On the c8-h3 diagonal, the Bishop controls the g4-square and the h3-square. Fianchettoed on b7, the Bishop would back up only the d5-pawn. The e6-Bishop can control space *and* defend the d5-pawn, resolving this question.

Why is defending the d5-pawn important? It is crucial for maintaining Black's majority. Black recognizes that the c7-pawn is a serious liability. The only way to make it a plus is to push it. Thus ...c7-c5 will become necessary. But the series of moves 11...c5? 12.dxc5 bxc5 13.Qxd5 would cost Black a pawn. By defending the d5-pawn, Black readies the big ...c7-c5 push.

Still, what about 11...Qe7-b4+? As before, this check carries no punch and would only benefit White. White would block with 12.Qd2, offering a Queen exchange. If he chose 12...Qxd2+ 13.Kxd2!, the ensuing ending would give White a large advantage. White's King would be in no danger in this position because no Black pieces could harass it. The critical factor would be Black's c7-pawn. After the further moves 13...c6 14.Ne5 Bb7 15.b4!, Black's majority would be restrained and become a liability.

Before playing a Queen check that results in an exchange of Queens, Black should first ask, "Whose Queen controls more space?" From that perspective, a Queen exchange in the current position would be to White's benefit.

Middlegame

12.Qa4!

This move further violates the opening principle of castling early and getting your King out of danger, but Fischer feels he can overstep this principle with impunity because Black's pieces are still far away from his King. Instead, the focus of White's position is to restrain the queenside majority. It seems a bit strange to develop the Queen early and *away* from the center. But the static position of the central pawns makes the wings, and especially the queenside, the main theater of battle. The text threatens b2-b4, which would restrain the c7-pawn.

Note that White would not profit from 12.Qc2, because the response 12...Rc8! would defend the c7-pawn and prepare ...c7-c5. The position of Black's h6-pawn explains White's hesitation to use this move. If Black hadn't put the question to White's Bishop back at move 6, the idea of 12.Qc2 Rc8 13.Bd3 would be tempting — White could develop his pieces with gain of tempo because of the threatened h7-pawn. The fact that Black's pawn is on h6 robs White of acting on this idea.

12...c5!

Black mustn't allow his majority to get stuck. Now is the time to strike out at White's center. Failure to make this freeing move would have given White a nice advantage through his control over the c-file.

With this move Black limits the c1-Rook. The c1-Rook no longer eyes the c6-square and the c7-square. Its space control has been reduced. Now Black is simply aching to play ...c5-c4 and to put his a7-pawn and b6-pawn into motion on the queenside. Naturally, White cannot allow that to happen.

13.Qa3

This move is what White had in mind when he made the Queen sally. Now the c5-pawn can't move forward because of the pin on Black's Queen. With this move, White threatens to capture twice and munch the c5-pawn.

13...Rc8

This is a protective move. Thus far, *all* the game's moves can be explained by standard opening theory — many games in chess have featured the diagrammed position. Here, Black avoids 13...Nd7?, protecting the c5-pawn because he anticipates that 14.Bb5! will be a strong move, increasing the pressure on the c5-pawn. It is interesting to see how the battle has shifted to the queenside, with both players concentrating their armies there. Again, the position revolves around the strength or weakness of Black's queenside majority. That is, will Black's majority become an advantage or a disadvantage?

14.Bb5!

The game's first nonstandard theoretical move is a very good one. The typical response would have been 14.Be2, followed by a quick castling. But White is apparently looking for an opportunity to trade his b5-Bishop for the b8-Knight. He thinks that the b8-Knight is far more useful as a defender of the queenside pawns, more important than the b5-Bishop's role as an attacker.

Fischer's move is far more subtle than it appears, however. If the idea of trading the Bishop for a Knight is so sensible, why shouldn't Black put the question to the Bishop with ...a7-a6 and force it to retreat? Why not, indeed! White's crafty point is that with ...a7-a6, this pawn will have been lured to a White square, which gives the White Bishop something to threaten.

14...a6

Black is falling in line with White's plans. (In the future, following this match, games will employ 14...Kf8!? or 14...Qf8!?, in both cases protecting the Queen, releasing the pin on the a3-f8 diagonal, and allowing Black to threaten ...c5-c4 to put his majority to work.)

But Boris Spassky is not to be faulted for the text because it contains a bit of poison. Because the a6-pawn is pinned to the unprotected a8-Rook, the threat to the b5-Bishop doesn't yet exist. Once the a8-Rook is protected, the b5-Bishop will be *en prise* — French for "in capture" — and will be forced to move. Black's little trick is the threat to protect the a8-Rook with ...Ra8-a7, which in turn would protect the e7-Queen. Black would then hold a double threat of ...a6xb5 and ...c5-c4, a big advantage.

15.dxc5!

Sidestepping Black's previously mentioned threat (...Ra8-a7), White makes sure that the push ...c5-c4 carries no punch. In fact, after ...b6xc5, Black will now try to avoid ...c5-c4 as the d4-square falls into White's mitt.

15...bxc5

This is the best recapture. After
15...Rxc5?, 16.O-O! would follow. Black
would not be able to capture the b5-
Bishop with either Rook or pawn because
of the pins by the a3-Queen. The text is
much superior because the c5-pawn and
d5-pawn control quite a number of
squares. Such pawns are known as
"hanging pawns" because neither pawn
is backed up or supported by another
pawn. They literally *hang together.*

Throughout chess history, great
debates have raged about the pros and
cons of hanging pawns. The debates are
nonsense; the answer is cut and dried. If
the pawns can be attacked and forced to
move forward, they are weak. If they can
be defended and remain where they are,
they are strong.

Thus a new battle is being formed.
The question of whether a pawn majority will push forward into a pawn storm
has been answered: White will fight
mightily to get *either* of the hanging
pawns to move forward. This would
leave crucial squares unprotected,
squares that White's pieces will pounce
upon. Equally determined, Black will dig
in his heels, fighting to keep the pawns
planted where they are.

16.O-O

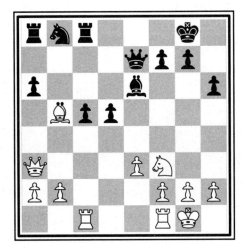

Castling at last! When grandmasters
wait for such extended periods before
castling, they really drive chess teachers
nuts. It's rough on teachers to see their
cherished principles flouted for too long.
But the time has come, and White tucks
his King behind a protective wall of
pawns. Now he hopes to play Rf1-d1, putting pressure on both of the hanging
pawns to force one or the other to move
forward.

16...Ra7?!

A controversial move — it leaves
Black's Queen in an awkward pin on the
a3-f8 diagonal. In his book on the match,
GM Samuel Reshevsky condemns this
move as a "serious tactical move [error]

from which Spassky never recovered." Reshevsky gives the move two question marks, an annotation usually reserved for moves that blunder and toss away material. Boris Spassky's second (or coach), GM Efim Geller, also considers the text a mistake, offering 16...Qb7 as an alternative.

Both Geller and Reshevsky are wrong. Spassky's move is actually *dubious* in merit. Reshevsky supports 16...Qb7, citing that "after its [b5-Bishop's] retreat, Black would continue ...Nb8-d7 and White could not post his Knight strongly on d4, as in the game." This annotation is shortsighted. Yugoslav GM Svetozar Gligoric critiques this move by posing an important question: after 16...Qb7 17.Ba4, what would Black do with his c5-pawn?

White's goal in Bf1-b5 (move 14) was to capture the b8-Knight, should it poke its head out. Therefore 16...Qb7 17.Ba4! leaves Black with problems concerning his c5-pawn. Black's best move would have been 16...Qa7!, which would have released him from the a3-f8 pin, defended the c5-pawn, and threatened the b5-Bishop. White could then consider the two retreats discussed next: 17.Ba4, or 17.Be2.

■ After 17.Ba4, keeping an eye on the b8-Knight, Black would continue with 17...a5! and threaten to develop his position with ...Nb8-a6-b4, blocking out the a3-Queen. Thus, through 18.Bb5 Nd7 19.Bxd7 Bxd7, White could accomplish his exchange, but the hanging pawns still wouldn't have budged. Black would again play ...Bd7-e6, planning to play ...d5-d4 to achieve a passed d4-pawn and an equal game.

■ The best scenario is 17.Be2 Nd7 18.Rc3 or 18.Rfd1, with continued pressure on the hanging pawns. But Black wouldn't have many worries in this line either, with 18...a5 planned as a counterattack against the b2-pawn.

Thus, by 16...Qa7 Black could achieve a comfortable position. The problem with Spassky's move is that Black's Queen remains in an awkward pin on the a3-f8 diagonal.

17.Be2

Now that the a6-pawn is no longer pinned, the b5-Bishop is well and truly en prise. The retreat 17.Ba4 also had to be considered. A line such as 17.Ba4 Nd7 18.Bxd7 Rxd7 19.Qxa6? Ra7 would have allowed Black to capture the a2-pawn with a comfortable game. White preferred the text, however, as the e2-Bishop greedily eyes the a6-pawn.

17...Nd7

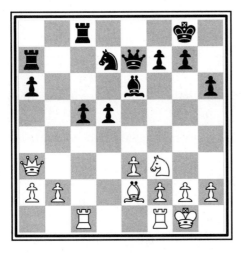

Black develops the Knight at last. Black realizes that his hanging pawns need protection. After this move, the d5-pawn can be protected by ...Nd7-f6. But since his failure on move 16, Black has discovered that he has problems. His most sensitive points are the a6-pawn and the c5-pawn. A Knight posted on f6 won't cover these two pawns.

18.Nd4!

An excellent move. We know that White must put pressure on the hanging pawns, yet the f3-Knight was not playing a role in attacking them. Taking advantage of the a3-f8 pin, White redeploys his f3-Knight.

18...Qf8?

Feeling the growing pressure against his center, Spassky now makes an error. All the previously mentioned annotators are unanimous in their criticism of this move, and they are correct. The text costs a tempo and places the Queen out of play on a bad square.

If he had chosen 18...Nf6, Black would have had to suffer an inferior ending, with White's response of 19.Nb3! attacking the c5-pawn. Black then could either defend the c5-pawn or push it. Defending with 19...Nd7 would allow the pythonlike grip of 20.Rc3! to close in, preparing to double on the c-file with Rf1-d1 and ultimately causing Black to lose either the c5-pawn or the a6-pawn.

Therefore, the best alternative would have been 18...Nf6 19.Nb3 c4 20.Qxe7 Rxe7 21.Nd4. White would have successfully implemented his strategy: one of the hanging pawns forced to budge and White's d4-Knight situated at a terrific outpost. But this ending would be far from lost for Black — he could play 21...a5! and then use the half-open b-file for counterplay.

19.Nxe6!

A praiseworthy strategic decision — at first blush, this exchange seems to strengthen the hanging pawns, especially the d5-pawn. While this is true, Fischer has more subtle plans. He knows that in open positions, Bishops operate better than Knights. So he stands to benefit in the *long term* as more pawns are exchanged. He also foresees setting his own pawn majority in motion.

This exchange is also made because other Knight moves wouldn't sufficiently pressure the hanging pawns. With 19.Nb3, Black could have shifted into the previously mentioned ending with 19...c4 or have done even better with 19...a5! because White's pieces wouldn't have been putting enough pressure on the c5-pawn and the d5-pawn.

19...fxe6

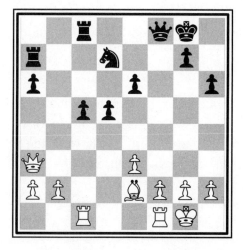

Spassky is happy to achieve a recapture, strengthening his center. Now if he can only get a chance to play ...c5-c4 and ...Nd7-c5, he will enjoy an active position. But with an opponent like Bobby Fischer, this may be like asking for the moon.

20.e4!

White thrusts powerfully at Black's center. Had Black played 18...Nf6, this key move wouldn't have been possible. Now Black realizes that he's in deep trouble.

The text had opened up the possibility of a sudden shift — perhaps Be2-g4 and Qa3-h3 — putting tremendous pressure on the h3-c8 diagonal. In fact, the threat of Be2-g4 appears so powerful, why didn't White play it at once? 20.Bg4 is only a one-move threat without any further piece coordination to back it up. After 20.Bg4 Qe7, Black could have continued with ...Nd7-f6, consolidating his position while attacking the g4-Bishop.

20...d4

A sad decision. Black is forced to move one of his hanging pawns forward, thus undermining their flexibility. However, this is because he is struggling amid a host of poor choices. His pawns are a wreck, and he can expect more problems.

He can see that White intends to swing his Queen to h3, pressuring the e6-pawn as well as threatening Be2-g4. What should he do?

The moves 20...dxe4 21.Rc4! Nf6 22.Rfc1 Rac7 23.Qxa6 would have won back White's pawn while attacking the e6-pawn. Offering a Queen exchange with 20...c4 21.Qh3! Qe7 22.exd5 exd5 23.Bf3 would hit the d5-pawn while pinning the d7-Knight to the c8-Rook. By further continuing with Rf1-e1, hitting Black's Queen, White's attack would quickly become decisive.

The aim of the text is to try to keep the position closed long enough to cover up the weakness in Black's pawn structure. The final defensive possibility, 20...Nf6, would have allowed White to put his kingside majority into motion: 20...Nf6 21.e5! Nd7 (after 21...Ne4 22.f3 Nd2 23.Rfd1 Qf4 24.Qc3, White would win material) 22.f4, now intending to use the h3-c8 diagonal. White would thus gain a powerful attack — analysis by GM Svetozar Gligoric.

While pushing the d5-pawn might be the least of the many evils Black faces, it does hurt the position. The hanging pawns have been forced forward, and now White gains the juicy c4-outpost for his e2-Bishop. The text also means that White has achieved his long-term strategy of *blockading* Black's majority. Now White can try to utilize his own kingside majority. Watch how with each move, Fischer tightens his grip.

21.f4!

White activates his majority. He is planning Be2-c4 and f4-f5 in order to win the e6-pawn. In addition to this threat, his f4-pawn controls the e5-square, limiting the d7-Knight. In fact, White's strategy will be to limit the d7-Knight's movement and to eventually entomb it.

Besides the sudden activation of the kingside, Black still has queenside difficulties. It shouldn't be overlooked that with b2-b4 White can undermine the support of the d4-pawn. Black faces problems everywhere!

21...Qe7

Black retraces his eighteenth move; the e6-pawn was calling out for help. Black is trying to do a little repair work and to cover his weak pawns. Now, if he can play ...e6-e5, Black can try to work on blockading White's majority.

22.e5!

This powerful move nails down the e6-pawn. White has a light-squared Bishop; by putting his pawns on *dark* squares, he gives the e2-Bishop a brighter future. Note that the text opens up the b1-h7 diagonal. If White can create a battery on this diagonal, Black could well be mated! Now the d4-pawn can only rely upon the support of the c5-pawn. If White can play b2-b4xc5, the d4-pawn will stick out like a sore thumb.

This current move, however, does have a drawback. If Black can maneuver his d7-Knight to the d5-square, it would take up a terrific outpost.

22...Rb8?!

Stopping a potential b2-b4, this move fails to address the problem of Black's d7-Knight. Most commentators rightfully felt that 22...Nb6 was necessary. Even with that alternative, however, the tactics would still favor White: 22...Nb6 23.Qb3 Nd5 24.f5! Rb7 25.Qh3! Rxb2 26.Bc4 Rd8 27.fxe6 Ne3 28.Rf7 — White's pieces would crash through on the kingside.

Spassky thought of variations like those just mentioned and felt that the Knight needed to stay close by, protecting his King. Besides, this proposed strategy would only have allowed his position to become entangled and too passive. The threats on the a2-g8 diagonal might have made it more prudent to play 22...Kh8, stepping off the diagonal. White would then have to decide whether to continue a kingside attack with Qa3-h3 or to try to break up the center with b2-b4. In either case, White would hold the *initiative*, but Black would be better positioned to confront White's threats.

23.Bc4!

Cracking the whip, Fischer is quick to take advantage of Spassky's last inaccuracy. Black has no time for 23...Nb6 because 24.Qb3! will pin the b6-Knight while hitting the e6-pawn as well. If White manages to employ the threat f4-f5, Black will be forced to vacate the diagonal.

23...Kh8

Black has no choice. Defending the e6-pawn with 23...Nf8? would have encouraged 24.f5 with f5-f6 to follow, collapsing the shield around Black's King.

24.Qh3!

The Queen has done a splendid job in restraining Black's queenside. Now is the time to exhibit its attacking skills as well by going after the Black King. White offers to trade his b2-pawn for the important e6-pawn.

24...Nf8

Black makes no trade because after 24...Rxb2 25.Bxe6 Nf8 26.Bc4, White would have a winning position. The difference is the pawn majorities. Black's c5-pawn and d4-pawn are firmly blockaded. The moment White plays Rc1-e1 and f4-f5-f6, it will be curtains.

25.b3

Slamming the door on the b8-Rook, the move emphasizes White's positional domination. Black's Rooks are ineffective, and a cursory comparison between the c4-Bishop and the f8-Knight speaks a thousand words. But there is a long distance between an effective move that flexes a little muscle and a won position! Although restricted, Black's position has defensive possibilities. How can he go about winning the diagram position?

Keep this in mind: not all winning positions present forced variations that win material and lead to technically won positions. Some won positions need to be nurtured. That is, a winning position can and has to be *improved and perfected* before material is won and it becomes a technical win. White has a beautiful position, but not all his pieces are coordinating well. Fischer needs to increase his spatial control by further utilizing his Rooks. Then, forced wins might present themselves.

25...a5

A sensible move. Black has no active plan and therefore waits in order to counter White's plans. The a6-pawn is a target for the c4-Bishop. Now the a6-pawn is out of danger, and with ...a5-a4xb3, Black might be able to open up the a-file, giving his Rooks some breathing room.

26.f5!

White's move activates the major pieces on the f-file. Black gets to trade off his weak e6-pawn, but White gets a powerful passed e5-pawn.

This subtle interplay of trading advantages and disadvantages makes chess a maddeningly complex game. Should White spend a tempo to stop Black's counterplay ...a5-a4 by playing

26.a4, or should he play for the attack? Fischer's whole career has featured a sharp attacking style of chess. Careful players would have played 26.a4, but Fischer goes for the jugular.

26...exf5

Black is forced to capture. White can't be allowed either f5xe6 or f5-f6, which would give him a win at once.

27.Rxf5

Now the Rooks emerge, omnipresent. The immediate threat is Rf5-f7, forcing the win of material because of the *skewer* of the a7-Rook. The f1-Rook suddenly controls six squares in the space count.

27...Nh7

Black uses tactics to stop the threat of Rf5-f7. Black hopes to trick White into 28.Rf7?, thus allowing a Knight fork by 28...Ng5 and then 29.Rxe7 Nxh3+ (check!) 30.gxh3 Rxe7 — Black would win the exchange.

In difficult positions, the defender often tries to jettison some material to relieve the pressure. But in attempting 27...Ng6 28.Rf7 Qxf7 29.Bxf7 Rxf7, Black would come up short: 30.Qe6 would secure a double hit to the f7-Rook and g6-Knight.

Blocking the c4-Bishop with 27...Ne6? 28.Bxe6 Qxe6 29.Rf8+ Rxf8 30.Qxe6 would cost Black his Queen for a Rook.

Endgame

28.Rcf1!

Continuing to build up the pressure, White reintroduces the threat of Rf5-f7. Black can't stop this threat by playing 28...Rf8 to contest the f-file because 29.Rxf8+ Nxf8 30.Qc8! would pin the f8-Knight, winning it on the next move.

28...Qd8

Black avoids the threat Rf5-f7, skewering the a7-Rook.

29.Qg3

In this simple but highly effective move, White continues to improve the position of his pieces before launching the decisive attack. The Queen is now repositioned to introduce the threat of Rf5-f7 and Qg3xg7 mate. Another possible idea would be to try Qg3-g6 in order to play Bc4-d3 and mate Black on the h7-square. Now *all* of White's pieces are poised for the attack, and he can try to conclude matters directly.

29...Re7

Black is unable to prevent White from penetrating. He can only hope that White will rush his attack and stumble in the process. While this could happen, the best way to unsettle the opponent is to give him something to worry about. I would have opted for 29...a4, hoping that this would cause White some distractions.

30.h4!

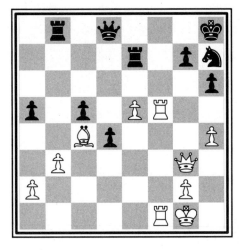

A real blow, this move takes away the g5-square for either the h7-Knight or the d8-Queen. Now the h7-Knight is stuck. The strength of this move is best revealed by thinking about 30.Rf7? Rxf7 31.Rxf7 Qg5! — which gives Black the opportunity for trading off a pair of Rooks.

30...Rbb7

Black is doing his best. The text guards against the invasion Rf5-f7. But in comparing the spatial control of the pieces, note how every White piece controls

more space than its Black counterpart. The only White piece that could be improved is the g3-Queen.

31.e6!

The passed e-pawn gleefully moves forward. Aaron Nimzovitch (1886–1935) described this move by saying, "The passed pawn lusts to expand." The e6-pawn is like a bone in Black's throat. If he doesn't get rid of it, he will choke. But how? With this move White opens up the possibility of centralizing his Queen. He also threatens the c5-pawn.

The only drawback of the text is that it allows the h7-Knight to crawl out by way of ...Nh7-f6. But as we shall see, Bobby is prepared to offer a decisive exchange sacrifice.

31...Rbc7

This move protects the c5-pawn. Black can't play 31...d3 32.Qxd3 Qxd3 33.Bxd3 Rxe6 because 34.Rf8+ Nxf8 35.Rxf8 results in mate. In this case, Black's airhole — the h7-square — hasn't helped.

32.Qe5!

Overwhelming centralization — now all of White's pieces radiate their maximum influence. Black is completely hogtied. White is now ready to pounce on the Black Knight if it should poke its head out of its hole: 32...Nf6 33.Rxf6! gxf6 34.Rxf6 (threatening Rf6xh6+ and Rh6-h8 mate) 34...Kg8 35.Rxh6 Rg7 36.e7+ — winning.

32...Qe8

Black is marking time with nothing to do. The moves 32...d3 33.R5f3 d2 34.Rd3 would cause only the loss of the d-pawn.

33.a4

Brutal. White is emphasizing his complete dominance by taking away all of Black's possibilities. By no means is Fischer rushing the attack.

33...Qd8

Black continues his waiting policy. Currently, he has all his weak points covered, so he leaves it up to White to find a way to crack his defenses.

34.R1f2

Fischer strives to place his pieces on the most effective squares before embarking on his decisive maneuver. Black has but one trump in the position: his passed d4-pawn. The text keeps a watchful eye on the d4-pawn. If Black were to try 34...d3, 35.Rd2 followed by Rd2xd3 would gobble up the pawn.

34...Qe8

Black still waits for events to offer him a chance to improve his position. Note that at no time could Black have played ...Kh8-g8 because Rf5-f7 would have been immediately decisive.

35.R2f3

White further improves the backup Rook. Now the d4-pawn is under lock and key. All the pieces are operating at their maximum, and White will start to look for the decisive blow.

35...Qd8

Black sticks to his policy of waiting for White to prove the win.

36.Bd3!

At last White begins the final maneuver. He anticipates creating a battery on the b1-h7 diagonal, setting up an h7-checkmate.

36...Qe8

Black attacks the e6-pawn and prevents Rf5-f7. The move 36...Qg8, covering the h7-Knight, would fail: 37.Rf7! Rxf7 (or 37...Nf6 38.R1xf6 to win) 38.exf7 Rxf7 (because 38...Qd8 39.Bxh7 would allow the f7-pawn to be promoted) 39.Bc4 would win an exchange after 39...Nf6 40.Qxc5 and Bc4xf7, with a technical win.

37.Qe4

This is the follow-up of White's previous move. White is ready to deliver a fearful mate on h7 after these moves: 37...Rxe6 38.Rf8+ Nxf8 39.Rxf8+ Qxf8 40.Qh7 checkmate. Therefore Black's Knight is forced to move. This allows an exchange sacrifice and a quick end to the struggle.

37...Nf6

Black moves in order to stop White's threat of Rf5-f8+.

38.Rxf6!

White has been preparing this exchange sacrifice for many moves now. The pawn shield is ripped away, unmasking the Black King.

38...gxf6

Black has no choice but to accept the offered Rook.

39.Rxf6

White snaps off the f6-pawn and threatens to chop off the h6-pawn with check, further denuding the Black King.

39...Kg8

There is no way to protect the h6-pawn. White would win in either of these scenarios: 39...Kg7 40.Rg6+ Kf8 41.Qf4+, or 39...Qh5 40.g4! Qxh4 (not 40...Rg7 because 41.Rf8+ Rg8 42.Rxg8+ — and g4xh5 would win the Black Queen) 41.Qa8+ Kg7 42.Qf8 checkmate—analysis by GM Samuel Reshevsky.

Spassky hopes to use his Rooks to block any frontal checks on the g-file. Fischer is quick to prevent this defense.

40.Bc4!

Very nice! The e7-Rook is frozen. If it moves, e6-e7+ would win immediately. Black's Rooks are unable to come to the rescue of their beleaguered monarch. The text also sets up the winning Rf6-f7.

40...Kh8

In another unhappy move, Black has to step off the c4-g8 diagonal. He hopes that the h6-pawn will tempt White into 41.Rxh6+ Rh7 42.Qe5+ Rcg7, prolonging the fight.

41.Qf4!

The final deadly move. The threat of Rf6-f8 will force 41...Kg8, and then 42.Qxh6 will leave Black helpless. He might try 42...d3, but 43.Rg6+ Rg7

44.e7+ will result in checkmate on the next move.

Black resigns.

This victory marked the first time that Bobby Fischer had gone up in the match. The score now became $3\frac{1}{2}-2\frac{1}{2}$ in favor of the challenger, and he never looked back. A stunned Boris Spassky joined with the audience after the game to applaud Fischer's victory. It was, after all, an extraordinary technical achievement. Fischer played perfectly throughout, topping the game off at the end with a prosaic exchange sacrifice. Around the chess world, grandmasters were awed at the simplicity and precision of Fischer's play. He became a chess legend.

Slaying the Dragon

F ollowing Bobby Fischer's dramatic World Championship victory in 1972, the chess world was abuzz. The new American champion captured worldwide interest: he enjoyed a New York City street parade, made a few appearances on TV shows, turned down a host of endorsement offers, and then . . . disappeared. The chess world was hopping up and down for another Fischer victory, but he was nowhere to be found. First one year, then a second year, and finally a third year went by without Fischer's pushing a pawn in public. As FIDE champion, he was obliged by the rules of chess's governing body to defend his title in 1975 against the new challenger.

But where was Fischer? Was he in deep preparation for his match? How was his training going? Why wasn't he competing? And finally, the crucial question: was Bobby going to defend or forfeit his FIDE crown?

In 1974 FIDE held an emergency meeting of its general congress. Fischer had sent FIDE his demands for the rules governing the 1975 FIDE championship. Since 1951, FIDE's rules for its championship were quite simple. The first player to score $12\frac{1}{2}$ points was the winner. If at the end of 24 games the match was tied 12–12, the champion retained the title, and the prize money was divided equally.

Fischer demanded that the rules for the 1975 match be the same as those used in 1886 for the match between Wilhelm Steinitz and Johannes Hermann Zukertort. Those rules, too, were eloquently simple. The first to win ten games would be champion. Draws didn't count. If the match was tied 9–9, it would be stopped and declared drawn, the monies would be split, and the champion would retain his title. For either champion *or* challenger to win the match, the minimum score necessary was 10–8.

At the 1974 FIDE congress, debates raged. Fischer's critics felt the ten-win system to be unfair. The moment that the champion won nine games, he couldn't lose his title. Fischer's supporters used the same spin to counter the criticism. Once the challenger won nine games, he couldn't lose the match either! Fischer had supported the ten-win system *prior* to the 1972 match with Boris Spassky. The 1972 match convinced Fischer of the correctness of his position.

In 1972, once Fischer had gotten the lead, he knew that all he had to do was draw some games and claim the title. With each drawn game, he would be one step closer, and Spassky would have one less opportunity to fight back. That's precisely what happened. Games 14 through 20 were all drawn! Seven games in a row. Fischer changed his style to suit the rules. He was no longer the warrior playing all-out in every game: he was a chess professional coasting to the title. This type of chess offended Fischer.

A parallel can be drawn between a boxing match and this type of chess. One fighter decisively wins the earlier rounds. Knowing that he is well ahead on points, he refuses to get into an exchange of blows that might get him knocked out and cost him the fight. Instead, the fighter who is leading on points runs around the ring, avoiding any risks and wins a decision — which is booed by the fans.

Fischer's supporters pointed out that a ten-win system forced the player who was in the lead to continue to play for the win. If draws didn't count, both players would have to play to win throughout the match.

While the intellectual debate between the two systems raged, a practical issue emerged. The organizers would have to consider the possible financial burden of an *unlimited* match. What would happen if neither player could prove his superiority? Suppose there was an endless series of draws? The costs could become staggering.

In 1974, the cold war was in full bloom. FIDE was composed of the national federations of the world, and as it did in the United Nations, the Soviet Union exercised enormous influence in FIDE's general assembly. If the Soviets were intent on blocking reform, the Western nations had little chance of securing Fischer's demands.

Much like a committee tasked with creating a horse, FIDE created a camel. They offered Fischer a must-win-six-games alternative. If a 5–5 score was reached, the next game would be decisive. Both players would have to reach six wins, draws not counting. FIDE hoped that Fischer would accept this compromise.

At this point, Philippine President Ferdinand Marcos offered a five-million-dollar match prize fund under the compromise of a six-win system. Fischer couldn't decline the opportunity to win millions of dollars, could he? Fischer could and did. He refused to play, forfeiting his FIDE crown in 1975. It wasn't until 20 years later, in 1992, that Fischer found a sponsor willing to support the ten-win system.

An Eastern Star

So, who would be the challenger for the 1975 FIDE match? The Soviet school of chess had nurtured a rising star, Anatoly Karpov. Karpov qualified for the FIDE candidates matches in the 1973 Leningrad Interzonal tournament. He then beat three Soviet players in succession: Lev Polugaevsky $5\frac{1}{2}$–$2\frac{1}{2}$ (Moscow, 1974), Boris Spassky 7–4 (Leningrad, 1974), and Victor Korchnoi $12\frac{1}{2}$–$11\frac{1}{2}$ (Moscow, 1974). The FIDE finals match in 1974 determined Bobby's challenger. Since there was no 1975 championship match, the FIDE candidates final match turned into a FIDE championship.

Anatoly Karpov's critics would point out that Karpov became the champion without leaving the bosom of Mother Russia. Many chess players refused to recognize Karpov as champion because he had never defeated Fischer, a monkey Karpov carried on his back throughout his career.

What Anatoly Karpov did to silence his critics was very simple: he won. He played all phases of the game — opening, middlegame, and endgame — superbly. He was exquisitely trained in the opening and rarely emerged with a bad game. His technical prowess was extraordinary. On top of this, he calculated well and won an enormous number of brilliant games. Gradually he won grudging admirers.

Karpov's year to shine was 1974. In the 1974 match, both he and his rival, Victor Korchnoi, knew they would be playing for the FIDE crown. It was a bitter, hard-fought duel. (A few years later Korchnoi would defect to the West.) The match had just started with a draw when Karpov drew first blood with this scorching victory, which would bring him to his goal of becoming FIDE champion.

■ ■ ■ ■ ■ ■ ■ ■ ■ ■ ■ ■ ■ ■

Sicilian Dragon

GM Anatoly Karpov
GM Victor Korchnoi
1974 FIDE Candidates Final (Game 2)

Opening

1.e4

Early in his career Karpov employed 1.e4 — a King Pawn Opening — exclusively. From the viewpoint of space and piece deployment, e2-e4 has to be considered the best opening move. The e4-pawn controls the f5-square and d5-square, the d1-Queen the h5-square, and the f1-Bishop the b5-square and a6-square for a space count of five. The f1-Bishop and d1-Queen are given diagonals on which to develop. In Fischer's words, e2-e4 "is best by test."

Especially in the eighteenth and nineteenth centuries, King Pawn Openings were considered the only way to open a chess game. They feature sharp, attacking games that are highly prized by chess lovers. Indeed, an extraordinary number of beautiful games begin with this first move.

Because King Pawn Openings have such a rich chess history, they have been extensively analyzed. Hundreds of encyclopedic books have attempted to map out Black's possible defenses. Today's grandmasters know that King Pawn Openings are incredibly sharp. A single misstep in the attack or the defense can lead to disaster. Learning the openings and defenses are a lifetime's work. If you aren't up-to-date on the latest wrinkle in a horrifyingly complicated variation, you may slip and lose.

The main feature of King Pawn Openings is a rapid development of the pieces in order to launch quick attacks. This fight for the initiative — the ability to make threats — is the decisive factor in the outcome of the opening.

1...c5

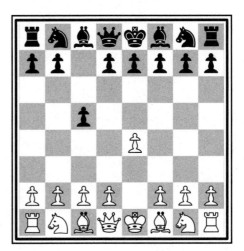

Black responds with the Sicilian Defense. The aim of the Sicilian Defense is to fight indirectly for control of the center. The text controls White's d4-square and b4-square. It doesn't help the development of

Black's pieces, noticeably the Bishops, but Black will slowly overcome this difficulty. First he means to keep an eye on the center by restraining White's control. Later he will go for a full-fledged center fight.

The Sicilian Defense is a relatively new one, only about 150 years old. (The oldest known chess openings began with 1...e7-e5, matching White's first move.)

2.Nf3

This is the most principled response. White wants to play d2-d4, opening the center and preparing for further piece development. The f3-Knight attacks the e5-square and g5-square while supporting the freeing move d2-d4.

One of the most dangerous gambits that Sicilian players face is the Smith-Morra Gambit. It starts with 2.d4 cxd4 3.c3 dxc3 4.Nxc3, in which White has sacrificed a pawn to bring two of his pieces into the game while opening up the center for his Bishops. Most Sicilian players eschew the gambit by playing 3...d5, fighting for development and center control as well.

2...d6

This move protects the c5-pawn, controls the e5-square, and opens up the diagonal for the c8-Bishop. On move 2, Black has many choices: 2...e6, 2...Nc6, 2...g6, and

2...Nf6 have all been played successfully. At this point, the defense is a matter of taste.

3.d4

With this thrust, White offers an exchange of pawns in the center, thus *opening up* the position. This move gives the opening its name, the Open Sicilian.

As the game continues, the name of the opening will become further refined. If White had chosen not to play d2-d4 but preferred, for example, 3.g3, fianchettoing his Bishop, the opening would be called the Closed Sicilian.

After d2-d4, it is easy to see that White has opened diagonals for his Bishops to be developed and enjoys a considerable increase in the space count. So why would Black play the Sicilian and allow White to be so active so early? Ah, the wonders of chess! The Sicilian Defense is most insidious. Black's idea is to *allow* White his piece activity. He seeks to *restrain* this activity while building up his own control of the center squares. Eventually, Black will try to catch up in development and activity to challenge the center. He may then win the initiative. Why? The answer lies in the pawn structure.

Because the center is so vital, having a center pawn — an e-pawn or a d-pawn — is crucial. With d2-d4, White offers to trade his d4-center pawn for a queenside c5-pawn. That leaves Black with two center pawns to White's lone e4-pawn. Black hopes to eventually utilize his *extra* center pawn to give him an advantage in the center. Black allows White the short-term activation of his pieces in exchange for the long-term advantage of having a preponderance of pawns in the center.

The exchange of the d4-pawn for the c5-pawn also opens up the files for the Rooks. Black gets the half-open c-file, and White gets the half-open d-file. Who benefits more? It is impossible to say at this moment. Each player will have to use his trumps as best he can.

Finally, what about the move 3.Bb5+, developing the Bishop with check? Actually, this is a well-known opening variation. I don't recommend it, believing it falls into the category of "Patzer sees a check, patzer plays a check."

Should the game continue with 3...Bd7 4.Bxd7+ Qxd7, White would develop Black's Queen with tempo. It would benefit Black more than White, though this often-played variation shouldn't be judged entirely on this short-term disadvantage to White.

3...cxd4

Black happily exchanges his wing c5-pawn for the central d4-pawn. Failure to

capture the d4-pawn would allow White the choice of d4xc5, or even d4-d5, clamping down the center.

4.Nxd4

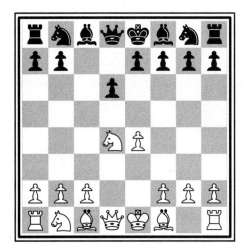

White moves the same piece twice in the opening. Opening principles generally dictate that moving the same piece early in the opening should be avoided, but in this case, White has the right to do so. Black too has moved his c-pawn twice, so White doesn't lose a tempo by moving his Knight twice.

Still, the recapture 4.Qxd4 looks awfully tempting, giving White three warriors in play to Black's lone d6-pawn. But the problem with 4.Qxd4 is that it would develop the Queen too early, making it a likely target for attack. Black could continue with either 4...Nc6 or 4...e5, forcing a response. Nevertheless, the advantages of 4.Qxd4 are obvious, and many grandmasters have tried this recapture instead of Nf3xd4. Though it is largely a matter of taste, Karpov's recapture 4.Nxd4 is the better choice. White brings his Knight to a more influential post, controlling squares b5, c6, e6, and f5. White has developed two members of his army to Black's one. Black must use his move to catch up in development.

4...Nf6

Black develops a piece while attacking White's e4-pawn. The text is considered the best move for two reasons. Black doesn't want to allow c2-c4, which would enable White to strengthen his control over the d5-square. Second, Black wants to induce Nb1-c3, which would put the c3-Knight on the half-open c-file. This would allow a potential exchange sacrifice ...Ra8-c8xc3, followed up with ...Nf6xe4. Such exchange sacrifices are a common tactical theme in the Open Sicilian.

From the point of view of developing with tempo, why not play 4...e5, attacking the powerful d4-Knight? For the short term, this would be a good idea. White would have to move his d4-Knight, and Black would have played the move ...e7-e5 for free. The drawback to 4...e5 is the *long-term* problem that this move would cause. The move ...e7-e5 would weaken the light squares in the center, most noticeably f5 and d5.

After 4...e5, White would want to exchange light-squared Bishops because this would make it easier for him to control the f5-square and the d5-square. Thus, 4...e5? 5.Bb5+! Bd7 6.Bxd7+ Qxd7 7.Nf5 — Black would force the d4-Knight onto a more dangerous square. Continuing with 7...g6 would further boot the Knight and induce 8.Ne3!, preparing a jump to the wonderful d5-outpost. The move ...g7-g6 is plainly bad. Let's continue in this line, and introduce some tactics:

- 4...e5? 5.Bb5+! Bd7 6.Bxd7+ Qxd7 7.Nf5 Nf6 (attacking the e4-pawn, which would support the f5-Knight) 8.Nc3 Nxe4 9.Nxg7+ Bxg7 10.Nxe4 d5 11.Bh6! O-O 12.Bxg7 Kxg7 13.Ng3 would produce an unclear position. Black's kingside defense would be compromised, but he would have a fine center pawn duo.

- White should be a bit more modest: 4...e5? 5.Bb5+! Bd7 6.Bxd7+ Qxd7 7.Nb3! This simple retreat would cause Black the most problems. Black would have a backward d6-pawn, and White would have a nice grip on the d5-square. By continuing with Nb1-c3-d5, White could secure a clear advantage.

5.Nc3

Karpov's choice is the main move in the Open Sicilian. He protects the e4-pawn and continues to control the d5-square.

White thus falls in line with Black's strategy as outlined in the previous note. Why? The question is how to defend the e4-pawn. With 5.Qd3 or 5.Qf3, White would develop his Queen too early, exposing it to possible attacks. In the first case, 5...Nbd7 would prepare ...Nd7-c5, forking the d3-Queen and e4-pawn; in the second case, Black could then play 5...Bg4, developing the Bishop with tempo.

Two other possible defenses could have been chosen.

■ A plausible move allowing development and defense would be 5.Bd3. It has a drawback: since the f1-Bishop has already moved, Black no longer fears Bd3-b5+. By continuing with 5.Bd3?! e5! 6.Nb3 (6.Bb5+? Bd7 7.Bxd7+ Qxd7 would leave the e4-pawn en prise) 6...d5!, Black would win the fight for the center.

■ White could try 5.f3!? to prop up the e4-pawn while preparing c2-c4. Many grandmasters have tried this reasonable idea — again, it is largely a matter of taste. The only drawbacks of f2-f3 are a weakening of the g1-b6 diagonal and a loss of the option f2-f4.

5...g6

The diagram position is probably the most complex in modern chess opening theory. Black has a host of possibilities: 5...e6 (the Scheveningen Defense), 5...a6 (the Najdorf), 5...Nc6 (the Rauzer), or the one Korchnoi chooses — the Dragon.

The Dragon's name derives from two factors: the g8-Bishop fianchettos itself on the long h8-a1 diagonal, breathing fire down the board, and Black's pawn structure — h7, g6, f7, e7, and d6 — resembles an outline of a dragon.

There is a lot to be said in favor of the Dragon variation. The fianchetto allows Black to build a *home* for his King on the kingside. Black's e7 and d6 pawns limit the effectiveness of the f8-Bishop. With the g7-Bishop, the pawns will play a robust role in the game by keeping an eye on the center e5-square and d4-square.

The Dragon is typical of the restraining center strategy introduced in the Sicilian. White controls more space, yet no outposts in the center are clearly visible. The d6-pawn prevents the move e4-e5, the f6-Knight hits the d5-square and e4-square, and the g6-pawn limits the d4-Knight by controlling the f5-square. In the long term, Black will try to utilize his extra center pawn. White must therefore look for some direct plan of action.

6.Be3

The player with more active pieces can easily create a plan of action; active positions usually offer a number of options, and White could have considered 6.f4, playing for e4-e5, or 6.Be2 and 6.h3, playing for g2-g4-g5. He could have played slowly, with 6.g3, fianchettoing his own Bishop, and continued with his plan of watching the d5-square. Instead, Karpov chooses the Yugoslav Attack against the Dragon — the most dangerous anti-Dragon weapon to be found.

The move 6.Be3 develops a piece while preparing to castle queenside. The move ...g7-g6 has weakened the h6-square, and this is compensated for by the fact that with a g7-Bishop, the h6-square is protected. The text sets up the idea of Qd1-d2, followed by Be3-h6, trying to exchange the fianchettoed Bishop. This strategy will lead to enormous complications, with both players castled on opposite sides.

6...Bg7

Black completes the fianchetto. He would have made a bad mistake by playing 6...Ng4?? to attack the e3-Bishop and open up the long a1-h8 diagonal. White could make the tactical shot 7.Bb5+!, followed by 7...Bd7 8.Qxg4! to take advantage of the pin to grab the g4-Knight.

7.f3

Preventing ...Nf6-g4, the text also reinforces the e4-pawn, precluding the sting of a possible c3-exchange sacrifice.

7...Nc6

As naturally as can be, Black continues his development. The d4-Knight is a powerful beast, so Black sets up an opportunity to exchange Knights.

8.Qd2

White too is implementing his plan. He prepares to castle queenside while setting up a battery for Be3-h6.

8...O-O

Battle lines are being drawn. Black has built a home for his King and will now turn his attention toward the center and queenside. Now that Black has committed his King, White knows where he has to attack.

9.Bc4!

A defining moment. This move initiates the Yugoslav Attack.

Practice has shown that after 9.O-O-O d5!, Black can strike out in the center and earn strong counterplay against White's King. The text is a harmonious move. White is planning to castle queenside and wants to make sure there are plenty of guards around for protection. After Bc4-b3, White cements the pawns around his King.

Also, Bf1-c4 fits nicely with the strategy of protecting the d5-square. This will rule out the countermove ...d6-d5, which would attack the e4-pawn. What treasure lies on the a2-g8 diagonal? Yes, indeed, the c4-Bishop looks directly upon the g8-King.

9...Bd7

Both players continue within the main line theory of the Dragon. The text fits in with one of Black's trumps: the half-open c-file. The c8-Bishop makes room for the a8-Rook to play ...Ra8-c8. Black would then be set up to take the initiative on the queenside.

10.h4!

This crucial link in White's scheme of development shows that he is committed to all-out war against Black's King. With this move, White burns his bridges and declares his intent. Once White castles queenside, the game will be decided by the player who gets to the opposing King first. Unfortunately for White, Black has a sizable lead in the race. The half-open c-file means that Black already has a highway to White's King. White therefore must open up a road for his pieces, especially the Rooks. White anticipates playing h4-h5 and h5xg6, weakening the pawn cover around Black's King. This idea of opening the h-file would cost White two tempi. In the meantime, Black's attack down the c-file is coming fast and furious. Who will get there first with the most?

10...Rc8

What could be sweeter? Black develops a Rook to his half-open c-file and introduces the threat of ...Nc6xd4, exposing the c4-Bishop.

11.Bb3

In view of the previously mentioned threat, White is forced to retreat the c4-Bishop. Although the retreat costs a tempo, White isn't completely unhappy. The b3-Bishop offers considerable queenside protection and is *x-raying* Black's King.

11...Ne5

An important decision — Black decides not to trade the d4-Knight. This means that the d4-Knight is *allowed* to stare at four squares (b5, c6, e6, and f5). Black decides to live with this pressure because the d7-Bishop also covers these squares. In Black's view, the b3-Bishop is a far greater threat to his position. His idea is to play ...Ne5-c4, blocking the b3-Bishop's diagonal and attacking White's Queen.

Practice has shown that this Knight maneuver is the best idea in the position. With the alternative 11...Nxd4 12.Bxd4 b5 13.h5! a5 14.hxg6 hxg6 15.a4 b4 16.Nd5, White's attack on the kingside would come first.

12.0-0-0

The players have now castled to opposite sides of the board. Such a position gives both players a free hand to go berserk against each other's Kings. Indeed, both sides are *forced* to go for broke in effecting the attack.

In such positions, fighting for the initiative will decide the winner. *Distracting* the opponent by creating threats helps an attack gain momentum.

White's plan is to play h4-h5 and then to utilize the half-open or open h-file to go after Black's King. For this reason, he needs to bring the a1-Rook into play. It may have a role on the h-file.

Black's plan is equally to the point. The half-open c-file is a natural gateway to White's King. Black will shift as many pieces as he can to the queenside. He will use his Rooks on the c-file as a battering ram against White's King. (The pros and cons of this position have been played out in hundreds of grandmaster games.)

12...Nc4

Black attacks the d2-Queen and the e3-Bishop.

In some scenarios, this move could make the b2-pawn vulnerable — it is easy to imagine a sequence in which Black sacrifices a Knight for the b2-pawn and then plays ...Rc8xc3, luring the White King onto the long diagonal. The g7-Bishop waits in its lair.

This game has gone far in changing the theory of the Dragon. Today's grandmasters consider 12...h5 to be the best move to prevent White's h4-h5 plan.

At the time this game was played, the text was the height of fashion.

13.Bxc4

White parts with a fine attacking Bishop and a noble guard to the White King. Though it would have been tempting to play 13.Qd3, preserving the b3-Bishop, Black would then reply with 13...Nxe3, robbing White of the possibility of Be3-h6. The importance of Be3-h6 cannot be overestimated. The g7-Bishop is a mighty defender. It is crucial that White be able to negotiate a dark-squared Bishop swap.

13...Rxc4

A triumphant recapture. Black needs two tempi for creating a decisive attack. With ...Qd8-a5 and ...Rf8-c8, a smashing sacrifice on the queenside could follow.

White has to prosecute this attack with vigor, or he will lose.

14.h5!

White sacrifices a pawn in order to break down Black's kingside fortress. Once the h-file is opened with Be3-h6 to follow, forcing checkmate will be a piece of cake.

White has to be careful of the many tactical pitfalls. One bad mistake would have been 14.Bh6? Rxd4!, taking advantage of the overworked d2-Queen. After 15.Qxd4 Bxh6+ 16.Kb1 Qa5, White would have lost material while his kingside attack came to a screeching halt.

Another attacking approach could have been 14.g4, aiming to play h4-h5 without sacrificing a pawn. Two possible countermoves from Black weaken this slower approach: the response 14...Qa5 15.h5 Rfc8 would prime Black's pieces for the attack. The second approach, 14...h5!?, could lead to 15.g5? — a horrible strategic error because after either 15...Ne8 or 15...Nh7, White would have closed the kingside, making Black's King safer. A better move would be 15.gxh5 Nxh5 when it isn't easy to break down Black's kingside. The text is the most straightforward and consequent line of play.

14...Nxh5

Victor Korchnoi keeps up his reputation as a fearless fighter. He often grabs an offered sacrifice and then tenaciously defends himself to emerge a pawn up in an ending.

A safer approach would have been 14...Qa5 15.hxg6 fxg6; by ...Rf8-f7, the f8-Rook could defend the h7-pawn. But in that case, White would not sacrifice a pawn, and Black's kingside pawn structure would have been breached.

The players are still following standard opening theory. The question is this: who is better prepared?

15.g4

A happy moment for White. He introduces the g2-pawn into the attack with tempo. The h5-Knight is given the boot, allowing the h1-Rook to operate on the h-file.

15...Nf6

The Knight has grabbed a pawn and quickly runs away.

Black doesn't fear 16.Bh6, for he has prepared a trick: 16...Nxe4! 17.Qe3 (the only move because 17.Nxe4 Rxd4 18.Qh2 Be5! 19.f4 Rxd1+ 20.Rxd1 Bh8 21.Bxf8 Qb6! attacking the b2-pawn would be good for Black) 17...Rxc3 (sacrificing an

exchange to ruin White's pawn shield) 18.bxc3 Nf6 19.Bxg7 Kxg7 20.Ne2 Qa5! with an unclear position — analysis by GM Alexander Matanovic.

For the second time we see that White mustn't be eager to play Be3-h6, going for a Bishop trade. He must watch out for the tactics against his d4-Knight.

16.Nde2!

Combining offense and defense, White loses a tempo to shore up the c3-Knight. While preparing to trade dragons with Be3-h6, White also prepares the sneaky tactic 17.e5 dxe5 18.g5, winning a piece because of the open d-file. Another reason for the retreat is that Black might try the defense ...h7-h5. The e2-Knight is now able to play Ne2-f4, pressuring the h5-square.

16...Qa5

Continuing to fight for the initiative, Black prevents the tactical shot e4-e5 because ...Qa5xe5 could snap a pawn. Black gets out of the way in order to double Rooks with ...Rf8-c8, going after White's King. The position is razor-sharp; the game hangs in the balance at every move.

17.Bh6

White completes the quest and tries to exchange dragons so that he can play Qd2-h6, sidling up to Black's King. Now that the h-file is open, this operation poses a grave danger to Black's King.

17...Bxh6

Korchnoi decides to keep his material.

Sacrificing the exchange with 17...Bh8 18.Bxf8 Kxf8 would be only slightly better for White, in the opinion of former World Champion Mikhail Botvinnik. I agree with this assessment and would add that sacrificing the exchange to retain the dragon h8-Bishop is a good way of minimizing White's kingside attack.

18.Qxh6

White introduces the lady and threatens a standard victory with Nc3-d5, removing the lone h7-pawn defender.

Middlegame

18...Rfc8

Both players have followed their strategies well. White is eager to do damage on the h-file; Black is poised for his blow along the c-file. The question is, who stands better? Up to now, the players have both followed standard chess theory.

19.Rd3!

Karpov uncorks a massive theoretical novelty — an extremely strong move.

White would have liked to play either 19.Nd5 or 19.g5 but isn't properly prepared. After 19.Nd5, White would be ready for either 20.Nxf6+ to munch the h7-pawn, or the simple 20.Nxe7+ to grab the c8-Rook. The problem is that Black's counterplay would be too swift: 19.Nd5? Rxc2+ 20.Kb1 Qb5! 21.b3 Qxe2 — Black's major pieces on the second rank would mate first. In a typical variation, 21.Nxf6+ exf6 22.Qxh7+ Kf8 23.Qh8+ Ke7, Black's King would skip away from the kingside.

The second attacking choice, 19.g5, also would miss the mark; the moves 19.g5 Nh5 20.Nf4 Rxc3 would lead to two losing variations for White:

■ Moves 21.bxc3 Qxc3 22.Rh2 Qe3+ 23.Kb1 Qxf4 would win material for Black and stop White's attack cold.

■ The sequence 21.Nxh5 Rxc2+ 22.Kb1 gxh5 23.Rxh5 Bf5! (covering the h7-pawn) 24.exf5 Qxf5 25.g6 Rc1 would lead to checkmate.

These variations show that sacrifices against the c3-Knight are the source of Black's counterplay. By overprotecting the c3-Knight, White stops Black's tactics. He intends to pursue his attack with g4-g5 and Ne2-f4 without distractions.

Recognizing that the move 19.Rd3 is a novelty, what had been previously analyzed as the best choice for this situation? GM Mikhail Botvinnik suggested 19.Rd5 Qd8 (of course 19...Nxd5?? 20.Qxh7+ Kf8 21.Qh8 would be a quick checkmate) 20.g5 Nh5 21.Nf4 Qf8! 22.Qxf8+ Kxf8 23.Nxh5 gxh5 24.Rxh5, winning back the pawn with a slightly better ending for White.

Karpov also thinks that this ending is better for White, and he aims for the same ending, but prefers that the d1-Rook go to d3 and not to the d5-square. An important nuance, as we shall see.

19...R4c5?

Black loses brilliantly. This single misstep is the only mistake of the game! It demonstrates the intense, keen-edged nature of the position and that of King Pawn Openings in general.

Black had to accept the disagreeable ending: 19...Qd8 20.g5 Nh5 21.Nf4 Qf8 22.Qxf8+ Kxf8 23.Nxh5 gxh5 24.Rxh5 Kg7 would have allowed White to continue with 25.Rh2, defending the c2-pawn and following with Nc3-d5. Besides this, the Rook on d3 would allow White to move Rd3-b3, swinging over to the queenside.

Black had to make the retreat ...Qa5-d8 and ...Qd8-f8 because of White's threat of 20.g5 Nh5 21.Nf4, thereby crashing through on the h-file. Besides securing this ending, White also would have a chance to use the d-file to win material.

GM Mikhail Botvinnik cites two variations, both of them satisfactory for Black, to follow 19...Qd8 20.e5!? dxe5:

- The sequence 21.Ng3 Qf8 22.Qxf8+ Rxf8! 23.g5 Bc6! 24.gxf6 exf6 would work well — Black would have three pawns and a whopping kingside majority for his piece. Botvinnik considers Black to have the edge in this variation.

- The sequence 21.g5 Nh5 22.Ng3 Qf8 23.Qxf8+ Kxf8 24.Nxh5 Bf5! 25.Ng3 Bxd3 26.cxd3 Rf4! would allow Black

two pawns and a Rook for two Knights. Botvinnik thinks this variation to be equal, but I prefer Black's position.

This tactical ploy of e4-e5 opening up the d-file often occurs in the Dragon variation.

Korchnoi's mistake — 19...R4c5? — was completely understandable. White's threat of g4-g5 is hanging over his position like the sword of Damocles. By preventing this move, it appears that Black has obtained a completely satisfactory game. Given time, he needs only to play ...Bd7-e6 to recharge his own queenside attack.

20.g5!!

A brilliant shot from out of the blue. Black's last move was specifically designed to stop this threat, but White carries it out anyway. White tries to lure

Black's c5-Rook off the c-file and onto the vulnerable g5-square. White would dearly love to play 20.Nd5, but as we've seen, 20...Rxc2+ would be good for Black.

21...Rxg5

Black has to accept the second pawn sacrifice. The alternative move would have been doomed: 21...Nh5 22.Nf4! Rxg5 (the pawn is captured anyway) 23.Ncd5 Rxd5 24.Rxd5 Qxa2 25.Rhxh5 Qa1+ 26.Kd2 gxh5 27.Rg5+, with mate at the next move.

22.Rd5!!

A marvelous follow-through. The Rook can now be captured in three different ways, but all captures losing for different reasons.

22...Rxd5

Black chooses the least of the three evils. The other two would have been more costly: 22...Nxd5? 23.Qxh7+, and mate would be next; 22...Qxd5? 23.Nxd5 would cost the Queen, and White's attack would continue.

All other moves, such as 22...Rc5 23.Qxg5 Nxd5 24.exd5, would cost Black a piece. White would then reset with Qg5-h6, producing a mate on the h-file.

This tactical explosion on the d-file recalls a comment made by Swedish GM Ulf Andersson, who is extraordinarily insightful concerning defense. When asked his opinion about the Dragon, he commented, "Black's d5-square is too weak." His words are prophetic.

23.Nxd5

At last — White has been itching to play this move. Now that Black's pressure on the c2-pawn has been neutralized, the c3-Knight springs into action. Black's sensitive f6 and e7 points need help.

23...Re8

This move protects the e7-pawn. Now the question of who has the initiative is no longer in doubt. Black has given up on his attack while White is still cranking up the pressure against Black's King.

Black would have dearly loved to play 23...Qxa2, munching a pawn while going after White's King. But 24.Nxe7+ Kh8 25.Nxc8 Bxc8 26.Nc3! Qa1+ 27.Kd2! Qxb2 28.Qf8+ Ng8 29.Qxc8 would cost Black a whole Rook.

The other defensive reaction, 23...Qd8, doesn't help either: 24.Nef4! Rc5 (trying to eliminate the d5-Knight) 25.Nxf6+ exf6 26.Qxh7+ Kf8 27.Nxg6+! (a tremendous blow — Black's King would no longer have a pawn shield) 27...fxg6 28.Qh8+ Ke7 29.Rh7+ (separating King from Queen). After winning Black's Queen, White's attack would continue.

24.Nef4!

Finely played — White would have been cashing in his chips early with 24.Nxf6+? exf6 25.Qxh7+ Kf8 26.Qh8+? Ke7. Black's King would have scampered

away, freed by the syndrome of "Patzer sees check, patzer plays check." Black's King is going nowhere, so White needn't rush matters.

Also note that the text rules out the defense 24.Nxf6+? exf6 25.Qxh7+ Kf8 26.Nf4, intending Nf4-d5 in anticipation of 26...Qg5! pinning the f4-Knight. White now intends to continue with a trade on f6 and then to play Nf4-d5, setting up all kinds of beautiful mates.

24...Bc6

Black desperately tries to prevent the previously mentioned threat. The other possibility would be neatly undone: 24...Be6 25.Nxe6! (threatening Qh6-g7 mate) 25...fxe6 26.Nxf6+ exf6 27.Qxh7+ Kf8 28.Qd7! with the threat of Rh1-h8 mate. Black is helpless — analysis by GM Mikhail Botvinnik.

Endgame

25.e5!!

Karpov uncorks a tactical shot to wrap up the game: another marvelous pawn sacrifice. This time White closes off the fifth rank preventing a ...Qa5-g5+ defense. As before, 25.Nxf6+ exf6 (threatening ...Qa5-g5) 26.Qxh7+ Kf8 allows Black's King an e7-square exit.

White could win an exchange with 25.Nxf6+ exf6 26.Nh5, threatening Qh6-g7 mate. But Black could play 26...Qg5+! 27.Qxg5 fxg5 28.Nf6+ Kg7 29.Nxe8+ Bxe8, and White would have won a battle but have lost the war. Black's kingside pawn majority would offer comforting compensation.

With the text, White simply threatens e5xf6, in which Black's King would be quickly mated.

25...Bxd5

Other captures all would have allowed mate:

- 25...dxe5 26.Nxf6+ exf6 27.Nh5! gxh5 28.Rg1+ and mate next move.
- 25...Nxd5 26.Qxh7+ Kf8 27.Qh8 — mate would be even quicker.

26.exf6

Once again White threatens Qh6-g7 mate.

26...exf6

This is the only way to stop mate. With ...Re8-e1+ subsequently, Black himself could now threaten mate! White is on the move and has to make everything count.

27.Qxh7+

White crashes through at last. Black's King is driven into the center of the board. This is the crowning achievement of a strategy nearly twenty moves old — it makes you wonder how far ahead grandmasters prepare their combinations!

27...Kf8

Will Black escape the kingside? He still has the miracle shot ...Re8-e1+ ready.

28.Qh8+

The final position.

Black resigns.

Korchnoi now gives up as he realizes 28...Ke7 29.Nxd5+ Qxd5 (or 29...Kd8 30.Qxf6+, and Rh1-d1 is an extra Knight for White) 30.Re1+ will force either the loss of his e8-Rook, or after 30...Qe5 31.Rxe5+, the loss of his Queen.

The game proved an impressive example of how to storm a fianchettoed King's position; following his loss, Korchnoi virtually gave up playing the Dragon for the rest of his career.

The tumultuous match itself set off a historical chain of events. Karpov went on to win the match 12½–11½ and became the FIDE challenger. After Bobby Fischer forfeited in 1975, Karpov was proclaimed the new FIDE champion. Several years later, Korchnoi would defect to the West.

Later, in 1978 and 1981, Victor Korchnoi again became the FIDE challenger to Anatoly Karpov. I joined Korchnoi's team as a coach for his 1981 match in Merano, Italy. While driving through the Austrian Alps, I asked him how history would have changed had he won the 1974 match. He told me that Karpov would be in the car.

■■■■ ▪▪▪▪ ▪▪▪▪ ▪▪▪▪ ▪▪▪▪ ▪▪▪▪ ▪▪▪▪ ▪▪▪▪ ▪▪▪▪

Sparkling Originality

A Dutch steel company, the Hoogoven Group, has sponsored an annual tournament in the Dutch coastal city of Wijk aan Zee for over 50 years. Only the Hastings tournament in England has a longer pedigree.

In 1976, two dynamically contrasting players settled down to battle in the Wijk aan Zee event. Playing the White pieces was the fiery, Yugoslavian attacking maestro Ljubomir Ljubojevic. Across from him sat the stoic master of defense, Sweden's Ulf Andersson — a classic matchup prized by chess lovers.

In that same year, I had broken into the chess master class and fancied that I had a good understanding of the game. This game taught me that I had a long way to go! I realized that chess isn't just about exploiting an advantage brought about by applying chess fundamentals. It is a clash of *styles* as well.

In annotating this game, I've relied upon the analysis of GM Jan Timman from his superb book, *The Art of Chess Analysis*.

■ ■ ■ ■ ■ ■ ■ ■ ■ ■ ■ ■ ■ ■ ■

Sicilian Defense,
Scheveningen Variation

GM Ljubomir Ljubojevic
GM Ulf Andersson
Hoogoven Tournament, Wijk aan Zee, 1976

Opening

1.e4

Although "Ljubo," as Ljubojevic is called, has experimented with other opening moves, 1.e4 has been his favorite. Indeed, 1.e4 is tailor-made for his swashbuckling attacking style.

1...c5

Andersson, on the other hand, chooses the Sicilian. This too is perfect for his style of chess — a defensive, counterattacking method designed to give the opponent just enough rope to hang himself.

2.Nf3

As in Game Two of this book, White is happy to lead the game into the channels of the Open Sicilian.

2...e6

Also mentioned in Game Two of this book, Black can employ a wide variety of defenses in the Sicilian. The text introduces the Taimanov System.

One of the great pluses of the Taimanov System — named in recognition of the many splendid ideas introduced by the Russian grandmaster Mark Taimanov — is its flexibility. Black might use the Taimanov move in order to transpose to another Sicilian Defense or to catch the unsuspecting in one of the many traps of this variation.

At this early stage, it is difficult to say how the opening will unfold. The aim of the last move was to protect the d5-square and the f5-square, making the push ...d7-d5 a possibility. Black also opens up the f8-Bishop. In an Open Sicilian, where White would play Nb1-c3, defending his e4-pawn, Black would have a chance for ...Bf8-b4, attacking the c3-Knight.

As we saw in Game Two, Black's central structure of the d6-pawn and the e7-pawn hemmed in his f8-Bishop. He therefore fianchettoed the f8-Bishop. In the Taimanov System, the c8-Bishop has the same problem, and once again the idea of a fianchetto, playing for ...Bc8-b7, would be the best way to activate this Bishop.

3.d4

White plays for an open attacking game. As in Game Two, White wants to develop his pieces as quickly as possible.

3...cxd4

Playing the trump card of the Sicilian Defense, Black trades his wing pawn for a center d-pawn.

4.Nxd4

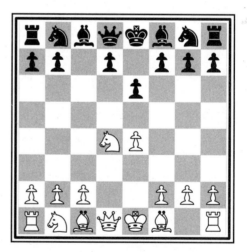

White sets up a powerful d4-Knight. At this point 4.Qxd4 would be a clear mistake because 4...Nc6 would develop with tempo.

4...Nc6

Black develops his position while putting pressure on the d4-Knight. The opening is still in a state of flux. A few more moves are necessary to determine the opening's name. Had Black played 4...Nf6 5.Nc3 (5.e5? would be premature because 5...Qa5+ would win the e5-pawn) 5...d6, the game would have developed into a Scheveningen Defense.

5.Nc3

White moves toward commitment as he voluntarily puts a Knight in front of the c2-pawn, denying himself c2-c4.

The most common line of play here would be to build up pressure in the center by erecting the Maroczy wall, that is, to have an e4-pawn and c4-pawn center. The most effective move order would begin with 5.Nb5, attacking the d6-square. White would move the same piece for the third time, breaking the principle of not moving the same piece more than once in the opening. He would do this for a specific strategic reason — to invade the d6-square, forcing Black to exchange the f8-Bishop. In the resulting trade, Black's dark squares in the center would be greatly weakened.

Thus 5.Nb5 d6 6.c4 would erect the Maroczy wall, named for the famous Hungarian grandmaster Geza Maroczy (1870–1951), who introduced this pawn

Ljubomir Ljubojevic

Ljubomir Ljubojevic, whose first name means "Gift of Love" in Serbo-Croatian, is in truth a gift to chess. He was born in Titovo Užice, Yugoslavia, on February 11, 1950. He became an international master in 1970 and an international grandmaster in 1971. "Ljubo's" fiery brand of chess captures the attention of the audience; he is a player who always goes for the gusto; and when he hits the mark, his achievements can be wondrous.

structure idea. He showed how White can utilize the spatial advantage that it gives him.

After 5.Nb5 d6 6.c4 Nf6 7.N1b3 a6 8.Na3, Black would chase the a3-Knight to a rather dismal square. In exchange, however, White would gain a solid grip on the d5-square and could hope to exploit the potential weakness of the d6-pawn. Many games have been played from this position.

5...Qc7

When *grandmasters* violate opening principles such as "Don't bring out your Queen early," these violations suddenly become "highly refined moves." Indeed, the text fits in well with Black's opening setup. The Queen covers the weak d6-square and

controls the e5-square, making the push e4-e5 less likely. Black can also prepare ...Bf8-b4 when the c7-Queen puts added pressure on the c3-Knight.

The drawback of developing the Queen too early is that it can then be attacked and thus be forced to move again and again — in which case, as the Queen flees its attacker, the opponent develops his pieces with tempo. Therefore, be warned about moving the Queen early in the game.

6.Be2

Rather than quietly developing his pieces as he does here, White could have tried to take advantage of Black's last move with 6.Ndb5, forcing ...Qb8 to push back Black's Queen. The problem is that White would have had no follow-through to his one-move attack. If he could continue with Bc1-f4, then the attack Nd4-b5 would be good. Black would have to play ...a7-a6, forcing the b5-Knight to retreat. He'd then play ...b7-b5 in order to develop the c8-Bishop. Black would therefore win back the tempo he lost in playing ...Qc7-b8.

The line 6.Ndb5 Qb8 7.g3 (in order to force Bc1-f4) 7...a6 8.Bf4? e5 would have been disastrous, placing two of White's pieces en prise.

6...a6

This extraordinary move is typical of Open Sicilians. Black spends an entire tempo in the opening to protect his b5-square. This move fits in with the idea of *restraining* White's pieces. Look at the center: you can see that Black does a good job of protecting his side of the board.

Black simply intends to develop the rest of his pieces while exchanging any enemy pieces that might launch an invasion. He will then try to utilize his extra center pawn. Another rationale behind playing ...a7-a6 is to continue with ...b7-b5 and a quick queenside fianchetto.

The question is, can Black spend a tempo on niceties while White is completing his development for attack?

7.O-O

White tucks away his King. He will see what Black intends to do with his own King before launching an attack.

7...Nf6

At last Black begins to develop his kingside forces. It would be a mistake to try to develop with tempo by playing 7...Nxd4 8.Qxd4 Bc5? because 9.Qxg7 would nip a pawn. However, Black's last move blocks the d4-g7 diagonal, making this scheme now possible.

8.Be3

White develops his position while preventing the scenario mentioned in the previous paragraph. One of the drawbacks of the earlier move ...a7-a6 is the weakening of the b6-square. With the text, White can envision trying to control b6 with a2-a4-a5 or even Nc3-a4-b6.

Although Bc1-e3 is a nice move, White would have liked to play something a bit more forceful such as f2-f4 and e4-e5, taking over the center. But the immediate move 8.f4?? would have been a disaster, since 8...Nxd4 9.Qxd4 Bc5! would win White's Queen. The text makes the idea of f2-f4 possible in the future.

8...Be7

A defining moment in the opening. After the text, the opening transposes into the Scheveningen Defense.

This defense is noted for its cramped but solid nature. Black takes a modest stance in the center and on the kingside. His counterplay will be on the queenside and along the c-file in particular.

If Black had played 8...Bb4, the game would have kept the characteristics of the Taimanov Defense. By pressuring the c3-Knight, Black could harry White's e4-pawn. But current opening theory maintains that after 8...Bb4 9.Nxc6 bxc6 10.Na4, White would have an advantage because of his control of the b6-square. Note that continuing this line of play would poison the e4-pawn: 10...Nxe4? 11.Qd4! would cost Black material.

Choosing 8...Bb4 or 8...Be7 is a matter of taste. Andersson prefers to have his pieces nicely packed together rather than a little bit dispersed as they would have been in the case of ...Bf8-b4.

A strategic error for Black would have been 8...Nxd4 9.Bxd4 Bc5? since 10.e5! would give White a large advantage in the center.

9.f4!

White sharpens the game. He threatens e4-e5, which would boot away the f6-Knight and effectively roll Black's pieces right off the board.

Black must therefore stop e4-e5 at all costs. Suddenly his earlier move 5...Qc7 makes much more sense. Black had *anticipated* this type of confrontation and had readied his defenses.

9...d6

Black parries with a forced and good reaction. Again, note how Black's pieces and pawns control a broad array of center squares, nearly all on his side! This means that the attacker will have to work twice as hard, spending extra tempi to move into Black's camp for a confrontation.

White's task will be as difficult as catching a mole that is making a mess of the front lawn. The animal burrows into its hole, making it a challenge for the attacker just to get a grip on it. A battle is fought simply to get the mole out of his hole. By the time that is achieved, the attacker is exhausted, and the mole is angry and ready to fight!

The point of this analogy is that White has to develop a strategic aim to avoid suffering a bruising counterattack. Think about *strategy* by forcing yourself to have a concrete goal. Abstract thoughts such as "I want to sacrifice all my pieces and deliver mate" or "If I can win a Rook, I'm sure I'll win the game" are meaningless.

Look back at the last diagram — it is much more vital to find the advantages and disadvantages of a given position. Black, although cramped, has no obvious weaknesses. The d6-pawn is a potential weakness, but Black can defend this pawn far more times than it can be attacked.

What about that word *cramped*? Black's pieces control less *space* than White's, and that is White's advantage. White should attempt to *increase* his spatial advantage. By developing and placing his pieces on better squares, he can then decide how to get at Black's position. Viewed from this perspective, White needs to involve his Queen and a1-Rook before taking a stab at Black's position.

10.Qe1

This is a standard maneuver in Open Sicilians. White repositions his Queen on an active square on the kingside in order to launch an attack.

10...O-O

Black tucks away his King. A good choice.

Going queenside isn't to be recommended at this point. After 10...Bd7 11.Rd1 O-O-O?, Black's King wouldn't have the necessary pawn shield. White could consider the immediate sacrifice 12.Ndb5 axb5 13.Nxb5 or the powerful 12.Qf2! to build a battery on the diagonal in preparation for Be3-b6. As a result, Black would face an unpleasant, though not impossible, defensive task.

11.Qg3

Now that Andersson has committed his King to g8, Ljubojevic readies his big guns.

And because he controls so much space, White has a number of options from which to choose:

- He can exchange Knights on c6 and continue with e4-e5. If the e3-Bishop can go to h6, a mate or a won exchange would be likely.

- He can play for f4-f5, in conjunction with Be3-h6 or even Qg3-h3, targeting Black's e6-pawn. In this case, White could create an e6-pawn weakness to exploit.

Having the room to choose plans is a real advantage.

11...Bd7!

Black has to keep a watchful eye on White's attacking ideas. The text connects the Rooks, preparing to make use of the c-file while keeping the e6-pawn protected.

Black's development doesn't permit him to aim for counterplay with ...b7-b5 because White's Bishops could exploit the resulting positions: 11...b5? 12.e5 dxe5 13.Nxc6 Qxc6 14.fxe5. Black would then suffer the double threat of Be2-f3 and Be3-h6, putting him in a rotten position.

The text is far better calculated. Black can prepare an exchange of Knights on d4 and play ...Bd7-c6, moving toward the center.

Middlegame

12.e5?!

Ljubojevic is eager to mix it up. As inspired as the move is, it is wrong. White hasn't completed his development — Ra1-d1 is missing — thereby setting himself up for an attacking failure.

Still, one can't be too critical of the move. At the board a player senses the nervousness of the opponent. If he thinks that a sacrifice might create particular problems for his opponent, bingo! He makes the sacrifice.

White's motivation for this pawn thrust is absolutely clear: he wants to open the board to his pieces as quickly as possible. But there are two drawbacks to this sacrifice. The first has been mentioned — the a1-Rook isn't participating. The second one is that after ...d6xe5, Black's e7-Bishop would be opened up. Note that White's King sits on g1. This makes the countermove ...Be7-c5 awkward to meet.

White should have prepared e4-e5 with either 12.Rad1 or 12.Kh1; then e4-e5 would have been more potent.

GM Jan Timman, from *The Art of Chess Analysis*, says it best: "In the present encounter, Andersson manages to show that the White action is premature. And a good thing too. My first reaction when I played over this game was, 'If this is good, then Black can't play the Sicilian anymore.'"

12...dxe5

Black naturally captures the pawn. The only other possible move would have been 12...Ne8 (12...Nd5? 13.Nxd5 exd5 14.f5 dxe5 15.f6 Bxf6 16.Rxf6 would be good for White); 12.e5 is justified because the f6-Knight has been forced to retreat.

13.fxe5

White follows up on his pawn sacrifice. He has burned his bridges since 13.Nxc6? Bxc6 14.fxe5 Ne4! 15.Nxe4 Bxe4 would be great for Black. He can defend his King with ...Be4-g6 when necessary, and his attack down the c-file is ready-made.

13...Nxe5

As before, Black is obliged to capture the offending e5-pawn.

If the f6-Knight moves, White's e4-e5 will have been justified. He has earned greater freedom for his pieces with ideas like Nc3-e4, Be2-d3 and Be3-h6. Here's the proof:

■ 13...Nd5? 14.Nf5! g6 15.Nh6+ Kg7 16.Nxd5 exd5 17.Nxf7! would net White at least a pawn. This tactic is based on a discovered check: 17...Rxf7 (White threatening Be3-h6+) 18.Rxf7+ Kxf7 19.e6+ picking up Black's Queen.

■ 13...Ne8 would be too passive. White could continue with 14.Nxc6 Bxc6

15.Bd3, aiming at Black's kingside. He could proceed with his sacrificial mode with 14.Ne4 Nxe5 15.Bf4 f6 16.Bg4, with a powerful attack.

■ Note that White's sneaky zwischenzug tactic after 13...Qxe5?? 14.Nxc6 Qxg3 15.Nxe7+! Kh8 16.hxg3 would gain a handful of extra pieces for White.

14.Bf4

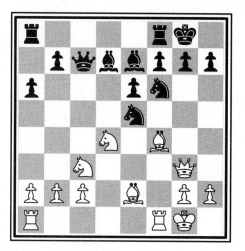

This was White's scheme: he has pinned Black along the h2-b8 diagonal. Black will suffer a congestion problem trying to break the pin and his play for the next few moves will be forced.

14...Bd6

This is the only way for Black to defend the e5-Knight.

15.Rad1!

With this powerful developing move, White aims squarely at the d6-Bishop that protects the e5-Knight. The piquant point is that White threatens the simple retreat Nd4-b3; then, after Rd1xd6 and Bf4xe5, Black would suffer material losses.

15...Qb8!

A marvelous defense. Black would like to move the e5-Knight, but the d6-Bishop needs protection. Protecting the d6-Bishop and then moving the e5-Knight would also lose. Thus the idea of being able to retreat by ...Bd6-c7 is forced.

Let's see what would happen if Black tried to move the e5-Knight:

■ 15...Nc4? 16.Bxd6 Qxd6 (16...Nxd6 17.Rxf6 would win a piece) 17.Bxc4 — White would win a piece.

■ 15...Nf3+ 16.Rxf3 e5 17.Bh6 Nh5 18.Qg5 exd4 19.Nd5 Qc5 20.Nf6+! — White would win the d7-Bishop — analysis by GM Jan Timman.

Another way to cope with White's threat of Nd4-b3 would be to block the d-file. GM Timman illustrates Black's problems:

15...Nd5? 16.Nf5! exf5 17.Nxd5 Qc5+ 18.Be3 Qc6 19.Nf6+ Kh8 20.Nxd7 Qxd7 21.Qxe5 — White thus would win a piece.

Following the text, Black's clever plan is to play 16.Nb3 Bc7! 17.Nc5 Bc6, neatly sidestepping all of White's threats. Black would like to solve his diagonal problems by protecting the c7-Bishop with ...Nf6-e8 and then playing ...Ne5-g6, to emerge a pawn ahead.

16.Rd3!!

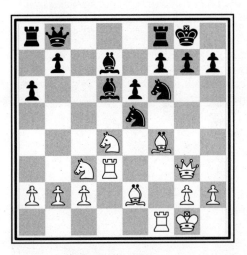

White makes a move of exceptional originality. He threatens Rd3-e3, "shish kabobbing" Black along the h2-b8 diagonal.

16...Ne8!

Stellar defense yet again. The d6-Bishop needs to be refortified so that the e5-Knight can move and break the pin. One nice touch is that 16...Nc4? 17.Bxd6 Qxd6 (17...Nxd6 18.Rxf6 wins a piece) 18.Rxf6 Qxg3 19.Rxg3! maintains the pin on the g-file, thereby winning a piece.

White has to continue to be creative in his attack, or else the loss of the e5-pawn will come back to haunt him.

17.Ne4

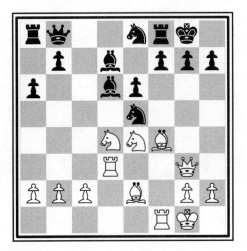

White attacks the d6-Bishop from another direction.

17...Bc7!!

Black was waiting for White's move and had his answer prepared. In accordance with the defensive scheme he had planned,

Black delivers a move of exceptional calmness and clarity.

It seems that no one has questioned the text. Neither GM Timman in *The Art of Chess Analysis* nor IM Srdjan Cvetkovic in *The Informator* considers 17...Nxd3!?, grabbing a Rook. Both annotators had registered 18.Bxd6 Nxd6 19.Nf6+ as winning for White and stopped. By no means is this the end of the line, however.

The variations that the annotators should have pointed out go as follows: with 17...Nxd3!? 18.Bxd6 Qa7!, Black takes advantage of a pin. In my note to White's 12.e5(?!), I pointed out that White's g1-King sits exposed to this type of a pin. That is why in many Open Sicilians, White often includes the tempo-loser Kg1-h1 within his attacks. Before reading any further, set up the position on a chessboard, and see what you would do as White to follow 18...Qa7, attacking the d4-Knight.

- 19.Bxf8 Qxd4+ 20.Kh1 Kxf8 21.Bxd3 Bb5! — trading pieces, White has insufficient compensation for his sacrificed pawn. He has to do better.

- With 19.c3!!, the position becomes pregnant with possibilities. What should Black do? Grabbing material with 19...Nxb2 20.Bxf8 Kxf8 21.Bh5 g6 22.Bxg6 hxg6 23.Qxg6

would allow White a vicious attack. Another capture, 19...Nxd6 20.Nf6+ Kh8 21.Bxd3 gxf6 (with 21...Bb5!? 22.Bxh7 Bxf1 23.Qh4 g5 24.Qh6, Black would be mated) 22.Qh4 f5 23.Qf6+ Kg8 24.Rf3 Rfe8 25.Qh6!, would result in unpreventable checkmate. Extraordinary variations! (Many thanks to American IM Nikolay Minev for spending an entire evening helping me with this position.)

Back to the text! Andersson certainly didn't analyze such a maze of variations. His intuition told him that he couldn't take the d3-Rook. With an extra pawn in his pocket, he didn't need more material. With 17...Bc7, he gets out of harm's way. Now the c7-Bishop is sufficiently covered, and the e5-Knight is raring to move.

18.Rc3!

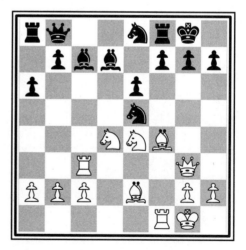

Sheer poetry! White keeps up the pressure by continuing to harangue the c7-Bishop. In fact, he has no other good moves.

18...Nc6!

I've known Ulf Andersson for nearly two decades and consider him to be an exceptional defender. Black can block the c-file with either 18...Bc6 or the text. As usual, Andersson has made the best choice.

Preventing Rc3xc7 by 18...f6? 19.Nc5! — immediately targeting the e6-pawn — would be a disaster. But 18...Bc6 seems to be an excellent move, except that Black's kingside would need more defenders. White could prepare a sacrifice on the e6-pawn. GM Timman is at his best as he points out two splendid wins for White:

■ 18...Bc6(?) 19.Ng5! h6 20.Ngxe6 fxe6 21.Nxe6 Rxf4 22.Rxf4 Nf7 23.Nxc7 Qxc7 24.Bc4 Qb6+ (necessary as 24...Ned6 25.Rxf7! would win) 25.Re3! Ned6 26.Bxf7+ Nxf7 27.Rxf7! Kxf7 28.Qf2+ — a devilish check. In this case, wherever Black moved his King, he'd lose his Queen to a discovered check.

■ Black could try to substitute 19...h6 with Bd6, but GM Timman's second illustration shows what would be Black's unpleasant fate: 18...Bc6(?)

19.Ng5 Bd6!? 20.Qh3 h6 21.Ndxe6 fxe6 22.Qxe6+, followed by Bf4xe5, wins for White.

In these variations we see White's pieces buzzing around Black's King like a swarm of bees. As he has done throughout his career, Andersson intuits the best defense.

19.Bxc7

It has been a struggle, but Black has managed to solve his problems on the h2-b8 diagonal. With the text, White has to accept that some pieces will be traded, reducing his initiative.

19...Nxd4!

Black shows that he can play tactically as well.

It would have been worse after 19...Qxc7 20.Nf6+! (the only way to win material) 20...Kh8 21.Qxc7 Nxc7 22.Nxd7 Nxd4 23.Rxc7 Nxe2+ 24.Kf2!. Black would have found himself having to lose either an exchange or a piece. In both cases White would gain excellent winning chances.

Now, Black would be happy to exchange Queens by 20.Bxb8? Nxe2+ 21.Kf2 Nxg3 22.Bxg3, since in this ending Black is a pawn up.

20.Bd3!

Excellent play — White knows at which address the Black King resides. The d3-Bishop now points itself in that direction.

20...Qa7!

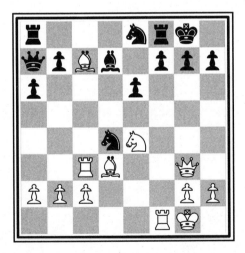

Thrust and counterthrust — Black now threatens a nasty double check by ...Nd4-

e2++, picking up White's Queen. It seems that Black has weathered White's attack; soon he will have an initiative.

Black has resisted the impulse to trade pieces. With 20...Nxc7? 21.Rxc7 Bc6? 22.Nf6+ Kh8 23.Nh5, White would win quickly because of the threats on the f7-pawn and the g7-pawn. By gaining the seventh rank with Rc3xc7, White would be handed concrete compensation for his sacrificed pawn.

21.Nc5!

Ljubojevic continues to play with fire. He is doing everything within his power to keep his attack alive. If White allows Black one moment to breathe by throwing away a tempo, the attack would be over.

If he had played 21.Kh1?! Nf5! 22.Qf4 Bc6! 23.Be5 f6!, White's attack would have hit rock bottom, because Black's King has plenty of faithful servants covering the entrances and exits.

The text, on the other hand, fits in splendidly. The d3-h7 diagonal is opened up, giving White the chance to relish a possible Bd3xh7+ and a quick battery on the h-file. Although Nc5xd7 isn't a threat yet, Black has to think about the a7-g1 diagonal.

21...Bb5?!

Oh, chess can be a sinister game! Sometimes the most natural move on the whole board is actually a howler. Black's move is as natural as a baby's smile. It is also a mistake. Black's motivation is clear — White's d3-Bishop is harassing the King, so he'll get rid of it. If Black can create a trade, ...Nd3-e2+ becomes a serious counterthreat.

Andersson should have taken the opportunity to get rid of the c7-Bishop. Because Rc3xc7 wasn't possible, now was the time. After 21...Nxc7! 22.Qxc7 Bb5!, Black would be doing very well. GM Timman's analysis continues with 23.Rf4 Bxd3 24.Rxd4 Rac8; the retreat ...Bd3-g6 would protect the King. GM Timman concludes that Black would thus stand better.

That being so, in the German chess magazine *Schach-Archive*, GM Ludek Pachman discovered a lovely way for White to save the game in spite of Black's fine move. He proposed 21...Nxc7! 22.Bxh7+! Kxh7 23.Qxg7+!! Kxg7 24.Rg3+ Kh7 25.Rh3+, securing a draw by perpetual check.

Fortunately for Andersson, the text is flawed only because it gives White a chance to attack yet again. It isn't a total howler after all.

22.Be5

White repositions his c7-Bishop also to aim at Black's King. Things are becoming distinctly unpleasant. Black would love to have his previous move back!

22...Nc6!

In this excellent retreat, Black avoids two traps in the position:

- 22...Nf5? 23.Bxf5! Bxf1 24.Be4 Bb5 (or 24...Rc8 25.Bd4 — threatening Nc5xe6 would be even better for White) 25.Qh4 f5 (not 25...g6?? 26.Qxh7+!; it would force mate in two) 26.Bxb7 would win back all White's sacrificed material with interest. White would gain a positional advantage.

- 22...Bxd3 23.Bxd4 Bxf1 24.Nxe6! fxe6 (mandatory, because 24...b6 25.Nxg7 would shatter the Black King's position) 25.Bxa7 Rxa7 26.Qb8 would snare the entangled a7-Rook — analysis by GM Timman.

Again, Black appears to be completely defended. If he can just play ...Bb5xd3, his extra pawn will tell. Unfortunately, all the previous complications have taken their toll on Andersson's clock. He is now under pressure with less time available to make extremely difficult decisions.

23.Bxh7+!

A picturesque sacrifice. Now that Black's pieces have been diverted to the queenside, White unleashes a barrage against Black's King. Since ...Bb5xd3 was threatened, this sacrifice was forced. The question is, will the sacrifice work?

23...Kxh7

Black continues to add to his collection of sacrificed White pieces. Black's morale is boosted by the fact that the c5-Knight is pinned and the c3-Rook has to play nursemaid to the Knight. Black is hoping White will simply run out of available attackers.

24.Rf4!

Ljubojevic continues to play all-out for the win.

American GM Lubosh Kavalek borrows a page from GM Pachman to point out that White has a perpetual check here: 24.Bxg7 Nxg7 (not 24...Rg8?? 25.Qh4+ Kxg7 26.Qg5+ Kf8 27.Rxf7+ Kxf7 28.Rf3+ Nf6 29.Rxf6+ — mate in one) 25.Qxg7+ Kxg7 26.Rg3+ Kh7 27.Rh3+, with the same perpetual as before.

64

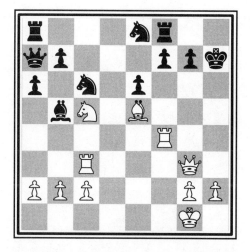

The idea behind the text is to set up a battery down the h-file by playing Rf4-h4+ and Qg3-h3. Although this is a disquieting threat, isn't that e5-Bishop left en prise?

24...f6!!

This is an extremely difficult defensive move to find. Once again, Black has several tempting choices, but, as we shall see, the text is brilliant. He plans to offer a safe landing for the King on the f7-square.

Two other possible moves seem to have endless ramifications. I like the text better than 24...f5, because on f6 the pawn acts as a better cover while attacking the e5-Bishop; in fact, 24...f5 has a direct refutation. The other defense, 24...Nxe5, simply captures all the things that White leaves en prise. Let's get a taste of what Andersson rejected:

■ 24...Nxe5 (a very consequent defense — one of the best ways to stop an attack is to capture the attacking pieces) 25.Rh4+ Kg8 26.Qxe5 (forced — the battery 26.Qh3 Ng6! is refuted by protecting the h8-square) 26...Qb6! (a suggestion by Yugoslav GM Dragoljub Velimirovic: Black readies ...f7-f6 but first defends the e6-pawn) 27.a4! (the only way to disturb Black's plan of ...f7-f6) 27...f6! (after 27...Bxa4 28.Qe4! f6 29.Qxa4 Qxb2 30.Qd4!, the dominating position of White's pieces gives him fine compensation for his two pawns — analysis by GM Jan Timman) 28.Qxe6+ Qxe6 29.Nxe6 — GM Timman considers this position to offer White a large advantage. I disagree. After 29...Bc6 30.Nxf8 Kxf8 31.Rd3 Kf7!, Black should draw this ending.

■ 24...f5!?—this defense becomes a mind-bender. Scores of GMs and chess clubs around the world have been attracted to it. I will skip the myriad number of side variations and just walk through its distilled main line. 25.Rh4+ Kg8 26.Qg6 (setting up for Rc3-h3 and Rh4-h8 checkmate; Black has to push away the g6-Queen) 26...Nxe5 27.Qxe6+ Rf7 (not 27...Nf7 28.Rch3 Qxc5+ 29.Kh1 — an Rh4-h8 mate is inevitable) 28.Qxe5! Rd8

29.Rch3 Rd1+ 30.Kf2 Rf1+ 31.Kg3 f4+ 32.Kg4 Nf6+ 33.Kg5. White's King survives, but Black's perishes — analysis by GM Timman. The final position from this line deserves an analysis diagram:

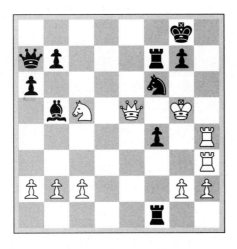

These variations indicate why chess is such a tough game. At some point general considerations, principles, and even tactics have to give way to concrete calculations. When to start calculating, and to what depth, requires judgment that shows chess to be an intuitive sport as well as a strategic one.

25.Rh4+

White moves to set up the h-file battery.

25...Kg8

Black is forced to retreat but knows he's ready for ...Kg8-f7 and a great escape.

26.Qh3

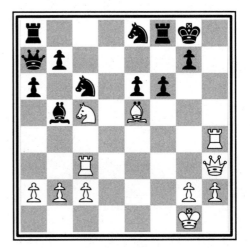

White pursues his strategy with dogged determination. He now threatens mate in three.

26...Nd8!!

This extraordinary move epitomizes Andersson's unique defensive style. Black burrows his pieces along the back rank. Covering the e6-pawn certainly looks like a sensible reaction.

In the postmortem, Andersson was critical of this move, pointing out that 26...f5 would have been better. White could not play Qg3-g6 because he has already committed his Queen to h3. Because of the threat of ...Nc6xe5, it seems that White would be compelled to make a perpetual check: 26...f5 27.Rh8+ Kf7 28.Qh5+ Ke7 29.Qg5+ Kf7. His c5-Knight and c3-Rook are almost completely knotted up. Playing for the win by 30.Bxg7? Nxg7 31.Rh7 Rg8 32.Kh1 Rd8! with a back-rank mating threat could easily rebound.

So, with 26...f5, Black could have made a draw. Does that mean that 26...Nd8 is bad? Not at all! The text doesn't spoil Black's position and in fact keeps his winning chances alive! After all, Ljubojevic has to prove the soundness of his sacrifices.

A winning attempt that Black should not make would be 26...Qxc5+ 27.Rxc5 Nxe5, gaining three minor pieces for the Queen. Normally this would be a good deal for the player getting the three pieces, but White has a combination to win a piece back: 28.Rh8+ Kf7 29.Rxf8+ Kxf8 30.Qa3!. Setting up a discovered check and taking advantage of the pin on the a-file to grab to the b5-Bishop, White would win — analysis by Henk Jonker.

27.Bd4

The drawback of Black's previous move is revealed. White's attacked e5-Bishop moves with tempo. White now threatens 28.Rh8+ Kf7 29.Rxf8+ Kxf8 30.Nxe6+ and Bd4xa7, winning Black's Queen.

27...b6!

A fine defensive reaction. Black blocks White's threat and attacks the c5-Knight. Also, Black's a7-Queen can now swing over to the kingside to save her monarch.

28.Nxe6

This move is forced. White would get nowhere by playing 28.Rh8+? Kf7 29.Qh5+ Ke7 30.Rxf8 Kxf8 31.Qh8+? Ke7 because he would run out of checks and attackers. Black's next move would be ...Nd8-f7, protecting the e7-King with tempo.

28...Nxe6

Black happily exchanges defender for attacker. White's threat had been Rh8xf8+, winning a Rook.

29.Qxe6+

Recapturing a piece with check is a good idea.

29...Qf7!

As advertised — Black has done a marvelous job in taking care of his King. But White isn't through yet. He still has plenty of tricks. Note that 29...Rf7? 30.Rch3! would get Black mated. Black had to counterattack the e6-Queen.

30.Qe4!

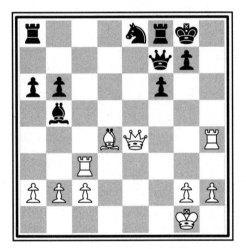

A crowning moment for Ljubojevic's play. He threatens both Qe4-h7 mate and the a8-Rook. Have all the sacrifices paid off?

Endgame

30...g5??

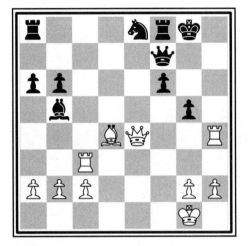

Time trouble rears its ugly head and produces a howler. It is this costly mistake that pitches the game. Jan Timman considers Andersson's mistake to be caused by the deep spell of White's attack.

The text seems so natural. Black prevents Qe4-h7 mate, while also attacking the h4-Rook. But it causes insurmountable problems in defending his King. The g7-pawn and f6-pawn act as a shield. The farther the shield goes from the body of the King, the weaker it becomes. With a cool head, not influenced by the ticking clock, Andersson would have realized that the best way to beat White's attack would be with one of his own. Black would be on the rampage after 30...Qxa2!! — escaping from the mate on h7 and offering White the a8-Rook. Black then would have deadly counterplay based on the threat of 31...Qa1+ 32.Kf2 Qf1+, flushing out the White King.

Could White withstand the attack and grab the Rook? Nope!

After 30...Qxa2!! 31.Qxa8? g5! (Black would play g5! before flushing out the White King to g3 to weave a mating net and deny White the possibility of Qa8-d5+: note that 31...Nd6? 32.Rh8+! would be good for White) 32.Rg4 (keeping a watch over the f4-square since 32.Rh6? Qb1+ 33.Kf2 Qf1+ 34.Kg3 [34.Ke3? Qe2 mate] 34...Qf4+, and it would be mate in two moves) 32...Nd6! (continuing to deny White the option of Qa8-d5+) 33.Qf3 Qb1+ 34.Kf2 Qf1+ 35.Kg3 Nf5+ 36.Kh3 Kf7!! — Black would set up a mate on the h-file — analysis by GM Timman. Because the counterattack is so strong, White would be obliged to force a draw with 30...Qxa2!! 31.Qh7+ Kf7 32.Qh5+ Kg8, accepting a perpetual check. Black would not be able to avoid the draw because 32...g6? 33.Qh7+ Ng7 34.Rc7+ Ke6 35.Re4+ Kd5 36.Re1 would be far too dangerous for him.

31.Rh6!

By this time, Ljubojevic too is struggling with time pressure. White is prepared for a decisive penetration down the h-file.

Another nice win would be found in 31.Rg3 Ra7 32.Rxg5+ fxg5 33.Rh8 mate, proving how badly the move ...g7-g5 has hurt.

31...Ra7

Black saves the Rook while threatening ...Ra7-e7 with powerful counterplay. Black is one move short, however, as White's threats come first.

32.Rch3

With this immediately decisive move, White threatens mate in two.

32...Qg7

A sad decision, but the threat of Rh6-h8 had to be stopped.

33.Rg6

Winning Black's Queen leads to an advantage in force and a technical win.

33...R8f7

Andersson is still trying to get in ...Ra7-e7, setting up counterplay. But the position is already beyond his formidable defensive capabilities.

34.c4!

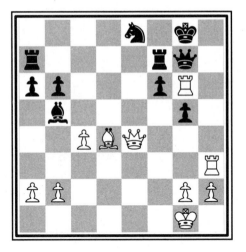

The last precise move. After 34...Bd7 (34...Bxc4 35.Qxe8+; 34...Ba4 35.b3; 34...Rae7 35.Rxg7+ Rxg7 [35...Nxg7 36.Qh7+] 36.Qd5+ — White would win a piece) 35.Rxg7+ Rxg7 36.Qd5+ Rf7 37.Rh8+ Kxh8 38.Qxf7, Ljubojevic would win.

Black resigns.

I'll quote Jan Timman's final tribute to this game from *The Art of Chess Analysis*: "On behalf of Raymond Keene, Ken Rogoff, and Gudmundur Sigurjonsson, who, when I showed them this game, followed it as avidly as I did when I first played it through, I want to convey the feeling that overcame us ... that this was the best game of the last twenty years."

Time-Trouble Misery

Following their 1974 match in Moscow, Anatoly Karpov and Victor Korchnoi were regarded as the two best *active* players of the day. The question of how Bobby Fischer would fare was constantly raised. After Karpov and Korchnoi's match in Moscow, cataclysmic changes affected both their lives. In 1975 Anatoly Karpov became the new FIDE champion by forfeit, and his stature in the Soviet Union grew enormously. He was to enjoy every benefit that the state could provide. Victor Korchnoi's life took another turn. He would soon defect to the West and settle in Switzerland, and the country of his birth would brand him a criminal.

From different sides of the world, the East and the West, these two men won the world's strongest chess events. As FIDE champion, Karpov awaited his eventual challenger from the FIDE candidate cycle. Korchnoi fought his way through the elimination matches with wins against Tigran Petrosian, Lev Polugaevsky, and Boris Spassky.

The 1978 FIDE championship match was played in Baguio City, the Philippines. The match, featuring a model sportsman of the Soviet Union versus a defector, soon became complete theater. There were protests and counterprotests over nearly everything. The players refused the ceremonial shaking of hands before the game.

In the book *Chess Scandals* by Ed Edmondson and GM Mikhail Tal, we're treated to an inside look at the rough-and-tumble world of championship chess. In his preface to game 17, Edmondson — one of the three members of the jury that handled player protests — offers this marvelous firsthand account:

"In a violent outburst beginning just three minutes before his clock was started, Korchnoi dug in his heels and refused to play unless Dr. Zoukhar was moved farther back in the hall from the fifth row seat he had occupied a few moments earlier. He angrily asked Dr. Filip, filling in again as chief arbiter in Schmid's absence, to summon one of the organizers to carry out his demand.

"Florencio Campomanes and the Chief Marshal quickly came to the stage and engaged the furious challenger in urgent conversation. By then it was 5:00 P.M. and Filip started White's clock. Karpov, playing Black, discreetly retreated to his dressing room; the surest way to preserve a certain degree of tranquillity, he evidently decided, was by avoiding any involvement in what threatened to become an ugly altercation.

"Korchnoi to Campomanes and Filip: 'No matter what your jury thinks the rules say, I tell you this man Zoukhar disturbs me. If he is not moved within ten minutes, then I will move him.' (Shaking a fist with obvious intent.)

"Campomanes unhesitatingly accepted Victor's word that he was disturbed and did his best to calm the situation. With spectators crowding around, he held an extremely impromptu jury meeting in front of the stage. Leeuwerik [chief of Korchnoi's delegation] and Baturinsky [chief of Karpov's delegation] were, as always, strictly at odds. The latter did suggest that Dr. Zoukhar might move if Korchnoi would forsake his dark glasses, but Campomanes replied that this was a separate issue on which the three arbiters had previously made a decision.

"Campomanes then asked we three neutral members of the jury (Lim, Edmondson and Malchev) whether we thought this emergency called for a decision by the jury or by the organizers. We were unanimous: 'The organizers. If either player later protests, then the jury must decide whether or not it is in agreement with the actions of the organizers.'

"The chief organizer then decided (for this game only) that no spectators would be allowed any closer to the stage than the seventh row. After everyone — including Zoukhar and Leeuwerik — had been moved back, Korchnoi made his first move with eleven minutes already gone on his clock."

Despite all the antics, the players still managed to play chess. It proved to be a heartbreaking match for Victor Korchnoi. He would lose 6–5 after 32 games.

When you lose a sporting contest by the narrowest of margins, you begin to think of all the earlier moments wherein you might have improved your performance. One of those earlier moments was game 17. This isn't so much a brilliant game as it is the strangest of the match. It offers a wealth of middlegame ideas, peculiar endings, and finally a finale so stunning that it left everyone in shock.

■ ■ ■ ■ ■ ■ ■ ■ ■ ■ ■ ■ ■

Nimzo-Indian Defense

GM Victor Korchnoi
GM Anatoly Karpov
1978 FIDE Championship
Baguio City (Game 17)

Opening

1.c4

Through most of his career, Korchnoi has preferred the English Opening move order, which will transpose into a Queen Pawn Opening.

1...Nf6

This has been Karpov's standard opening move when facing either Queen Pawn or English openings. Black develops his position while controlling the e4-square and d5-square.

2.Nc3

In turn, White develops and controls the same squares.

2...e6

This move opens the diagonal for the f8-Bishop. Black likewise could have played 2...e5 with a transposition to a reversed Sicilian, a defense that Karpov has played on many occasions.

3.d4

A bit of a surprise — Korchnoi usually favors 3.Nf3 to keep his options open. The text is a direct transposition into a Queen Pawn Opening. To keep the original flavor of the English, 3.e4 d5 4.e5 d4 is a popular alternative.

3...Bb4

Black pins the c3-Knight in order to double White's pawns by ...Bb4xc3+ or simply to keep pressure on the center, particularly the e4-square.

This opening defense was devised by Aaron Nimzovich (1886–1935) and is called the Nimzovich Defense. With a name like that, it understandably was quickly nicknamed *the Nimzo*. At the time that Nimzovich introduced his defensive strategy, his peers were less than enthusiastic. The advantage of the two Bishops was revered, and preparing to give one away so early in the opening was distrusted. Today's GMs consider the Nimzo to be a first-rate defense against the Queen Pawn Opening.

4.e3

This move — the Rubinstein Variation of the Nimzo Defense — was introduced by Akiba Rubinstein (1882–1961). It is also known as the Rubinstein Complex. This opening attempts to prevent Black from being allowed to double White's queenside pawns by 4.Qc2, 4.Qb3, or 4.Bd2, all preparing a2-a3 and to recapture on c3 with a piece.

At first the move e2-e3 appears to be unduly modest. White blocks in the c1-Bishop before it develops; thus, 4.Bg5 would be a popular move. This move received a lot of attention after a series of notable victories by Boris Spassky. It is called the Nimzo-Indian, Spassky Variation, or sometimes the Nimzo-Indian, Leningrad Variation. (A discussion of 4.Bg5 would take us too far astray.)

The Rubinstein Variation (4.e3) has concrete aims. White intends Bf1-d3 and Ng1-e2, preparing to recapture on c3 with the e2-Knight. After this operation, White would continue with e3-e4 with a

Victor Korchnoi

Victor Korchnoi was born on March 23, 1931, in Leningrad. His life has been very difficult; he just managed to survive World War II. He became an international grandmaster in 1954. Perhaps his harsh life's experience has molded his style of play. His tenacious defense, combined with a fine counterattacking style, has made him a feared competitor. He won the Soviet championship three times before defecting to the West. He was the challenger for the FIDE championship in 1978 and 1981 and lost the candidates final in 1974, which served as the FIDE championship match.

massive center. Black could not expect to control the center using only his pieces. He would have to employ his center pawns, too.

4...O-O

Black safeguards his King before taking concrete action in the center. Black has a host of alternatives — 4...c5, 4...b6, 4...d5, or the offbeat 4...Ne4 have all been extensively used.

5.Bd3

Bringing out the Bishop to a nice diagonal, White tries to regain control over the e4-square. This is important — he wants to build up an imposing pawn center by e3-e4.

5...c5

Striking back in the center, Black doesn't want to allow White a free hand to play e3-e4.

Black had two other main choices. 5...d5 would stop e3-e4 directly; Black would usually follow up with ...c7-c5, continuing to challenge White's center. The other choice would remedy the problem c8-Bishop. Black could try 5...d6 in order to continue with ...e6-e5, with play in the center. At such an early stage, which defense to play is a question of taste.

6.d5?!

With this bold yet reckless move, White tries to put a central clamp on his opponent. The d5-pawn, if maintained, would seriously impair Black's piece mobility. The problem is that White's pieces aren't exactly well placed to support this advance. The c3-Knight is pinned, and the d1-Queen is blocked.

Nevertheless, the move can't be completely condemned. Psychological reasons motivate it. Korchnoi has spent countless hours studying Karpov's games and his style of play. He knows that Karpov doesn't like to play cramped defensive positions, the kind of position that d4-d5 would produce if White is allowed a free hand. This means that Black has to undertake rigorous action to avoid falling into a passive position because of White's pawn center. To refute the text, Karpov would have to *risk* something — that is the psychological twist. With the correct forceful action, Black will get a fine game.

6...b5?!

This interesting error is produced by psychological factors. To stop White from achieving a central *pawn wedge*, Karpov knows he has to react forcefully. By offering a pawn sacrifice, Black will get good play for his pieces, and the decision is made.

The alternative was 6...exd5 7.cxd5 Nxd5 8.Bxh7+ Kxh7 9.Qxd5, restoring the material balance. An unusual posi-tion would be reached. Black would have good play in the center and with the two Bishops. On the other hand, his kingside pawn shield would be compromised. And this was Korchnoi's second discovery. Like most GMs, Karpov jealously guards the pawn shield protecting his King. Korchnoi has discovered that Karpov was willing to sacrifice pawns and pieces before compromising his King's position.

With 6.d5, Korchnoi gambled that Karpov wouldn't compromise his King and would sacrifice a pawn instead. With 6...d6! 7.Ne2 Nbd7! (threatening ...Nd7-e5 and the *purchase* of the d3-Bishop) 8.f4 exd5 9.cxd5 Nxd5! 10.Bxh7+ Kxh7 11.Qxd5 Nf6, Black would have excellent central play, while his compromised King position would be just a bluff. There are no White pieces in the vicinity. After the further moves 12.Qd3+ Kg8 13.O-O d5!, Black would have the advantage.

The sacrifice ...b7-b5 has much to be said for it. In return for a pawn, Black gets the chance for a mass of center pawns and fluid play for his pieces. Not a bad deal, right? Not exactly — a pawn has value. To get concrete compensation for the pawn, Black will have to find a target in White's position. Game 7 of this 1978 match featured the same opening. In that game, Karpov kept on sacrificing material to maintain a dwindling initiative. He was lucky to save his skin.

7.dxe6

White shows his determination to accept the pawn sacrifice. Clearly bad for White would be 7.cxb5? — either 7...exd5 or 7...Nxd5! would give Black a big advantage in the center.

7...fxe6

A rather automatic recapture. Black *captures toward the center*, thereby increasing his ability to control that area. You can see a swarm of central pawns forming for Black. From the point of view of piece mobility, Black gets to employ his f8-Rook on the half-open f-file.

Besides the automatic ...f7xe6, an interesting try would be 7...bxc4 8.exf7+ (the only way to win a pawn — after

8.exd7?, Bb7! would give Black good development) 8...Rxf7!? 9.Bxc4 d5, with sharp but probably unsound play for the pawn.

The text is the most consistent move, wherein Black builds up a big pawn center.

8.cxb5

Korchnoi has achieved what he hoped for: he has won a pawn. "Chessically" speaking, Korchnoi has been known to be willing to walk on hot coals for an extra pawn. Karpov also knows that Korchnoi is at his happiest when he is ahead in material. Karpov hasn't sacrificed a pawn with a light heart — he has a new plan in mind.

Middlegame

8...a6!?

This is Karpov's new idea. In game 7 of this match, he had played 8...Bb7, forcing 9.Nf3, and after 9...d5, a difficult game had ensued. In that game, Korchnoi was able to play Nf3-g5-e6-c7xa8! — quite a journey. Karpov wasn't anxious to force White to play Ng1-f3.

The text is a page out of the Benko Gambit (1.d4 Nf6 2.c4 c5 3.d5 b5 4.cxb5 a6) in which Black gambits a queenside pawn to gain time to bring his c8-Bishop to the a6-square.

In the opinion of Danish GM Bent Larsen, allowing White to play Ng1-e2 is quite nice for the first player. In this way, he can avoid problems related to ...d7-d5 and ...e6-e5-e4, forking the d3-Bishop and the f3-Knight. I agree with Larsen and am not convinced that 8...Bb7 is not the better move.

9.Ne2

White happily develops his kingside. As is the case when up in material, White needs only to develop and then start trading all the pieces to realize the advantage of his extra pawn.

9...d5

The point of Black's pawn sacrifice — Black enjoys a nice wedge of central pawns. Black's strategy will be equally simple. He will move his center pawns as far as possible. This will keep White's pieces cramped. From a position of greater mobility, Black will then search for an attack from either wing of the board.

10.O-O

There's a story about a trainer of the Soviet Women's Olympic Chess Team. Because of nervousness, he arrived late to a round. Upon entering the tournament hall, he asked a spectator if all the members of his team had castled. When the answer for some members was affirmative, he sagely nodded his head and said, "That is good." For those who had failed to castle, he would shake his head sadly and say, "We have to work harder."

Korchnoi does a good thing. He tucks his King away to bed and starts to turn his attention to the queenside. Why?

Because you should *try to create play on the side of the board on which you have the advantage.*

10...e5!

With this consistent follow-up of his previous play, Black's center acts to confine White's pieces. Because of his space and superior mobility, Black will try to launch a kingside attack. He has various piece placements to choose from. He can try ...Bc8-b7, ...d5-d4, and ...e5-e4. Or he can try to play for ...e5-e4, cutting off White's defenders and going after the h2-pawn with ...Nf6-g4 and ...Qd8-d6.

In his plan of attacking White's King, Black has a problem: what to do with the b8-Knight. It would take a lot of tempi to bring it to the kingside, not to mention the problem of where to put it once it got there. Black does have a plus regarding the a8-Rook. It is easy to visualize a variation that would make a Rook lift by ...Ra8-a6 and swing to the kingside.

11.a3

The right idea — White puts the question to the b4-Bishop. Although it is sitting out on the b4-square, Black could reroute the b4-Bishop toward the kingside by ...Bb4-d6 after playing ...c5-c4. It is a good idea to get Black to commit himself to a course of action.

11...axb5?!

This misguided move helps White by clarifying the picture on the queenside. Black prevents the threat to his b4-Bishop with the pin on the a-file. The best move would have been 11...Bxc3 12.Nxc3 (12.bxc3 c4! 13.Bc2 axb5 would win back the pawn) 12...e4! 13.Be2 d4 14.Bc4+ Kh8 15.Ne2, with a difficult position to access. Black has been able to push his center, but it isn't clear whether the pawns are strong or overextended.

Another possibility would be GM Mikhail Tal's suggestion of 11...Ba5!? — keeping the Bishop. In this case, White could return the pawn by 12.b4!? cxb4 13.axb4 Bxb4 14.Qb3, with the intention of e3-e4 to harass Black's center. White would have the advantage.

12.Bxb5

White finds the proper way to recapture. White escapes both ...c5-c4 and ...e5-e4, attacking the d3-Bishop.

12...Bxc3?

This move is inconsistent with Black's last one. Black had played ...a6xb5 to pin the a3-pawn, taking away the threat of a3xb4. With his last move Black made it appear as if the threat a3xb4 was real. It would have been better to play, for example, 12...Bb7, awaiting 13.Bd2 (now the threat a3xb4 would be made real) 13...Bxc3. Here the d2-Bishop would not be so wonderfully placed.

In any case, Black has no real opportunity for equality. 12...Bb7 13.Rb1! Ba5 (13...Bxc3 14.bxc3, opening up the b-file, would be good for White) 14.b4 would be advantageous to White, because he would be able to utilize his extra queenside pawn. Black's best option was probably 12...Ba5, planning ...Ba5-c7 to aim at White's King. The immediate response 13.b4?! Bxb4! would not work for White. He might consider 13.Na4 as an alternative.

13.bxc3!

Karpov had clearly underestimated this excellent move. One of the best ways of dealing with a pawn storm — in this game, a *central* one — is to get pieces out

of the way. In this case, by refraining from 13.Nxc3, White doesn't put his pieces in harm's way. Now the impact of Black's potential ...d5-d4 or ...e5-e4 has been neutralized. Although White injures his queenside structure by accepting *split pawns*, the c3-pawn does a great job of halting Black's center.

Now White has a ready-made plan in which a3-a4 and Bc1-a3 hit the c5-pawn. Black's dreams of launching a piece attack on the kingside have gone up in smoke. From now on, Black will be thrown on the defensive.

13...Ba6

Black develops the queenside pieces at last, although he has a number of problems to worry about. The moves a3-a4 and Bc1-a3 by White can cause the c5-pawn trouble. He can chip away at the

Black center by playing c3-c4 or f2-f4. Black has to keep a vigilant eye on all of these possibilities. The only way to address these problems, however, is by developing his own position. The b5-Bishop is doing good work, so Black decides to get rid of it.

14.Rb1!

Now an exchange of Bishops results in the White Rook's being brought to Black's b5-square, allowing Black's c5-pawn to be harassed. Note the simple principles that White is following. Move Rooks to open files; play on the side on which you have the advantage. Sound, classical play.

14...Qd6!

Black makes a good move in a difficult position. It is by no means clear what Black should do. Indeed, it seems anything he tries to do will only help White.

After 14...Bxb5 15.Rxb5 Nbd7 16.a4, Black would be under pressure. With 14...Nbd7 15.Bc6! Bxe2 (the only possible move, since 15...Ra7 16.Bxd5+ would win a pawn with check) 16.Qxe2, Black must surrender another Bishop. The text keeps an eye on the entire Black center — remember all of White's possible undermining moves. Black's move also prepares for ...Nb8-d7 when Bb5-c6 is no longer possible.

This type of move is one of Karpov's hallmarks: he has the ability to remain calm under pressure and create the stiffest resistance in difficult positions.

15.c4!

Korchnoi is truly an agent provocateur. With an extra pawn in his pocket, he thinks, "Black's only compensation is his nice pawn center — let's destroy it!" He intentionally lures the center pawns forward in the hope that the unprotected squares that they leave behind will become possible outposts.

This approach is justified. After 15.a4!? Nbd7 16.Ba3 Rfb8 17.c4 Bxb5 18.Rxb5 Rxb5 19.cxb5 Nb6!, Black would have managed to stall White on the queenside.

15...d4

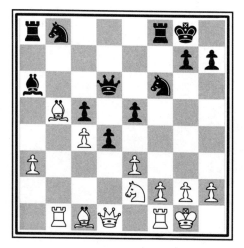

Black has no choice. His trump is his mighty pawn center. If he were to allow c4xd5, both the c5-pawn and e5-pawn would become isolated and weak.

16.Ng3

White aims for the e4-square and the f5-square.

GM Mikhail Tal, in his notes from *Chess Scandals*, considers that the more undermining 16.f4(?) would be a mistake because 16...d3! 17.fxe5 dxe2 18.Qxd6 exf1=Q+ 19.Kxf1 Ne8+ would allow Black to emerge a piece ahead. Tal also suggests that after 16.f4, Bb7 wouldn't be bad; he cites 17.fxe5 Qxe5 18.exd4 Qe4, hitting the b1-Rook and the g2-pawn, as good for Black.

Both variations, although nice, result from White's being a bit too cooperative.

In fact, 16.f4! would be the critical move. With c2-c4, White was trying to lure Black's center forward so that he could destroy it. The move f2-f4 would do precisely that. If White could play f4xe5 and e3xd4 in succession, he would not only win a pawn, he would destroy Black's only trump and emerge two pawns to the good! I think that 16.f4! would be an excellent move to destroy Black's position. Let's look closer at the two lines given by Tal:

■ After 16.f4 Bb7 17.Rb3! — preventing ...d4-d3 renews the threat of f4xe5's winning a pawn. Momentarily, Black is unable to create a Queen and Bishop battery on the a8-h1 diagonal. Even if he could, White now has the defensive resource Rb3-g3. Let's continue our analysis: 17...Nc6 18.fxe5 Qxe5 (with 18...Nxe5? 19.exd4 Neg4 [19...cxd4 20.Qxd4 wins a pawn] 20.Bf4, then d4-d5 wins) 19.exd4 Nxd4 20.Nxd4 (20.Re3 Ne4! allows Black good piece activity) 20...cxd4 21.Bb2 — White emerges with the two Bishops and an extra pawn in an open position.

■ But I'm being unfair to Tal. His actual preference was 16.f4 d3! in which the only consideration is for 17.fxe5, which loses. White has a good position after 16.f4! d3! 17.Ng3! e4, the only move to stop the center from collapsing.

White has successfully enticed the center forward. 18.Bb2 Bxb5 (White threatened Bb2xf6; thus 18...Nbd7? 19.Bxd7 Qxd7 20.Bxf6 wins the e4-pawn) 19.cxb5 Nbd7 20.Qb3+ Kh8 21.a4!? is strong for White. Black's pawns are further advanced, but they are blocked. At some moment the sequence Bb2xf6 and Qb3-c4 will be good for White.

We can conclude that far from being a mistake, 16.f4 would've been good for Korchnoi.

16...Nc6!

The Knight finds the right square. Black intends ...Nc6-a5, not only blockading White's a-pawn but also putting considerable pressure on the c4-pawn.

17.a4

White moves in order to activate the c1-Bishop.

17...Na5

Complementing his previous move, Black immediately attacks the c4-pawn. Trying to block the b-file by 17...Nb4? 18.Ba3! would be bad for Black.

18.Qd3

Now a tense struggle revolves around the fate of White's c-pawn. If Black can win it, he will have excellent chances. Conversely, if White can hold it, he will have the advantage.

18...Qe6

Black continues to hound the c4-pawn. GM Tal suggests 18...Bb7!? to gain counterplay on the a8-h1 diagonal. But after 19.f3!, it's not clear what Black could hope to accomplish.

19.exd4

In order to prevent ...Na5xc4, White now exchanges pawns.

19...cxd4

There was no choice. After 19...exd4 20.Ba3! Rfc8 21.Rfe1! Qf7 22.Nf5, White could have siezed the initiative.

20.c5

By this maneuver, White gets to keep his c-pawn.

20...Rfc8

An awkward move. Black would prefer to develop his a8-Rook, but 20...Rac8?? would leave the a6-Bishop en prise. 20...Bxb5? 21.axb5 would give White connected passed pawns and a winning game. Going after the c-pawn by 20...Qd5 21.Rfe1! Qxc5? 22.Ba3 would result in getting skewered.

21.f4

At last, White brings about the collapse of Black's center and thereby earns a clear advantage. All the annotators were unanimous in their praise.

■ White could have considered 21.Rfe1, intending Qd3xd4. For example, 21.Rfe1 Rxc5 (21...Qd5 22.Nf5 Qxc5 [22...Kh8 23.Qg3] 23.Ba3 Qc3 24.Qxc3 Rxc3 25.Bb4 would eventually emerge in an ending with an extra pawn) 22.Qxd4 exd4 23.Rxe6; then Black could play 23...Bxb5 24.axb5 Nb3 25.Ra6! Rac8, preserving the balance. Korchnoi likely saw these endings but felt that Black's open King position would offer favorable attacking possibilities.

■ A move that White properly avoided was 21.Ba3? Nd5! with possibilities of ...Nd5-f4 and ...Nd5-c3.

21...Rxc5

Black wins back the pawn, if only temporarily.

22.Bxa6?!

This move is inconsistent with White's plan.

GM Tal, a master of the initiative, points out that 22.fxe5 Rxe5 23.Bf4! would give White a sudden and dangerous attack. Tal is right on the money with this one. I'd add only that 23.Qxd4 would regain a healthy extra pawn in a position where the two Bishops can operate.

After the text, White has the better ending, but Black has resources in this ending. It would have been much better to go for the attack.

22...Qxa6

A forced recapture. After 22...Rxa6? 23.Rb8+ Kf7 (23...Rc8 24.Rxc8+ Qxc8 25.fxe5 would win Black's center) 24.Ba3 Rc3?? 25.Rf8, checkmate would appear on the board. Again, because of his exposed King, Black is happy for the opportunity to trade Queens.

23.Qxa6

Korchnoi has seen a favorable ending and doesn't hesitate to go for it.

23...Rxa6

A relief — Black knows he's in an inferior ending, but White will have to show good technique to win the advantage.

Endgame

24.Ba3

Developing with tempo, White now hopes for 24...Rc3? 25.Bb4 Re3 26.Bd2 with the threats f4xe5 and Bd2xe3, through which White would win material.

24...Rd5

The only way for Black to protect the e5-pawn.

25.Nf5!

When playing 21.f4, this was the position Korchnoi had in mind. White introduces his Knight into action with the threat of Nf5-e7+, forking King and Rook.

White correctly rejected a series of checks by resisting 25.Rb8+ Kf7 26.Rf8+ Ke6 27.f5+ Kd7 28.Rf7+ Kc8! 29.Rxg7 (29.Rc1+? Rc6 would get nowhere) 29...e4! in which Black's connected passed pawns would give him the advantage. A rather advanced case of "Patzer sees a check" — in fact, a whole series of them.

Now Black will have an impossible time keeping the material balance. White has two threats, the fork on e7 and the trade f4xe5, ...Rd5xe5, Nf5xd4, swiping a pawn.

25...Kf7

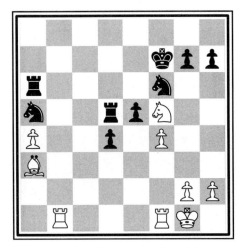

Black continues a brave march forward. Karpov realizes that he's about to lose a pawn and therefore seeks piece activity as compensation. In the ending, the King can become an aggressive fighter, not just a worried general in need of protection. Meeting the threat of Nf5-e7 isn't easy.

Perhaps Black should have sacrificed the exchange with the speculative 25...e4!? 26.Ne7+ Kf7 27.Nxd5 Nxd5, hoping that the connected passed pawns could save the day.

26.fxe5!?

Korchnoi is being taunted by opportunity.

Amusingly, of the many annotators to this game, only GM Miroslav Filip of the Czech Republic considers 26.Ne7, giving it a dubious mark because in his estimation

27...e4 would offer Black compensation. Was 25...Kf7 the best move? If Karpov had played 25...e4, then 26.Ne7+ Kf7 would have given a direct transposition to GM Filip's line.

The other try for White after 25...e4!? 26.Rb8+ Kf7 27.Rf8+ Ke6! 28.Nxg7+ Kd7 29.Rf7+!? Kc8 would leave him in a similar situation to the "patzer sees a series of checks" variation. Black has a dangerous pair of pawns.

So was 25...e4!? Black's best move? The answer must lie with 26.Ne7+ winning the exchange. This is what I meant about Korchnoi's being taunted. Instead of the text, in which he wins a pawn, could play 26.Ne7, winning the exchange. Let's check out the compensation: 26.Ne7!? e4 27.Nxd5 Nxd5 28.Rb5! forcing either 28...Nc3 or 28...Ne3, since 28...Ke6? 29.f5+ Ke5 30.Bf8! Ra7 31.Bc5 Ra6 32.Bxd4+ Kxd4 33.Rd1+ would win for White. Let's look at Black's two alternatives:

- After 28...Nc3 29.Rf5+ Kg6 (29...Kg8?? 30.Rf8 mate! or 29...Ke6 30.Re5+ Kd7 31.Bb4 Nc4 32.Rc5 would be good for White) 30.Rg5+ Kf6 31.Bb4 Ne2+ (31...Nc4 32.Bxc3 dxc3 33.Rc1 would be good for White — in principle, whenever White can split up the passed pawns, Black is doomed) 32.Kf2 Nc6 (32...Nxf4? 33.Rxa5 wins) 33.Kxe2 Nxb4 34.a5 Rc6 35.Rd1, the extra exchange is greater than the passed pawns. White should win.

■ After 28...Ne3 29.Rc1! Nac4 30.Bc5 d3 31.Bxe3 Nxe3 32.Rc7+, White has all the winning chances.

That's quite a jumble of variations to calculate! It's made even more difficult by the fact that Korchnoi has been playing for several hours already. Now Korchnoi begins to face his bête noire — time trouble.

Both players are allowed two and a half hours to complete their first 40 moves. Failure to do so means a forfeit on time. Korchnoi was down to his last ten minutes of the first time control. Understandably, he sidesteps this complicated morass and plays to keep it simple.

26...Rxe5

Naturally, the f6-Knight can't move because of the discovered check on the f-file.

27.Rb5?!

Further inconsistency.

Being short of time, White's task would have been a lot simpler if he had played 27.Nxd4, grabbing a pawn while it was hot. After 27.Nxd4 Re4, the simplified nature of the position might lead to a draw, in the view of GM Tal. Although it is true that Black would have drawing chances, White, a pawn ahead, would have winning chances. Furthermore, because of his time trouble, White would reduce his risk of missing a tactic.

White is expecting 27...Rxb5 28.axb5 Rb6 29.Nxd4, in which the a4-pawn becomes a more dangerous-looking b5-pawn.

27...Nc4!

Black makes a strong and practical decision. Since Korchnoi is running short of time, Karpov is happy to activate his a5-Knight and create some unusual tactics.

Keeping the position *alive* by refusing to simplify is an excellent way to take advantage of your opponent's time trouble. Black intends to meet 28.Rxe5 Nxe5 29.Nxd4 Rxa4, making a comfortable draw.

28.Rb7+!

This is the only way for White to play for a win. The trick 28.Nd6+? Rxd6 29.Rxe5 would boomerang to 29...Nxa3!, allowing Black to win material. Here, White flushes out the Black King with a series of checks.

But who is actually on the attack? Will White win because Black's King is exposed, or will the active Black King become a strong piece?

28...Ke6

Black centralizes the King. 28...Ke8?? 29.Nxg7+ Kd8 30.Bc1 would have been a horrible error — Black would have put his King in a great deal of danger by going to the back rank.

29.Nxd4+

White grabs the right pawn. If he had played 29.Nxg7+? Kd5!, Black's d4-pawn would have become the strongest pawn on the board, while White's army is a bit far-flung and in disarray.

Because the a3-Bishop is en prise, White could also consider 28.Bf8, trying to weave a mating net. But with the level-headed response 28...d3! (not 28...Rxf5? because 29.Re7+ would win the f5-Rook), White would come a cropper. Black's d-pawn would be far too potent.

29...Kd5!

Proving that the King can be a powerful piece, Black's King bravely marches into the center of the board. Now two White pieces are en prise.

30.Nf3!?

This move is not a bad decision but an unduly sharp one. After 30.Nc2! Rxa4 (30...Nxa3? 31.Nb4+ would fork King and Rook) 31.Bf8, White would still have the better chances because of the exposed Black King. White is anticipating giving up his two minor pieces for the e5-Rook along with a couple of pawns — a reasonable approach given that White takes no risk in such endings.

30...Nxa3

Black is happy to grab the a3-Bishop. After the moves 30...Re2 (30...Re8 31.Be7 Kc6 32.Rfb1 would be excellent for White) 31.Bf8, Black would have fallen into grave difficulties.

31.Nxe5

White implements his plan of getting the e5-Rook.

These types of endings are very easy to misjudge. Because of the open position, White's Rooks operate at full power. But to win the game, White will have to advance his pawns, trying to win one of Black's Knights in the process. Therein lies the difficulty. When play is devoted to a single side of the board, the Knights' cavalry can leap about, causing a lot of confusion. In grandmaster experience, the Knights draw far more often than lose.

In his work *Karpov versus Korchnoi: The World Chess Championship, 1978*, GM Bent Larsen points out that after 31.Rd1+ Kc6! 32.Rb3 Re4 33.Rxa3 Raxa4 34.Rc3+, Black would draw without difficulty, even though his King is on the wrong side of the board and not supporting his g7-pawn and h7-pawn.

31...Kxe5

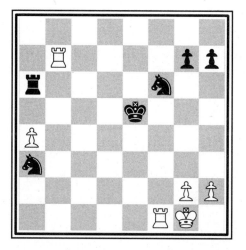

Now the endgame battle has taken shape. White will try to win all the pawns on the kingside, while Black will try to coordinate his forces to prevent White from mobilizing his kingside pawns.

32.Re7+!

In time trouble, the natural inclination is to check the opponent and think about it later. Here the check works well.

White needs to drive the Black King away from the kingside, in order to win the g7-pawn and h7-pawn. 32.Rxg7? Ke6! 33.Rg3 Nc4 34.Rgf3 Kf7! would allow Black to crawl back and keep things together on the kingside.

32...Kd4

Black chooses the best square, as 32...Kd6 33.Rxg7 would interfere with the a6-Rook's ability to protect the f6-Knight.

With 32...Kd5, Black's King would step onto a square that the f6-Knight might want to go to. It's important to mobilize your pieces without interfering with their ability to move to the best squares.

33.Rxg7?!

White makes another rushed and ill-considered move.

For the last dozen moves or so, I've been critical of Korchnoi's moves. He'll put a logical plan into effect and then switch horses. White should have driven Black's King as far away from the king-side as his previous move intended. The smart thing to do would have been 33.Rd1+ Kc3 34.Rc7+! Kb3 35.Rxg7, driving Black's King to the far side of the board. White could then have tried to work on winning the h7-pawn.

33...Nc4!

Black brings the Knight back into the game. Black needs only to establish his Knights on f6 and e4 to create a fortress and make a draw. The text brings the a3-Knight back into play in order to establish such a fortress.

34.Rf4+?!

GM Tal is critical of this check, suggesting it should have been left alone. I agree.

If White had played 34.Re7 in order to play Rd1+ and drive Black's King away, he could still have hoped to keep Black's forces from coordinating. Korchnoi was down to his last six minutes for six moves.

34...Ne4!

Black's move fits the motto "Time above material" — GM Tal. Undoubtedly this move came as a shock to Korchnoi. Instead of grittily holding on to his last pawn, Black makes a cohesive force from his remaining army.

35.Rd7+

White shows doubts about grabbing the h7-pawn. After 35.Rxh7 Nd2!, Black could plan ...Ra6xa4 and ...Kd4-e3 in order to harass White's King. The effect of this piece deployment would leave the f4-Rook without a future. So White first decides to involve his f4-Rook before biting the h7-pawn.

35...Ke3!

Instead of being stuck in a galaxy far, far away on the queenside, Black's King has snuggled up to the kingside, where he can help torment White's King.

36.Rf3+

White decides that on f3, the Rook will play a more active role.

36...Ke2

A forced and good move! Black's King is uncomfortably close to its counterpart.

37.Rxh7

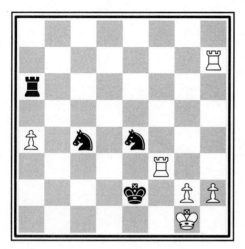

White zaps Black's last pawn. With that done, White is now certain that he can't possibly lose. But how will he win? Black's army is well poised to attack White's King. Indeed, remove the a4-pawn, and Black can threaten mate in two!

37...Ncd2!

Black sets White up for a very subtle trap.

After the expected 37...Rxa4 38.Rf1 Ne3 39.Rb1, Black's active pieces would have allowed him to make a repetition by 39...Nd2 40.Rc1 Nb3 41.Rb1 Nd2, with a draw. Thus when Karpov played the text, he knew he had a draw in hand! Instead, he chose to explore *his* winning chances!

38.Ra3?!

With his f3-Rook and a4-pawn under attack, White's first impulse is to save both!

Being in time trouble, a safe way to force the draw would have been to play 38.Rhf7 Rxa4 39.h3 Nxf3+ 40.Rxf3, with a book draw. Black's Knight could stop White's pawns from running too far.

38...Rc6!

Black threatens mate. Again, with no time to think, a player's first impulse is to cover the first rank.

39.Ra1??

White falls headlong into the crafty trap.

The best move would have been 39.g3! Nf3+ 40.Rxf3 (40.Kg2 Ne1+ 41.Kh3 [41.Kh1 Rb1 would have spelled trouble] 41...Ng5+ would have walked into a Knight fork) 40...Kxf3 41.Rf7+, resulting in a drawn position.

39...Nf3+!!

A shocking move. After 40.gxf3 Rg6+ 41.Kh1 Nf2, White will find himself mated.

White resigns.

As a postscript to this game, I offer a quote from Ed Edmondson from *Chess Scandals*: "It took Petra [Leeuwerik], [GM] Yasha Murey, [GM Michael] Stean and [GM Oscar] Panno five minutes to recover sufficiently to rise from their seats. As this group slowly left the hall, the three players shook their heads over the way Korchnoi had blown what they all thought was a win."

A Sunny Moment

I hope, dear readers, that you will be tolerant with me concerning my next choice. It features one of my own games. My opponent was the FIDE World Champion Anatoly Karpov, and the game was played in London in 1982. I wrote an article about the game for *The Seattle Weekly*, and my notes to the game as well as this preface appeared around the world. For this book I've embellished upon my earlier writing.

I met Karpov for the second time across a chessboard during the April 1982 Phillips and Drew Masters International in London. Playing the World Champion again was enough to get my blood pumped up. But if there was a need for additional motivation, I found it in the memory of our first meeting two months earlier during a tournament in Mar del Plata, Argentina. I had him down and wounded then but let him slip away with a draw.

He too remembered that event, I was sure. And that thought kept me in bed a moment longer when I awoke on the morning of the match. The truth was, though, I enjoyed my nervousness. I was happy to be fighting the World Champion — win, lose, or draw, I would be doing something that I had dreamed about.

I prepared for Karpov by spending several hours the night before with Victor Korchnoi, three-time challenger for the World Championship. Korchnoi, who had become my close friend during the time I helped him train for his unsuccessful assault on Karpov, is a Soviet refugee who loathes the Soviet system and the chess players it turns out. He knew that one of Karpov's strengths was a strong finish. We agreed it would be important psychologically to force Karpov to adopt a passive system — in particular, the T.M.B. Variation of the Queen's Gambit. This system was introduced by Savielly *T*artakower, improved by Vladimir Andreevich *M*akogonov, and refined by Igor Zakharovich *B*ondarevsky is a great favorite of Karpov's. The T.M.B. was hotly disputed in the 1981 World Championship in Merano, Italy, where Karpov scraped by with two draws from miserable positions against Korchnoi. We hoped he would be stubborn and try once again to prove it sound.

Walking to the tournament hall, I met Boris Spassky, a former World Champion and a fellow countryman of Karpov's. "Enjoy your day in the sun," Spassky said.

I was late. Karpov seemed ready — certainly the photographers and television crew were. The experience could have been unnerving, but I knew I belonged in the arena of professional chess. My clock began ticking and the world disappeared.

■ ■ ■ ■ ■ ■ ■ ■ ■ ■ ■ ■ ■ ■ ■

T.M.B. Queen's Gambit Declined

GM Yasser Seirawan
GM Anatoly Karpov
Phillips and Drew, 1982 (Game 11)

Opening

1.Nf3

This crucial opening move is important in inducing Karpov to play the T.M.B.

If I had adopted the English 1.c4, I would have had to be prepared for the active rejoinder 1...e5, which Karpov chooses upon occasion. The straightforward Queen Pawn 1.d4 would allow the Nimzo-Indian and Queen's Indian systems of which Karpov is a renowned master.

1...Nf6

With Karpov's most standard rejoinder, systems with ...e7-e5 are out of the way. Now for the next hurdle.

2.c4

I was now concerned that Karpov might play 2...b6, transposing into a Queen's Indian Defense (Q.I.D.).

The Q.I.D. has a solid reputation. In that defense, Black takes a restrained role in the center, fianchettoing his Queen's Bishop. He develops his kingside with ...e7-e6 and ...Bf8-e7 or ...Bf8-b4, giving the opening a Nimzo-Indian character. I was begging for the Queen's Gambit.

2...e6

So far, so good. The text is a prelude to ...d7-d5.

3.Nc3

After 3.d4, I'm sure Karpov would have chosen a Q.I.D. The text is my best chance to get him to play the Queen's Gambit. He has two choices that he has played quite often, 3...c5 and 3...Bb4, which would keep an English flavor to the opening. I haven't committed myself to d2-d4, which gives him a number of other options.

3...d5

Thank you. I'm now in the opening that I spent hours preparing for the night before.

4.d4

This move matches Black in the center. We're now in a direct transposition from the move order 1.d4 d5 2.c4 e6 3.Nc3 Nf6 4.Nf3, while narrowing Black's range of defenses.

4...Be7

Black makes the best choice. The Vienna Variation, with 4...Bb4!? 5.Bg5, would offer sharp play almost immediately, but Karpov prefers a slow buildup of his position before forcing complications.

5.Bg5

As in Game One of this book, I choose the same move that Bobby Fischer used. A comforting thought! A few more moves, and we'll reach the positions that Korchnoi and I have prepared.

5...h6

As we've seen in other games, Black puts the question to my g5-Bishop.

Interestingly, chess opening theorists have begun to argue whether this move should come before or after Black has castled. It seems to me to be a question of taste.

6.Bh4

A popular alternative would have been 6.Bxf6 Bxf6 7.Qd2, getting ready to castle queenside. In this case, the idea is to continue with g2-g4, h2-h4, and g4-g5 after Black has castled kingside.

6...O-O

Lucky me — Karpov has chosen his favorite defense, and I get the chance to spring an interesting new idea on him.

7.Rc1!

This move initiates a key position to the T.M.B. I plan to delay the move e2-e3 in order to retain the possibility of a kingside fianchetto. This may seem strange with a h4-Bishop, but I have some specific ideas about initiating an early queenside attack.

A safer move would have been 7.e3, as in Game One.

7...b6

Karpov repeats the variation that he played in the FIDE World Championship in Merano in 1981.

Now I had to recall our analysis from Merano. To prepare for this game, I had concentrated on Karpov's most recent treatment, 7...dxc4, liquidating the central tension. Korchnoi and I had spent half the night worrying about this.

Black would prefer to refrain from ...d5xc4 because if White then was able to play Bf1xc4, White could benefit by rapidly developing his pieces. The sample line 7...dxc4 8.e3 c5 9.Bxc4 cxd4 10.exd4 Nc6 11.O-O Nh5 shows Black forcing the trade of a pair of minor pieces, but White would then have an advantage in space, giving him a slight pull.

I think that curiosity got the better of Karpov in this game. He was aware that I was a coach for Korchnoi in the 1981 match, and he wanted to test the strength of our preparation. As we shall see, Karpov wasn't idle. He and his team of coaches had worked for many days on this variation.

8.cxd5!

I open the c-file for the c1-Rook.

8...Nxd5!

This step is necessary because White has an early advantage in space; it is important for Black to exchange pieces to make room. This same trading device was used by Boris Spassky earlier in Game One.

9.Nxd5

Consequent follow-up, in which I am creating a leading role for my c1-Rook.

9...exd5

In view of the threat to the c7-pawn, this recapture is forced.

10.Bxe7

Everything is proceeding according to my plan.

10...Qxe7

Reaching a standard position in the T.M.B., Black hopes to make use of his queenside majority as well as the half-open e-file.

11.g3!?

This little nuance is actually a big deal.

If I had played 11.e3, the game would have directly transposed into the opening of Game One. In studying that game, you might have noted the difficulty that White had in utilizing his f1-Bishop. In a hanging-pawn position, the f1-Bishop has an awkward task in pressuring the d5-pawn. With the text, White anticipates a hanging-pawn position in which the fianchettoed Bishop could flex its muscles. We're still in standard opening theory; the extent of our homework is about to be revealed.

Middlegame

11...Re8!

Here is Karpov's improvement, for which Korchnoi has prepared a novel response.

In Merano, Karpov had tried 11...Bb7?! and received a bad position for his effort. The text is far more sensible. Black utilizes the half-open e-file in order to pressure the e2-pawn. In this way he hopes to demonstrate that the kingside fianchetto was ill advised.

12.Rc3!

This is Korchnoi's idea! Its advantages are deceptively subtle:

- White adds a measure of protection to the Nf3; for example, 12...c5? 13.dxc5 Bb7 14.cxb6 d4 15.Qxd4! grabs the loot.

- White will neutralize Black's pressure on the e-file by Rc3-e3.

Note that the immediate 12.Bg2 Ba6! would have undone White's strategy. The e2-pawn would have become a sensitive point. With 13.e3, White's King would be stuck in the center because of the influence of the a6-Bishop.

Sufficiently impressed with myself, I meandered around the stage awaiting Karpov's reply. As impressed as I was, I had certainly assumed that my move would be at least as much of a surprise to Karpov. It was I who was surprised to see his reply so speedily forthcoming.

12...Na6?!

Karpov played after only 11 minutes of thought!

Most grandmasters, when confronted with a novel idea, stew for about one hour in order to double-check the road ahead for possible ambushes. Once convinced that their position is sound, they react. Karpov's quick reaction caused a warning light to go off in my head. I was beginning to smell a rat.

Naturally, Korchnoi's team had prepared for everything — everything except 12...Na6?!, which we had all rejected outright. The saying "Knight on the rim deserves a trim" had prejudiced us into underestimating the move. I stared at Karpov's icy exterior and didn't discern anything. This was especially annoying. If your opponent maintains such grimness, it's hard to get excited about your own position.

What Black wants to achieve is the freeing move ...c7-c5. He then plans to answer d4xc5 with the recapture ...Na6xc5, bringing his Knight to a strong square. Even if this Knight recapture ends up with the loss of the d5-pawn, Black isn't worried. His compensation after ...Bc8-b7 and ...Ra8-c8 will be tremendous.

13.Qa4!

I enjoyed my thoughts for 24 minutes before selecting this move. It is the most challenging. The intended break ...c7-c5 is stopped because Rc3-e3 is a tremendous threat. I now expect hysterics:

■ 13...Rd8? 14.Ne5 would be masochistic.

■ 13...Qe4 would surprisingly rebound after 14.Nd2!! Qxh1 (14...Nc5 15.Rxc5) 15.Qxe8+ Kh7 16.Qxf7, giving White the upper hand. In this line, the plight of the a6-Knight is comical: 13...Qe4?! 14.Nd2 Bd7! 15.Qxd7 Qxh1 16.Qa4! lets White win two pieces for a Rook.

■ Finally, 13...Bb7 would be no bargain: 14.e3! Qe4! 15.Bg2! Qb1+ 16.Kd2! Qxb2+ (16...Qf5!?) 17.Rc2 Qb4+ 18.Qxb4 Nxb4 19.Rxc7 Ba6 20.Rb1 would allow White to win material.

Believing Karpov to be in a heap of trouble, I began to walk to calm my fraying nerves. GM Efim Geller, a roly-poly grandmaster with tremendous international experience, was intently watching the progress of the game when I strolled by him. Geller had excitedly grabbed GM Jan Timman — the world's second-highest-rated player — by the arm and exclaimed, "...c5!" Pretending I hadn't overheard, I continued my pace. "...c5! — doesn't that lose a piece?" I thought. Geller, as Karpov's chief trainer, was obviously very familiar with the position.

13...c5

When I saw this move, my heart sank into my shoes. "Oh, [bleep]!" I thought. I had obviously fallen into *his* preparation. Karpov had foreseen my strategy and had prepared a piece sacrifice. White's

threat is Rc3-e3, and Black has chosen to ignore it. Karpov doesn't sacrifice his pieces based on intuition, but rather when he is 99 percent sure that the sacrifice is correct. He had called my bluff. I thought for 15 minutes about declining the sacrifice with 14.e3 c4 or even 14.Re3 Be6 15.Bh3, but in both cases I would be worse off!

The text drew a great murmuring from the audience that packed the Greater London Council Chambers for the daily games. I could see them gawking at the demonstration board, excitedly pointing out that I could win a piece.

14.Re3

Since I have no choice, I might as well ride the tiger and go for the gusto. At times like this, when a player is nervous about falling into a losing trap, the solace provided by having some extra material in hand is rather comforting.

14...Be6

Black can't move his Queen because his e8-Rook would be captured. This text, while forced, leaves the a6-Knight hanging.

15.Qxa6

This move is not a happy decision. I am sweating bullets looking at my poor King, which is stuck in the center. Despite my frantic analysis, I didn't see a winning line for Karpov.

15...cxd4

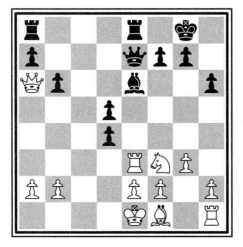

Having sacrificed a piece, Black is eager to open the position in order to expose my King. He intends to use the c-file to invade with his Rooks. My immediate problem is dealing with ...Qe7-b4+, which could harass my King.

16.Rb3

Preventing ...Qe7-b4+ is priority number one.

So far everything has been forced. Certainly Karpov had prepared the sacrifice, but he now surprises me by thinking for 34 minutes! Was the sacrifice correct after all? My moves have been good, solid, forceful ones. Thus the sacrifice was bogus! What has Karpov seen?

Black has three choices: 16...Qc5, 16...Rac8, and 16...Bf5.

■ With 16...Qc5 17.Qd3! (scurrying back to the defense, White prevents ...Qc5-c1 checkmate) 17...Qa5+ (17...Rac8 18.Nxd4 Qa5+ 19.Rc3 would save White's skin) 18.Qd2 Qxa2 19.Nxd4 Rac8 20.f3!! (making room for Ke1-f2, escaping to the kingside) 20...Qb1+ 21.Kf2 Rc1 22.Nxe6! fxe6 23.Qd3! Qa1 24.Ra3!, White wins.

■ With 16...Rac8 17.Nxd4! Rc1+ 18.Kd2 Rc4 (18...Qc5? 19.Rc3! wins) 19.Nxe6 fxe6 20.e3, White emerges a piece ahead.

Or . . .

16...Bf5!

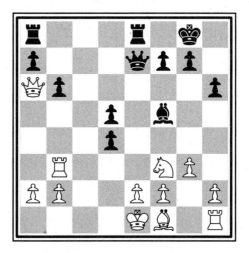

Karpov finds the best move. Since the other two alternatives would both lose for Black, he tries to rescue his game by winning back some material. Black prevents the defense Qa6-d3 and at the same time plans ...Bf5-c2, attacking the b3-Rook that inhibits ...Qe7-b4+.

Although the text is the best move, it came as a bit of a relief. Black has to waste tempi on the maneuver ...Be6-f5-c2xb3, which gives me just enough time to save my King.

17.Bg2

The Bishop moves in order to exit stage right. If I can sprint my King to safety, the material that Black has sacrificed will leave me with a technically won game.

17...Bc2

Black has no choice but to pick off the b3-Rook. His other options would produce the following unprofitable results:

- With either 17...Qc5 or 17...Rac8, 18.-O-O can calmly stroll away from an invasion down the c-file.

- Black's trick 17...d3, threatening ...Qe7xe2 checkmate, would be a mistake. After 17...d3? 18.e3 d4 19.Nxd4 d2+ 20.Kxd2 Rad8 21.Rd1, all of Black's threats would be finished. White would consolidate his King's position and pocket the point.

18.Nxd4!

Karpov clearly missed this move in his preparation. He thought White would be forced to play 18.O-O, which would allow 18...Bxb3 19.axb3 Qxe2 20.Qxe2 Rxe2 21.Nxd4 Rxb2, with a rough equality. But if I can retain the e2-pawn, all endgames will be winning for me.

18...Bxb3

Black wins a Rook for two pieces.

In general, such a trade is favorable for the winner of the two pieces: a Rook is worth five points, but the pieces are worth three each, for a total of six points. This particular position will favor the pieces over the Rooks. Why? The answer concerns files.

In this position, only the c-file is open. Black will find his operations along the e-file to be blocked. Once Black takes control of the c-file, it will be difficult to coordinate an attack. That's because White doesn't have any weak pawns.

But that is a principled view. From the specific point of view of this game, Black has several weak pawns, especially the isolated d5-pawn and the a7-pawn. If Black is unable to bother White's King, his position will slowly worsen.

19.Nxb3

I make the only possible move. After 19.axb3??, Qb4+ would win the d4-Knight.

19...Rac8!

In this natural move, Black quickly puts a Rook on the open c-file.

Black must not be beguiled by 19...Qb4+? since 20.Kf1 Rac8 21.Bf3 and Kg2 would give White a decisive advantage; Black would have misplaced his Queen and left his a7-pawn unprotected. This type of maneuver — Ke1-f1-g2 — is known as *castling by hand*. White must make three moves to bring his King to safety, but once he gets to the g2-square, he will be very comfortable.

Endgame

20.Bf3!

The final point — without sacrificing the e-pawn by 20.O-O, I achieve a technically winning position.

It was only at this point that Karpov allowed his poker face to slip. GM Efim Geller, who had been immersed in his own game, now surfaced to see Karpov's miserable position. As Geller stared in open astonishment at the position, Karpov's face suddenly turned crimson. He fixed Geller with a long scornful stare. The suggestion was clear: "Comrade, when we return to Moscow, we shall talk!" Geller hurried away. Karpov again returned to the board to think. I felt exalted and couldn't sit still. It was still necessary to keep my killer instinct pumped up.

In the postmortem, Karpov, commenting on his preparation, explained that he had overlooked White's Bg2-Bf3 possibilities, a deadly mistake. The protected e2-pawn completely neutralizes Black's battery on the e-file. Black will have to spend tempi to bring his major pieces into play.

20...Rc2?

In this final mistake, Black intends to capture the b2-pawn, but the Rook will be woefully misplaced.

The only hope for Black to prolong the game would have been 20...Qf6! 21.O-O Qxb2, at which point the Black Queen would have a chance of causing some damage.

21.O-O

What a pleasure to castle out of danger!

At the point that Karpov sacrificed a Knight, I could only hope for such a possibility. With my King tucked away, I can refocus my thoughts upon winning. The first order of the day will be to improve my pieces. I'll do that by bringing them to strong positions where they can control space.

21...Rxb2

Collecting as much wood as he can, Black hopes for an ending without Queens, which would improve his survival chances.

When you are in a bad position, it is a good rule of thumb to capture as much as you can! You never know — maybe your opponent will run out of troops.

22.Rd1

This move is not such a clear choice. It would be very tempting to play 22.Rc1, gaining control of the c-file. I choose the text because I want to win back some material, specifically the d5-pawn.

22...Rd8

Black hopes for 23.Rxd5 Rxd5 24.Bxd5 Rxe2, whereby he can trade his weak d5-pawn.

23.Nd4!

Very nice. The Rook on b2 is completely dominated. Black's Queen must stand guard to prevent Qa6-a3, which would snare the quarry. The Rook on b2 will be a constant tactical target. Black must also watch out for Nd4-c6, which would fork Queen and Rook. With these threats, the rest of Black's pieces cannot prevent White from making inroads.

23...Rd7

The first order of the day is to save material. Black gets out of the threatened fork and protects his attacked a7-pawn.

24.Nc6!

My position is a picture of harmony, but how can I win?

Because the b2-Rook lacks protection, I devoted a lot of time to trying to coordinate an attack on the g7-pawn with an attack on b2 before discovering the above move. For instance, 24.Nf5 Qe6 25.Qc8+ Kh7 26.Qc3 looks like a win. But Black could intervene with a timely ...Qe6-f6, stopping the threats. While searching for the most exact win, I found a remarkable piece sacrifice, again based on the hanging b2-Rook.

24...Qe8

Black does his best to save material.

If he had moved 24...Qc5, 25.Qc8+ would pick up the d7-Rook. The check Qa6-c8 can't be allowed, so Black blocks it. After 24...Qf8, the simple 25.Bxd5 would win a pawn because Black's Queen is no longer attacking the e2-pawn.

25.Nxa7!

The point is grabbing pawns! I now threaten Na7-b5, a2-a4, Qa6xb6, harvesting the queenside.

My main line is a piece sacrifice, which leads to a forced win: 25...Qa8 26.Rc1! Qxa7 27.Rc8+ Kh7 28.Qd3+ g6 29.Qd4 (threatening the b2-Rook and Rc8-h8 checkmate; play remains forced) 29...Rb1+ 30.Kg2 f6 31.Qxf6 Rg7 32.Qf8 g5 33.Qf5+ (33.Bh5), and Qxb1! would win a Rook and the game.

25...Rc7

With this move, Karpov regains his poker face. Too late! He has already revealed himself. Besides, I have worked out a forced win.

26.a4!

Once more I challenge Black to accept the piece. If he doesn't, it will take only Na7-b5 and Qa6xb6 to complete the harvest.

I didn't want to play 26.Rxd5 Rb1+ 27.Kg2 Rcc1 with counterplay against my King because I had seen a trick — 28.h4?? Rh1! with the threat ...Rb1-g1 checkmate — which gave me a shudder.

26...Qa8

At last the piece sacrifice becomes irresistible to Black. If he had chosen 26...Rb4, 27.Nb5 Rcc4 28.Nd6 would win material.

27.Rxd5

I had this move in mind when my Knight went hunting. The Rook blasts its way into the game.

27...Qxa7

Black captures the offered sacrifice with a heavy heart. The Knight has given his all and will be redeemed by getting the Black King.

Black's counterattack 27...Rc1+ 28.Kg2 Rbb1 29.Rd1 would get him a lost ending, whereas 27...Rxa7? 28.Qd3 followed by Rd5-d8+ would cost him the Black Queen. Karpov prefers to go down fighting.

28.Rd8+

With this most forcing move, I will weave a mating net that Black will have to walk into.

28...Kh7

It is a lucky thing that Black had made luft at move 5. Review the notes to Game One about the importance of making luft *before* the middlegame begins.

29.Qd3+

The audience is becoming noticeably agitated. They can see that although I'm the exchange down, White is now winning.

29...f5!

Karpov is still kicking. He can't play 29...g6 30.Qd4 Rb1+ 31.Kg2 f6 32.Qxf6 Rg7 33.Qf8 g5 because White would have mate in two moves.

30.Qxf5+

I pick up a pawn with check. Black is forced to loosen his pawn shield just a little bit more. If at this moment I hadn't calculated a forced win, then 30.Ra8, trapping Black's Queen, would have been the best move.

30...g6

This is the only way for Karpov to block the check. Before reading further, can you spot the win? Warning — it is trickier than you think!

31.Qe6!

I avoid the trap.

I stayed away from 31.Qf6? because 31...Rc1+ 32.Kg2 Qg7! would give Black a chance at survival. Now I am faced with 31...Rg7 32.Qe8 g5 33.Be4+ or 31...Rc1+ 32.Kg2 Qg7 33.Rd7, winning the Queen.

Black resigns.

Karpov stopped the clock, shook my hand, and congratulated me. I have watched Karpov lose four games — two to Victor Korchnoi in Merano in 1981 and two in Mar del Plata in 1981 — but I had never seen him resign. This historic moment was the first time in 27 years that a reigning FIDE World Champion had lost to an American in tournament competition. In his whole career, Bobby Fischer wasn't able to defeat a reigning FIDE World Champion before his 1972 match with Boris Spassky.

Suddenly I was showered in warm applause and received a mighty embrace from Korchnoi, who had watched the whole game. I was immediately enrolled in the rather exclusive $400 Club. To become a club member, you have to beat Karpov in tournament play. A check for $400 then arrives with compliments from Victor Korchnoi.

▀▄▀▄▀▄▀▄▀▄▀▄▀▄▀▄▀▄▀▄▀▄▀▄▀▄▀▄▀▄▀▄

Olympian Effort

F rom the time that Bobby Fischer stopped tournament competition, two players, Anatoly Karpov and Victor Korchnoi, had dominated the two top rungs
of the chess ladder. But time doesn't stand still. Younger players were beginning to make an impact on the chess hierarchy. The best of the pack was a relentless
tactician from the city of Baku in Azerbaijan. His name was Garry Weinstein. In
1975, at the age of 12, he had changed his name to Garry Kimovich Kasparov.
Kasparov was to blaze his name across the chess heavens, a meteor that still shines
as brightly today.

At the time the following game was played, Victor Korchnoi was still considered
the second-best player of the day. The young wolves were still jostling for position.
This game was played at the 1982 Lucerne Chess Olympiad. The olympiad is played
every two years. In the 1994 Moscow Chess Olympiad, more than 120 men's teams
and 80 women's teams competed for medals.

In the 1982 olympiad, one single game stood out above all the others as a great
brilliancy; even today its complexities are still being debated. The experienced Soviet
defector Victor Korchnoi, representing the Swiss team, was playing against the
Soviet Union. We had all expected Anatoly Karpov to be Korchnoi's opponent. But
for this game, Karpov demurred and was replaced by the fiery Garry Kasparov. We
all watched transfixed as the players uncorked a masterpiece.

■■■■■■■■■■■■■
Modern Benoni A64

GM Victor Korchnoi
GM Garry Kasparov
1982 Lucerne Chess Olympiad

Opening

1.d4

Korchnoi momentarily puts aside his foxy English Opening, opting instead for a straight Queen Pawn Opening. Kasparov already had a growing reputation for playing sharp, risky defenses as Black. Korchnoi was interested in testing one of them out.

1...Nf6

Kasparov doesn't show his defense yet.

In those days Kasparov often played the classical Tarrasch Defense of the Queen's Gambit Declined — 1.d4 Nf6 2.c4 e6 3.Nc3 d5! 4.Nf3 c5!?. Korchnoi had spent most of his career combatting such classical defenses. It was more likely that Kasparov would choose something a little more modern, trying to sidestep Korchnoi's advantage of experience.

2.c4

White plays the most standard response.

The alternative Trompovsky Attack, 2.Bg5!?, is enjoying a resurgence of interest among today's grandmasters.

2...g6

Black still masks his intentions.

Two of Kasparov's favorite defenses are the Grunfeld Defense and the King's Indian Defense. This kingside fianchetto opens the door to either one. From the games that we've already played through, we've seen how a kingside fianchetto can keep a King well protected. With the text, Black shows he isn't interested in fighting for the center from the opening move. He aims to put his Bishop on the long diagonal, to build a home for his King, and to castle. Once that has been done, only then will Black begin a direct challenge in the center.

Although popular, such modern strategies are dismissed by classical players; they hold that while Black is busy building a safe house for his King, White is taking over the center. By the time Black is ready to turn his attention to the center, it is too late. White's grip has grown too strong, and Black will be squeezed for space and be slowly pushed off the board. Believe me, countless games have been played to discover who is right and who is wrong. The jury is still out.

3.g3

Here's a surprising countermove by Korchnoi. The text aims to achieve the same benefits as Black's fianchetto. With his center pawns already developed, White fianchettos as well and builds a home for his King.

Korchnoi has built an exalted career with 3.Nc3, playing for a big center with e2-e4. Kasparov would in response have to declare his defense, either playing 3...d5 for the Grunfeld Defense or 3...Bg7 4.e4 for the King's Indian Defense.

3...Bg7

Black completes his chosen method of opening the game.

4.Bg2

White does likewise and prepares to take a bigger bite out of the center with e2-e4.

4...c5

A defining moment. Black decides the time has come to attack White's center.

White must decide how he wants to resolve the d4-c5 pawn tension.

5.d5

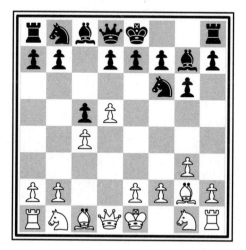

Advancing in the center, White expects that his central pawn wedge will give him a spatial advantage that will cramp Black's pieces.

- ■ A less satisfactory choice would be 5.dxc5? Na6! 6.Be3?! Qa5+ 7.Qd2 (7.Nc3 Ng4 causes problems for White) 7...Qxd2+ 8.Nxd2 Ng4! — Black thereby advantageously wins back his pawn.

- ■ A tame response would be 5.Nf3 cxd4 6.Nxd4 O-O 7.O-O d5 8.cxd5 Nxd5, resulting in a symmetrical position. White would have a small advantage because he is on move, but the position is actually quite balanced.

Weighing the pros and cons of White's d4-d5 isn't a simple matter. The position is extremely dynamic. White has a beautiful d5-pawn that makes it difficult for the b8-Knight, and by extension the c8-Bishop, to find a square. On the other hand, White has blocked the long diagonal for his g2-Bishop while opening up the long diagonal for the g7-Bishop. White has a static advantage — the d5-pawn — but Black has the dynamic potential of using his g7-Bishop. This defensive setup is known as the Benoni Defense.

The plans of both players can be quickly outlined. White will try to keep his static advantage, the d5-pawn; Black will try to nibble away at White's center, looking for opportunities to play tactically. White will develop his pieces behind the broad front that the d5-pawn provides; Black will work around the d5-pawn, trying to find one good square for each of his queenside pieces.

5...d6

Preparing to develop the c8-Bishop and the b8-Knight, Black also prevents the future possibility of d5-d6.

6.Nc3

White develops his pieces and reinforces the d5-pawn.

The text also provides an important service by preventing a possible ...b7-b5. We know that Black wants to remove the d5-pawn. One way to do that is to get rid of its supporters! The c4-pawn is a loyal backup. If Black can engineer a ...b7-b5 break, the d5-pawn could become vulnerable. After White's move, Black will have to try a little harder if he intends to play for ...b7-b5.

This idea of ...b7-b5 is not an inconsiderable point. Remember that when the center is closed or locked because of the central pawn structures, the players find it difficult to create a plan of action in the center. That said, their attention turns to the wings, both queenside and kingside. The player who can develop an initiative on one of the wings will gain the advantage.

6...O-O

Mission complete. Black's King makes a nice picture of safety. His other pieces are cramped and not faring so well however. Black will need to address the issue of what to do with them.

7.Nf3

White develops his position and prepares to build his own home.

Another possibility would be 7.e4, playing for a central grip. One variation, 7.e4 Nbd7 8.Nge2 Ne5 9.b3 Bg4 10.O-O Nf3+ 11.Kh1 Nxe4!?, would yield sharp play. Continuing this idea with 12.Nxe4 Bxa1 13.h3 reveals that Black's attack might be premature. Although continuing to grip the center with e2-e4 is strategically justified, White feels it would be better to castle and complete his development. Within this scenario he's doing well enough in the center as it is.

7...e6

Black begins to chip away at White's center. The e7-pawn controls none of White's squares; thus it has no import in the space count. On the other hand, the d5-pawn controls two in the space count. Black intends to knock off the d5-pawn and reduce White's advantage in the space count.

This is a smart idea for two principled reasons:

■ When you have a cramped position, trade material, especially pieces.

■ When you don't know which pieces or pawns to trade, just ask yourself which piece or pawn controls more space.

The idea ...e7-e6 becomes quite suggestive.

8.O-O

White's King is now happy, too.

White has worked hard, spending two tempi to get a d5-pawn. He isn't eager to spoil his hard work by playing 8.dxe6 Bxe6 9.Ng5 Bxc4! 10.Bxb7 Nbd7, in which he would win an exchange but give up his central grip and his fianchettoed Bishop. Both players were aware that a number of games have continued with 8.dxe6, but neither player considers the resulting position to be dangerous for

111

Black. The text is the most consequent course of action.

8...exd5

Trading the less powerful e6-pawn for White's d5-pawn, Black aims to reduce White's space advantage.

9.cxd5

White replaces the d5-pawn with the c4-pawn.

At first blush it looks better to use the d5-square as an outpost for pieces. After 9.Nxd5 Nxd5 10.Qxd5, White's Queen would take up a powerful outpost. But this is an illusion. With 10...Nc6 and the immediate ...Bc8-e6, White's Queen would be forced to move. The c4-pawn would be a target, and Black's Bishops could rake the board.

Capturing with 9.Nxd5 would be fundamentally wrong for another reason: space! If White were to allow a trade of Knights, there would be fewer Black pieces on the board that are cramped. White's d5-pawn is intended to make life awkward for Black's pieces to find squares. If Black were allowed to trade pieces, the cramping d5-pawn would lose its effect.

Black has accomplished what he could in the center. His attention now turns to the wings. Which side will he play on?

There is no use in disturbing the kingside because such play might expose his own monarch. Therefore the time has come for the battle to shift to the queenside.

9...a6

Black makes a difficult decision.

Black is longing for ...b7-b5-b4, which would create an initiative on the queen-side. But it isn't easy to achieve such a pleasant prospect. Kasparov had to wrestle with the idea 9...Na6 10.h3 Nc7 11.a4 a6 12.e4 Bd7 13.a5 Nb5, with combative play on the queenside and in the center. In his preparation before the game, Kasparov had made this decision of 9...a6 or 9...Na6. We are still in the early stages of opening theory. Both players have come prepared, and they intend to uncork their novel ideas later.

10.a4

This move stops ...b7-b5 and could help in planning a4-a5, taking charge of the b6-square.

White is satisified with his central grip. If he can command events on the queenside, victory will be easy. He is as safe as a bug in a rug on the kingside.

10...Re8

Black makes a standard move in the Benoni Defense. He has achieved a half-open e-file and therefore puts his Rook on it to gain space. If Black can next play ...Nf6-e4, he could earn some desired trades while opening up the long diagonal for his g7-Bishop.

11.Nd2!

This move prevents ...Nf6-e4 and at the same time eyes the b6-square. White in turn is eager to improve his possibilities in the queenside theater. He plans a4-a5, Nd2-c4-b6 to establish a chokehold on the position.

11...Nbd7

Black momentarily covers the b6-square. He needs to develop his pieces, and this is the only available route. Again White's d5-pawn gives White an enjoyable benefit. Black is having trouble with a clutter of pieces.

12.h3

With this careful move, White awaits further developments.

The text takes the g4-square from Black's pieces. Its advantage is best revealed in the plays 12...Ne5? 13.f4! (forcing Black to go back) 13...Ned7 14.e4! — White could thus establish an impressive pawn center.

12...Rb8

Black combines his central play with his queenside majority. He is now prepared for ...b7-b5-b4 and to gain the initiative.

13.Nc4

White stops ...b7-b5 because of the attack on the d6-pawn.

A principled reaction would be 13.a5, preparing en passant in case of ...b7-b5. Theoreticians have debated the resulting position 13.a5 b5! 14.axb6 Nxb6, in which both players could claim they had improved their games. White's a1-Rook is developed *without having moved*, making the a6-pawn vulnerable. Black has stopped Nd2-c4, while putting the b8-Rook on the half open b-file. This is a difficult position to assess.

13...Ne5

Black defends the d6-pawn and offers an exchange of Knights. White faces a dual strategic threat in ...b7-b5 or ...Ne5xc4.

14.Na3

White addresses both threats but relegates the a3-Knight to inaction.

White isn't too concerned about the misplaced a3-Knight because he is winding up for a big central pawn push. His first blow will be f2-f4, bumping the e5-Knight out of the way. He can then play Na3-c4, leaping back into the fray, or play e2-e4, anticipating e4-e5. Black's pieces face the bleak prospect of being pushed back into oblivion.

14...Nh5!

This ungainly move stops f2-f4 because of the weak g3-pawn.

Black is desperate to gain a foothold in the center. He intends ...f7-f5 in order to challenge e2-e4. Once that has been done, Black's e5-Knight will be able to retreat to the f7-square. That would be an important strategic achievement, in light of the fact that the d6-pawn is covered and neither of Black's Bishops will have their diagonals blocked. In this way, Black hopes to be able to *play around* the cramping effects of the d5-pawn.

Middlegame

15.e4!

Each move increases the tension!

White could win a piece in one of two ways:

- 15.g4 Bxg4! (15...Nf6? 16.f4 Ned7? 17.e4 — the Black pieces would be routed) 16.hxg4 Nxg4 — the a3-Knight would be far, far away from protecting White's King.

- 15.f4? Nxg3 16.fxe5 Bxe5!

In both cases, Black would have a powerful attack against White's King. Note that Black's Queen would be ready to join the battle by ...Qd8-h4.

The text fits perfectly into White's plans. Now that the d1-Queen covers the g4-square, the threat of g3-g4 becomes far more serious.

15...Rf8!

This fantastic idea came from GM Jan Timman.

Previous games had continued with 15...f5 16.exf5 Bxf5 17.g4, winning a piece. Supporters of the Benoni would choose to sacrifice not one but two pieces by continuing with 17...Bxg4 18.hxg4 Qh4 19.gxh5 Rf8! in order to threaten ...Ne5-g4 — Black would have to stop Bc1-f4 by defending the h2-square. Two pieces ahead, White would be prepared to give some of his bounty back: 20.h6! Bh8 21.Nc4!! (an idea of Yugoslav GM Vlado Kovacevic) 21...Ng4 22.Qxg4 Qxg4 23.Nxd6; White would gain three pieces for his Queen. The theoreticians decided that the resulting position would ultimately favor White, and the whole variation fell into disrepute.

The point of the text is to once again prepare the advance ...f7-f5, now that the Black Rook is better placed on the f8-square. The tempo loser ...Rf8-e8-f8 seems to weave mockingly to and fro. White, already in possession of a big center, would be given an extra move.

16.Kh2

With this sensible move, White protects the g3-pawn in order to play f2-f4, booting the e5-Knight.

The immediate 16.g4? Qh4! 17.gxh5 Bxh3! 18.h6 Bh8 19.Ne2 f5! gave Black a winning attack in the game between Jan Timman and Peter Scheeren at the 1980 Dutch championship. We are still in the thick of opening theory for this line of the Benoni. Both players have yet to play their novelties.

16...f5

Black has no time to lose. He must play this critical break, or else f2-f4 will render him helpless.

In his book *Fighting Chess*, Kasparov gives detailed notes to this game, from which I now liberally borrow. He considers the text to be inexact, citing 16...Bd7 17.f4 b5! as favoring him because ...b5-b4 would be such a strong threat. This is indeed true, but after 16...Bd7 17.a5!, Black would face the same problems as before. The sting of ...b7-b5 would be

missing. A probable continuation would be 17...Qxa5 18.f4! (18.g4 Nf6 would be weaker since Black would sacrifice a piece on the g4-square) 18...b5 19.fxe5 Bxe5 (19...b4 20.Nc2 Qb6 21.Ne2 Bxe5 22.Nf4 would yield insufficient compensation for the piece) 20.Bf4!, ending with advantage for White. Far from being inexact, Kasparov's move is the most consequent course of action.

17.f4!

A real clash of opening ideas! Either Black's pieces will be driven back, or his hordes will rule the day on the kingside because of the missing stallion on a3.

17...b5!!

Fantastic! The whole board is in flames. The fight is carried on in every sector: queenside, center, and kingside.

Strategically, the text is an absolute necessity. Black can't afford to retreat in the center, and at the moment he can't make progress on the kingside. If 17...fxe4 18.Nxe4! Nf7 19.Nc4! b5 20.axb5 axb5 21.Na5! Bd7 22.Nc6 Bxc6 23.dxc6, White would have a huge advantage. Black's kingside attack would be snuffed out, and White would be prepared for Qd1-d5 or Ra1-a7, making serious inroads on the queenside. Black could get flattened.

The text, on the other hand, also completely confuses the issue. Black introduces the potent threat of ...b5-b4 or even ...Ne5-c4, moving forward instead of backward. If Black can involve his dormant b8-Rook in a kingside sweep by ...Rb8xb2, the b5-pawn would become an honored martyr.

18.axb5!

Korchnoi is at his happiest when devouring his opponent's pieces. By snapping off the offered b5-pawn, he knows he has the game in the bag. With an advantage in the center and an extra pawn, he must only make sure his King doesn't bite the dust.

White therefore avoids the greedy 18.fxe5 Nxg3! 19.Kxg3 Bxe5+ 20.Kf2 (20.Bf4? Qg5+ wins) 20...Bd4+ with its annoying problems. After 21.Be3? Bxe3+ 22.Kxe3 Qg5+ 23.Kf2 b4, Black would

regain a piece with a strong attack. White doesn't want to disturb matters on the kingside. Making big gains on the queenside will be quite sufficient.

18...axb5

Black renews the threat of ...b5-b4, which would win a piece.

19.Naxb5

The a3-Knight is happy to be reemployed. Already he is kicking up a fuss by attacking the d6-pawn. With Nb5-a7-c6, further gains could be made.

The only disadvantage to winning the b5-pawn is that the b8-Rook will barrel down the b-file. The b5-Knight may have to stay put to neutralize the pressure; this in turn would keep the c3-Knight stuck on guard duty.

Kasparov later explained that 19.fxe5? Bxe5 20.Ne2 Nxg3! 21.Nxg3 f4! was his intention, with a fine attacking display in sight.

19...fxe4

Black's move is well timed. Now that the c3-Knight is stuck in the defense of the b5-Knight, White can't recapture with Nc3xe4, which Black had previously feared.

20.Bxe4!

This move was Korchnoi's novel idea.

Previously in the same year, the plan 20.Na7 e3!? 21.Qe2 Nxg3! 22.Kxg3 g5, with a razor-sharp position, had been tried by Lev Alburt versus Helgi Olafsson at Reykjavík. Korchnoi had been present for that game and had participated in the postmortem. From this exchange of ideas, Korchnoi had determined that the text would put Black back on his heels.

20...Bd7!

Black responds, blow for blow.

As usual, the retreat 20...Nf7? 21.Bg2 Nf6? 22.Na7 would leave Black with a miserable game. The tricky 20...Qd7, attacking the h3-pawn and the b5-Knight, would continue with 21.Bg2 Rxb5 22.Nxb5 Qxb5 23.fxe5 Bxe5 24.Rxf8+ Kxf8 25.Qf1+ and result in an endgame that, because of the threat of Ra1-a8, would favor White.

Now White faces a critical choice: should the b5-Knight retreat, plunge ahead, or receive protection? The decision requires a mixture of calculation, intuition, and luck.

21.Qe2(!)

The exclamation mark is Kasparov's; he considers it the right move.

In games of this complexity, I've learned to question all moves, especially those bearing an exclamation mark! My view is that White misses an opportunity for an advantage with this move.

■ I agree with Kasparov that 21.fxe5? Bxe5! would only favor Black. Black's attack against White's King with ...Qd8-h4 would be overwhelming.

■ Also, moving ahead by playing 21.Na7? Ra8!, threatening ...Qd8-b6 to win the a7-Knight, would be good for Black.

■ The complicated 21.Nxd6?! Rb6! 22.fxe5 Bxe5 23.Nc4 Bxg3+ 24.Kg1 (24.Kg2 Bxh3+) 24...Rbf6! would make harrowing threats against White's King.

■ All the variations with f4xe5...Bg7xe5 would work splendidly for Black, giving him the sudden coordination of the offside h5-Knight and the e5-Bishop, poised to mash the g3-pawn.

Of far greater interest is the passive retreat 21.Na3!, which would ask Black what he intends to do with his kingside attack. I think this is the question that White should be posing: I'm a pawn up on the queenside and your pieces are hanging in the center — how are you going to prove your attack?

■ In *Fighting Chess*, Kasparov offers a fiery continuation: 21.Na3 Qc8 22.Bg2 (don't even *think* about capturing the e5-Knight) 22...Bg4! 23.Qd2 Bf5 24.fxe5 Bxe5 25.Ne2 Rb3! with strong threats. There are several problems with this offering:

■ The invasion ...Rb8-b3 would be very strong and should not be allowed.

■ The analysis focuses upon f4xe5, which we've seen should be avoided.

■ White's best choice in fact would be 21.Na3! Qc8 22.Bg2 Bg4 23.Qc2! Bf5 24.Ne4! — a simple way to counter the attack on the g3-pawn. Black would then have but two key choices:

■ In 24...Rb4?! 25.Nxd6! (this is White's threat) 25...Bxc2 26.Nxc8 Bd3 27.Ne7+ Kf7 28.Re1, White emerges with advantage because of the two extra White pawns.

■ With 24...Nf7 (at last! — Black has been forced to retreat) 25.g4 Bxe4 26.Bxe4 Nf6 27.Bf3!, White again has the advantage. White has two promising ideas: Na3-c4 to centralize and g4-g5, intending Bf3-g4-e6.

The conclusion that we can draw is that 21.Na3! would give White an advantage and put this continuation of the Benoni into doubt. The text is not a bad move, however, as White can include Qe2-g2 as a defensive idea.

21...Qb6!

Black puts more pressure on the b5-Knight and also covers the d6-pawn.

22.Na3

White is forced to make the retreat Nb5-a3 anyway. The question is, which side gains from the inclusion of the Queen moves?

22...Rbe8!

Black does! He immediately places his Rook opposite the White Queen on the open e-file. Black is trying to scare up opportunities based on the tactic ...Ne5-g4+, with a discovered attack on the e2-Queen once the e4-Bishop has moved.

23.Bd2?

This is a poor follow-up to White's previous move. The c1-Bishop has been performing an important role in covering the b2-pawn, but not anymore.

■ According to Kasparov, White should be protecting his King with 23.Qg2! Nf7 24.Nc4 Qb8 (24...Qb4!?), making the position dynamically balanced. Black's pieces are well placed, whereas White will have to work hard to realize his extra pawn.

■ Kasparov explains why it would be a mistake to capture the e5-Knight: 23.fxe5? Bxe5 24.Bf4 (24.Nc4 Bxg3+ 25.Kg2 Qd8 offers a strong attack) 24...Nxf4 25.gxf4 Bxf4+ 26.Kg2 Qd8, giving Black many advantages on the kingside.

■ GM Jan Timman offers another scheme of development: 23.Qc2 Qb4 24.Bd2 Qd4 25.Rae1, thus completing development and keeping an eye on the center.

Either 23.Qc2 or 23.Qg2 would be better than the text, which is based on an oversight. Note that 23.Qc2 would mean a loss of tempo, however, thereby undoing 21.Qe2.

23...Qxb2!!

A valiant foot soldier just got the ax. This brilliant shot visibly rattled Korchnoi. The b2-pawn was the *extra* pawn that held the queenside pieces together.

24.fxe5?

Stunned by his tactical oversight, Korchnoi commits another one.

He had intended to play 24.Rfb1, which would appear to trap Black's Queen, but 24...Nf3+!! would not only rescue the Black Queen, it would also win! Frustrated that the e5-Knight has been leading such a charmed life — it has been en prise for an eternity — Korchnoi decides he can't stand it anymore and thus removes it. But as we've seen, its

removal can lead to a replacement by a far more dangerous piece.

The choice 24.Ra2 Qb8! 25.Qg2 Nf7 was necessary, though offering advantage to Black. Now that White is missing his b2-pawn, his position is a lot looser.

24...Bxe5

All of Black's pieces are participating in the kingside attack. White's pieces on the queenside are congested, giving no aid to their monarch. Despite being a piece down, Black maintains a powerful attack, with the fireworks still to come.

I had been watching this game in progress from the American tables in the olympic hallways. Even from that distance, I could see from Kasparov's face that he was delighted with his newfound situation.

25.Nc4

There is nothing else to be done. Black's threats of ...Be5xc3 or ...Nh5xg3 are too strong. At least White can try to get the a3-Knight back into the game.

25...Nxg3!

The point! Black leaves his Queen en prise to go after his opponent's one, with discovered check to boot.

26.Rxf8+

White gets out of the threat ...Ng3xf1 with double check, winning a whole Rook!

26...Rxf8

Black takes over the open f-file.

27.Qe1

This is a disappointing retreat. White has to deal with the double threat of ...Ng3xe2+ as well as ...Qb2xa1, winning a Rook. The text does both.

27...Nxe4+

Black reaps the harvest of his efforts. His army is a model of coordination.

28.Kg2!

White makes the best practical decision. Although White's once-proud home has been torn asunder, he can still cling to the hope of Nc4xb2, winning the lady. A quick loss would follow the choice 28.Nxe5 Nxd2 29.Nxd7 Nf3++ 30.Kh1 Qh2, with checkmate.

28...Qc2!

It all works like a charm. Black is ready to play ...Be5xc3, winning a piece.

29.Nxe5

White removes the most potent threat.

After the moves 29.Qxe4 Qxe4 30.Nxe4 Bxa1 31.Ncxd6 Bd4, Black would be an exchange ahead with a winning ending.

Olympian Effort

29...Rf2+?

After conducting a flawless attack, Kasparov makes an error under the pressure of his ticking clock. He had been faced with two tempting choices: 29...Nxd2 or 29...Rf2+, going after White's King.

This check appears to make a forcing finish. In fact, it offers White an amazing chance to climb right back into the game. After 29...Nxd2!, Black could have won without trouble: 30.Qc1 Qxc1 31.Rxc1 dxe5, with an extra piece; or 30.Nxd7 Nf3+ 31.Qe2 Nh4+! 32.Kg1 (32.Kg3 Qxc3+ 33.Kxh4 Rf4+ wins; also 32.Kh2 Rf2+! wins) 32...Qxc3 33.Qe6+ Kh8 34.Nxf8 Qg3+ 35.Kf1 Qg2+ 36.Ke1 Nf3+ 37.Kd1 Qd2 checkmate — analysis by GM Kasparov.

30.Qxf2!

Alert defense! Kasparov had only counted on 30.Kg1 Rxd2 31.Nxe4 Rg2+ 32.Kf1 (32.Kh1 Rh2 is mate next move) 32...Bb5+! — a sneaky check that would bag the game. Instead, Korchnoi sacrifices his Queen to start an attack of his own against the Black King! The spectators are buzzing in delight. Both players are now in time trouble, having but a few minutes each to make the time control at move 40. Who's winning now?

Endgame

30...Nxf2!

Facing a most difficult decision, Black intuits the right choice. His problem is that his d7-Bishop is en prise.

It would seem natural to get the Bishop out of capture, with check at the same time. Kasparov shares some lovely variations: 30...Bxh3+? (the problem with this move, as we'll see, is that by opening the seventh rank, White's Rook is able to give perpetual check) 31.Kg1! Nxf2 32.Ra2! would drive the Queen away from the d2-Bishop. Black's Queen would have *two* available squares:

- 32...Qf5 33.Ra8+ Kg7 34.Ra7+ Kg8 (if the King steps onto the f-file, Ra7-f7+ will win Black's Queen) 35.Ra8+ with an immediate draw by perpetual check.

- 32...Qb3 33.Ra8+ Kg7 34.Ra7+ Kf8 (34...Kg8 would acquiesce to a draw by perpetual check; too dangerous is 34...Kf6 35.Nf3, threatening Kg1xf2 and Bd2-g5+, with Black in serious trouble — for example: 35...Bg4 or 35...Ng4 36.Bg5+ and Ra7-f7 would be mate; 35...Nd1 36.Bg5+ Kf5 37.Rf7+ Kg4 38.Rf4+ Kg3 39.Ne2 would be checkmate, whereas 35...Nd3 36.Ne4+ Kf5 37.Nxd6+ Kg4 38.Nh2+ Kg3 39.Ne4+ Kh4 40.Rxh7 would be mate) 35.Bh6+ Ke8 36.Ra8+ Ke7 37.Bg5 checkmate!

Thus the move 30...Bxh3+? would allow White a draw, and if Black isn't satisfied with that, he'll find himself mated. This again demonstrates that in sharp positions, it is not enough to play natural moves. One must calculate the myriad of variations. In this case, sensing that White mustn't be allowed Ra1-a8+-a7+ kept Black's winning chances alive.

31.Ra2!

A critical resource. Black's Queen is far too deadly and must be driven away. Any move that allows ...Qc2xd2 would be curtains.

31...Qf5!

Despite his time trouble, Black plays well.

The choice 31...Bxh3+? 32.Kg1 would only transpose to the above note, whereas 31...Qb3 32.Nxd7, would leave the b3-Queen in a passive position.

32.Nxd7

White tries to trade pieces by 32...Qxd7 33.Kxf2 Qxh3. In the resulting position, White's Rook, Knight, and Bishop offer excellent compensation for the Black Queen. Because of the strong d5-pawn, White should have little difficulty drawing the game.

32...Nd3!

Black maintains his Knight. Black readies either ...Qf5xd7 or ...Qf5-f2+, which looks tough to meet.

The next diagram shows the position, with White to move. His position looks hopeless, but he has a hidden resource. Can you find it?

33.Bh6?

In desperate time trouble, Korchnoi tosses away the draw.

White should have used the same perpetual check idea of his Rook on the eighth and seventh ranks. He could have done this by 33.Ra8+ Kg7 34.Ra7!! (setting up a discovered check) 34...Qf2+ 35.Kh1 Qf1+ 36.Kh2 Qf2+ 37.Kh1 Qxd2 (Black has nothing better as 37...c4 38.Nc5+ blocks the attack on the a7-Rook) 38.Ne5+ Kf8 (38...Kf6? 39.Ne4+ forks, as does 38...Kh6? 39.Ng4+ Kh5 40.Rxh7+ Kg5 41.Ne4+, clipping the Black Queen) 39.Ra8+ Ke7 40.Ra7+ Kd8 41.Ra8+. Black can't "escape" with 41...Kc7 because 42.Nb5+ will win the game for White by a fork or a checkmate — analysis by GM Kasparov.

After missing this last opportunity, Korchnoi and Kasparov blitz out their next few moves.

33...Qxd7!

For the first time, Black takes a lead in force. He now threatens ...Qd7-b7, which will keep the a2-Rook out of play.

34.Ra8+

The only remaining hope is that White can generate some cheapos — lucky tactical shots — against Black's King.

34...Kf7

Forced — Black's King tries to make a run for the center. If he can play ...Kf7-f6-e5, he will not only be safe, but he will also become a tower of strength.

35.Rh8?

It's not Korchnoi's day. His best chance was 35.Ne4, preventing the King from slipping away.

After 35.Ne4 Qe7! 36.Ng5+ Kf6, Black would win, but he would have to discover 35...Qe7 rather than what Kasparov had intended: 35...g5?! 36.Rf8+ Ke7 37.Nxg5, with White still kicking.

35...Kf6!

Simple and elegant. Black guards his h7-pawn and prepares to sprint his King to

the d4-square. The Soviet olympiad team can at last breathe easier.

36.Kf3?

A complete collapse in time trouble.

36...Qxh3+

White resigns.

It is hard to recapture the excitement and tension that this game generated among those who watched it — a truly Olympian clash.

▀▄▀▄▀▄▀▄▀▄▀▄▀▄▀▄▀▄▀▄▀▄▀▄▀▄▀▄▀▄▀▄▀▄▀▄

Experienced Hands

In the 1983 FIDE candidate cycle, 62-year-old Vassily Smyslov of the Soviet Union surprised everyone. The former chess World Champion — he had won the championship in 1957 and lost it the next year — managed to qualify for the candidate matches. He won his first match in the quarter-finals against Robert Hubner of Germany. That match had had a storybook finish: neither player could prove superiority, and the match was tied. The rule called for the drawing of lots. Since the match was sponsored by a casino, the players decided to play roulette. The first spin produced a double zero. Green! The ball was spun again and landed on one of Smyslov's numbers. He advanced to the semifinals against Hungarian Zoltan Ribli.

One brilliant game stood out in that semifinal match and will be replayed for countless generations to come. In annotating this game, I've relied upon Smyslov's discussions in *Chess Informant* 36.

■ ■ ■ ■ ■ ■ ■ ■ ■ ■ ■ ■ ■ ■

D42 Queen's Gambit Declined, Tarrasch Defense

GM Vassily Smyslov
GM Zoltan Ribli
London, 1983 (Match 5)

Opening

1.d4

Smyslov has had such a long and illustrious career, he can play any opening move. At this point in time, Smyslov prefered Queen Pawn Openings.

1...Nf6

By virtue of its flexibility, this is perhaps the most frequently chosen first move of modern grandmasters.

2.Nf3

The moves 2.Nf3 and 2.c4 seem almost interchangeable. Through this move order, White avoids the three B's: the Benko, Benoni, and Budapest Defenses.

2...e6

Adopting the Nimzovitch Defense that we've seen.

3.c4

With this most tried and trusted move, White develops a pawn that can take part in the central battle.

3...d5

This move transposes back into the Queen's Gambit Declined. With 3...b6, we would be in a Queen's Indian, or with 3...c5, in a possible Benoni.

4.Nc3

Just as in Game One.

4...c5

The Tarrasch Defense, named after the German player Siegbert Tarrasch (1863–1934), unfolds.

Vassily Smyslov

Vassily Smyslov was born in Moscow on March 24, 1921. He became an international grandmaster in 1951 and defeated Mikhail Botvinnik in the 1957 World Championship match, $12^{1}/_{2}$–$9^{1}/_{2}$. He lost the title to Botvinnik in the following year. Smyslov brings a wonderful light touch to the game. His play is fluid and smooth, and his sterling qualities include a tremendous grasp of the ending. In fact, he coauthored the classic *Rook Endings* with Grigory Levenfish. Smyslov still competes often, creating a stream of interesting games. He attributes the longevity of his career to his easy way of life and spiritual happiness.

Tarrasch introduced ...c7-c5 to opening theory. He considered it absolutely necessary that Black attack White's center as quickly as possible. Black's idea is straightforward. He intends to match White in the center early, and after a clash and an exchange of pieces, to equalize the game, thereby negating White's advantage of playing the opening move.

5.cxd5

Tournament practice has shown the text to be the only chance for an advantage. After 5.e3 Nc6, the position would be symmetrical, with White having only the advantage of the move.

5...Nxd5

This is the best way to recapture. After 5...exd5 6.Bg5!, White's annoying pin on the f6-Knight would lead to pressure against the d5-pawn. With the text, Black avoids this pin and offers an exchange of Knights, reducing the armies on the board.

6.e3

This move is a bit too modest for my taste. White is not trying to win the game from the opening. All he wants is a quiet start: developing pieces, castling early, and only then beginning a plan of action.

I think that 6.e4 Nxc3 7.bxc3 cxd4 8.cxd4 Bb4+ 9.Bd2 Bxd2+ 10.Qxd2 would have offered White the best chance for an opening advantage.

6...Nc6

Developing and putting pressure on the center squares, Black intends to make the d4-pawn his object of attack.

7.Bd3

Now that the f6-Knight is absent, White develops his f1-Bishop in hope of putting pressure on the h7-pawn. Another variation would be 7.Bb5, pinning the c6-Knight and intending to continue with Nf3-e5. Again, a question of taste determines the opening.

7...Be7

Black prepares to castle. The more active 7...Bd6?! would not complement Black's development scheme. With the text, he can later play ...Be7-f6, putting pressure on the d4-pawn.

8.O-O

White brings his King to safety, following one of the guiding principles of the opening.

8...O-O

Black agrees and follows suit.

9.a3

White puts forth a useful preventive move.

White wants to prepare either Qd1-c2 or Bd3-c2 and then Qd1-d3, setting up a battery on the b1-h7 diagonal. In both cases, White doesn't want to be bothered by ...Nc6-b4, which would interfere with the plan. White also prepares 10.Nxd5 exd5 11.dxc5 Bxc5 12.b4, followed by fianchettoing the c1-Bishop. Note that White has refrained from Nc3xd5 ...e6xd5, as the c8-Bishop would then have an easy time developing. White has also avoided d4xc5, since ...Nd5xc3 b2xc3 ...Be7xc5 would leave White with split queenside pawns.

9...cxd4

In view of the previous move, Black resolves the tension in the center.

Middlegame

10.exd4!

This move sets up one of the most intensely debated middlegames in chess, the case of the so-called isolated pawn.

The d4-pawn is referred to as an isolated pawn or an *isolani*, since none of White's pawns are on the adjacent e-file or c-file: the d4-pawn is isolated from its fellow pawns. The debate centers on whether the isolani is weak because it is separated or strong because it supports outposts on the key c5-square and e5-square.

Besides the issue of its vulnerability to attack, and hence its need for piece protection, the isolani has another failing: the square directly in front of the isolani is an ideal outpost for the opponent's pieces because another pawn can't budge the opposing piece. In this case, the d5-Knight has a terrific outpost.

A number of books have been written on the study of isolated Queen Pawn positions. As *Winning Chess Strategies* taught, a few principles can guide you in play with isolated pawns:

- The fewer the pieces that are on the board, the weaker the isolani becomes.

- The player that has the initiative will have the advantage.

- If the player that is playing against the isolated pawn can find an effective development for his queenside pieces, he will normally win.

- The player with the isolated pawn must be prepared to attack, which often means sacrificing. If you are not prepared to sacrifice, don't play with an isolated pawn!

10...Bf6

This move immediately pressures the d4-pawn.

Another possibility would be 10...Nxc3 11.bxc3 b6 in order to fianchetto the c8-Bishop. In this case, the d4-pawn would be reinforced, no longer isolated. White would then have a slight advantage, and Ribli isn't anxious to let his opponent off the hook.

11.Qc2!

This was Smyslov's novelty: by immediately hitting the h7-pawn, White can force a weakness in Black's pawn shield. Previously, 11.Be4 followed by Qd1-d3 was considered best.

A deeper point is the question of what White wants to do with his Rooks. Practice has shown that the ideal locations for the Rooks are the d1-square and the e1-square. Black favors the c8-square and the d8-square for his Rooks. By vacating the d1-square so quickly, White is hoping to play Ra1-d1 soon.

11...h6

A tough choice. After 11...Nxd4?! 12.Nxd4 Bxd4 13.Bxh7+ Kh8 14.Be4, Black would not be a happy camper because his King's position would be compromised. The other choice, 11...g6 12.Bh6 Re8 13.Rad1! indirectly protecting the d4-pawn, would allow White to achieve the ideal setup for his Rooks.

12.Rd1

This is not the ideal formation that White wanted, but the d4-pawn requires protection.

White should have considered 12.Be3, playing for Ra1-d1. White wants to develop a kingside attack using the d4-pawn to mask his plan; thus he wants to shift as many pieces as possible to the kingside.

12...Qb6!

Black goes after the d4-pawn with a vengence! He momentarily neglects his queenside development in order to vacate the d8-square for the f8-Rook.

A safe alternative would be 12...Nce7 (12...b6? 13.Nxd5 Qxd5 14.Be4 wins the c6-Knight) 13.Qe2 b6 14.Qe4 Ng6, setting up a tense game. Black would be ready for ...Bc8-

b7, whereas White would have managed to shift his Queen to the kingside.

13.Bc4

White is being distracted from his king-side threats because of the weak isolani.

13...Rd8

This tactical flurry convinced Black not to take the d4-pawn: 13...Nxd4? 14.Nxd4 Bxd4 15.Na4! (the key move, the b6-Queen, is chased away) 15...Qc7 16.Rxd4 b5 (the only way to win the piece back) 17.Bxh6! results in a winning attack. Moves such as 17...f5 18.Rxd5! or 17...bxc4 18.Rg4! would win material for White.

The text fits into Black's strategy of bringing his Rooks to the d-file and the c-file. With the d5-Knight protected, White has to worry about his d4-pawn again.

14.Ne2!

This fine move demonstrates Smyslov's experienced hand. He knows that in isolated pawn positions, trading pieces benefits the player who is facing the isolated pawn.

This move is based on the principle that the player who has more space tries to keep pieces on the board. Although isolated, the d4-pawn does control the c5-square and the e5-square. By avoiding ...Nd5xc3 swaps, White intends to bring his pieces to the kingside. White avoids 14.Qe4 Nxc3 15.bxc3 Ne7!, in which ...Qb6-c6 or ...Bc8-d7-c6 could boot the e4-Queen.

14...Bd7

Black is close to completing his development. If he plays ...Ra8-c8, dangerous threats down the c-file will follow.

15.Qe4!

White continues his policy of shifting to the kingside.

Although White had set up the battery Qc2/Bd3, he now intends to reverse the battery Bd3/Qe4 and invade the h7-square. Because the h6-pawn sticks out, Black is denied the defense ...g7-g6, as that would hang the h6-pawn. Not coincidentally, White vacates the c-file quickly.

15...Nce7!

Ribli is up for the defensive challenge. The c6-Knight had been in the way of Black's queenside operations; now the Knight performs some key defensive tasks.

White's kingside attack would have sputtered out before it achieved lift-off.

16.Bd3

This move completes the battery. White is ready to thrust; Black is ready to parry. A charged tension has arisen. Which defense will be chosen?

16...Ba4?

This constitutes a very bad move on two levels, the tactical and the strategic. The move deserves two question marks, but because it doesn't lose material, it gets only one.

Black sees the threatened Qe4-h7+ but isn't intimidated. He rejects blocking the diagonal: 16...g6? 17.Bxh6; 16...Nf5? 17.g4 would help White accomplish his goal; 16...Ng6!? 17.h4! Bb5 18.h5 Bxd3 19.Rxd3 Nge7 20.Ne5 would lead to a situation in which, in the words of Victor Korchnoi, Black would begin to "experience unpleasant sensations."

In fact, Ribli's deeper consideration of the position precipitated this mistake. He asked himself, is Qe4-h7+ dangerous? He came to the surprising conclusion that it wasn't. After 17.Qh7+ Kf8 18.Qh8+ Ng8 19.Bh7 Ke7, Black would threaten ...g7-g5, trapping White's Queen. Once Ribli had convinced himself that Qe4-h7+ wasn't a threat, he began to look at his own queenside play. He then decided to move his d7-Bishop — to the wrong square!

It is not difficult to realize that White's d3-Bishop is more potent than the d7-Bishop. (It controls more squares.) Therefore Black should try to trade Bishops.

After 16...Bb5! 17.Qh7+ Kf8 18.Ng3 Bxd3 19.Qxd3 Rac8 20.h3, the position would be equal — analysis by GM Smyslov.

So Black misses the opportunity to trade Bishops and achieve equality. Why is it so bad to attack the d1-Rook? The answer lies in the strategy for the Rooks I have outlined before. On d1, the Rook is a defender. By pushing it to the half-open e-file, it becomes an attacker. Just watch!

17.Qh7+

White does not wait for a second invitation.

17...Kf8

Scooting away, Black welcomes 18.Qh8+? Ng8 and anticipates the chance to trap White's Queen.

18.Re1!

An important strategic shift has taken place. It is time to count the number of White pieces hovering around Black's King: their presence is alarming. Now that the d1-Rook is moved away from the threat of attack, it can play a role in catching the Black King in a cross fire on the e-file.

18...Bb5!

This move is the best chance. Black has to trade pieces as quickly as possible.

It is interesting to muse that this same position could have occurred with the e1-Rook on the d1-square. This little nuance makes a huge difference. After all, if your opponent doesn't make a mistake, it is impossible to win!

19.Bxb5

White can't prevent a piece trade from occurring. After 19.Bc2 Bxe2 20.Rxe2, Black would trade. White wants to keep his e2-Knight because the maneuver Ne2-g3-h5 will increase the pressure on the kingside.

19...Qxb5

Black gratefully recaptures the Bishop. If Black can engineer a Queen exchange

by ...Qb5-f5 or ...Ra8-c8 and ...Qb5-b3-c2, his King will be safe, leaving him with a fine game.

20.Ng3!

White is not waiting. He mustn't allow Black to exchange Queens. By opening up the e-file and preparing Ng3-h5, he places Black's King under heavy fire.

20...Ng6

This move prevents Qh7-h8+ and blocks the h7-Queen from retreating.

Black is still entertaining ideas of trapping White's Queen. White's attack arrives first; after 20...Rac8 21.Nh5 Qb3, 22.Bxh6! would attack the g7-pawn.

With 22...gxh6 23.Qxh6+ Ke8, 24.Nxf6+ would win two pawns.

21.Ne5!

Utilizing the e1-Rook, White threatens Ne5xg6+ to win a pawn.

21...Nde7

Black protects the g6-Knight.

Black can't implement his idea of trapping White's Queen: 21...Bxe5 22.dxe5 Ke7 23.Qxg7 Rh8, intending ...Ra8-g8, would win for Black. But 24.Nf5+! exf5 25.e6! refutes this idea with a winning attack — analysis by GM Smyslov.

Black can't protect the g6-Knight by playing 21...Ndf4 22.Bxf4 Nxf4 23.Nf5! exf5 (23...Ng6 24.Nxh6! Bxe5 25.Qg8+ wins) 24.Nd7+ Rxd7 25.Qh8 checkmate.

The e1-Rook controls the e7 flight square. This variation is the nicest illustration of the importance of the Rook's being on the e1-square. Also, 21...Nxe5 22.dxe5 Bg5 23.Bxg5 hxg5 24.Ne4! would win some of Black's kingside pawns for no compensation.

The text is the most challenging move. Black attacks the d4-isolani, which is the supporting backbone of White's attack.

22.Bxh6!

The Bishop enters the game with fearful effect. It is immune from capture because of Qh7xf7 mate.

22...Nxe5

The only possible move.

White would sacrifice an exchange after 22...Bxe5 23.Rxe5! Nxe5 24.Qxg7+ Ke8 25.dxe5, emerging with a winning attack — analysis by GM Smyslov.

23.Nh5!!

White plays a classic haymaker.

White would achieve nothing from 23.dxe5 Bxe5 24.a4 Qd5 because he wouldn't win material. The text introduces threats to the f6-Bishop and g7-pawn and a possible capture of the e5-Knight, putting more pressure on the f6-Bishop.

23...Nf3+!

Black refuses to go down without a fight and addresses his problems as best as he can. Since a piece is going to be captured, Black gives it back in a way that will wreck White's kingside pawn structure.

Other moves would lose quickly: 23...gxh6? 24.Qxh6+ Ke8 25.Nxf6 would result in mate; 23...Nf5 24.Nxf6 Nxh6 25.dxe5 Nf5 26.Rac1 would doom Black. White has development, attack, and an extra pawn on his side.

24.gxf3

White has to make a capture.

After 24.Kh1? Qxh5! 25.Bxg7+ Bxg7 26.Qxh5 Nxe1 27.Rxe1 Rxd4, White would have given up too much material, and Black would gain the advantage.

24...Nf5!

Ribli proves himself to be a scrappy fighter. He covers his g7-pawn and attacks the h6-Bishop.

At this point, 24...Qxh5? would be a mistake. After 25.Bxg7+ Bxg7 26.Qxh5, White would be winning because he has retained both his Rooks.

25.Nxf6

White removes a primary defender. The attack would quickly boomerang if White were to retreat with 25.Be3? Ke7! 26.Nxf6 Rh8, which would trap White's Queen!

25...Nxh6

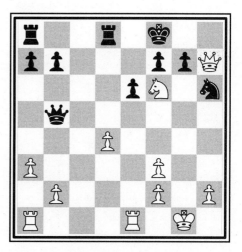

Black recaptures the piece.

After this flurry of forced moves, it looks as if Black has weathered the storm. He threatens ...Qb5-g5+ or ...Qb5-f5 with advantage. With 26.Qh8+? Ke7 27.Qxg7 Rg8! 28.Nxg8+ Rxg8 — surprise! — Black would win!

26.d5!!

Beautifully done — White cuts Black's Queen off along the fifth rank, preventing his threats while introducing a brutal threat of his own. His plan is 27.Qh8+ Ke7 28.Qxg7 Rg8 29.Rxe6+!, which would win at once because of the pin on the f7-pawn.

26...Qxb2

Black tries to support his King by getting on the long diagonal.

In the following beautiful, clear analyses, GM Smyslov shows what he had planned against two other defenses:

- 26...Nf5 (defending the g7-pawn) 27.Qg8+ Ke7 28.Rxe6+! fxe6 29.Qxe6+ Kf8 30.Nh7 checkmate.

- 26...gxf6 27.dxe6! (27.Qxh6+ Ke7 28.dxe6 is also convincing, but Smyslov believes the text is even stronger) 27...Qg5+ 28.Kh1 fxe6 (White threatens e6-e7+ to win the d8-Rook) 29.Rg1

Qf4 30.Rg7 (setting up Qh7-h8 checkmate — no matter how Black twists and turns, he can't prevent his fate) 30...Qxf3+ 31.Kg1 Rd1+ 32.Rxd1 Qxd1+ 33.Kg2 Qd5+ 34.f3 Qd2+ 35.Kh3 — Black has run out of useful checks.

27.Qh8+

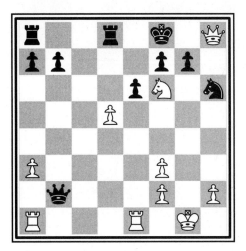

This is the start of a beautiful combination that will win Black's Queen. Before reading further, can you discover what White is up to?

27...Ke7

Black makes the only possible move. He is now ready to pounce upon the f6-Knight.

28.Rxe6+!

Ever since being pushed from the d-file to the e-file, White's Rook has dreamed of being such a hero.

Note that 28.Qxg7?? Qxf6 (not 28...Rg8?? because 29.Rxe6+ would win for White) was the defense that Black had counted on. The moves 29.Rxe6+ Qxe6! 30.dxe6 (30.Qg5+ f6! 31.Qg7+ Qf7 32.Re1+ Kd7 would win) 30...Rg8 would make Black the winner.

The text neatly uncovers Black's pawn shield. Now the g7-pawn will be exposed with check.

28...fxe6

Black is once again left with no choice.

29.Qxg7+

White rescues both his Queen and his Knight. Black's King is placed in check.

29...Nf7

Like a bad dream that won't stop, Black is again forced to dance to the tune of White's moves.

After 29...Kd6? 30.Ne4+ Kxd5, 31.Qxb2 would win Black's Queen. It now seems as if White has run out of material and won't be able to checkmate Black's King. Being a Rook ahead, Black should win, right?

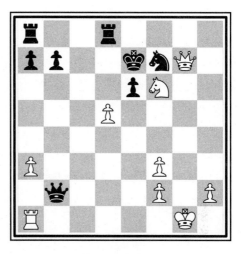

Endgame

30.d6+!

White delivers a beautiful clearance tactic on the long diagonal in order to pick off Black's Queen with Qg7xb2.

The problem is that the f6-Knight doesn't have a good square for a discovered check. After 30.Ng8+? Rxg8, White's Queen would be pinned to his King! Now the d5-square has been *cleared*.

30...Rxd6

Ribli must feel terrible — he now realizes that he is on the losing end of a brilliancy, with nothing to do. With 30...Kxd6 31.Ne4+, matters would grow worse.

31.Nd5+

With the scorpion's sting at the end of the combination, the long diagonal is neatly uncovered. White wins material.

31...Rxd5

Black makes White pay as dear a price as possible for the loss of the Black Queen.

32.Qxb2

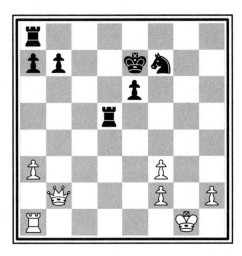

White completes the masterstroke of the combination.

The game has now reached a technical phase: White has a Queen (9), a Rook (5), and four pawns (4); Black has two Rooks (10), a Knight (3), and three pawns (3). Thus White has a material advantage of 18–16 points. His position is worth two extra pawns, a huge advantage at the grandmaster level.

In such technical phases, the easiest way to win the game is to trade pieces. In this case, White has an additional advantage, because Black's King is exposed. White can start a direct attack with Queen and Rook. Lack of a pawn shield means doom; Black's pieces can't cope against the powers of the Queen.

32...b6

Black saves his b7-pawn.

There was no reason to allow Qb2xb7+, which would lose the pawn with check. It was possible to throw in a check with 32...Rg8+ 33.Kh1, but Black would have no follow-up, and he would still have to worry about the b7-pawn.

33.Qb4+

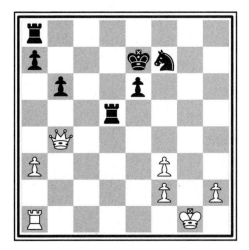

White begins his attack. His first aim will be to determine what Black intends to do with his King: will he stay in the center by interposing a piece, or will he move his King to the kingside?

This is the very essence of chess. You have to determine your target, and then you harass the target until it falls.

33...Kf6

Black makes perhaps the best decision.

After either 33...Nd6 or 33...Rd6, Black would be pinned. White would play 34.Rc1! preparing Rc1-c7, with decisive penetration. If Black were to abandon the e6-pawn by playing 33...Ke8, 34.Re1 Ne5 35.Qf4! would mean the loss of the e6-pawn.

34.Re1

White activates the Rook at last. Now White can consider Re1xe6+ with a combination designed to pick up the a8-Rook. He is also poised to play Qb4-h4+ to harass the Black King further.

34...Rh8

Black tries to prevent Qb4-h4+.

A check along the g-file with either 34...Rg8+ or 34...Rg5+ would be futile. After Kg1-h1, White's King would be perfectly secure. Black would like to create some kind of counterplay based on ...Nf7-e5, but 34...Ne5? 35.Qf4+! would mean the loss of the Knight.

35.h4!

The text robs Black of the g5-square, thereby incarcerating the f7-Knight; it also pushes a passed pawn, which ties down Black's pieces. In short, the text restrains Black's pieces while using one of White's trumps, the passed h-pawn.

Chess is a game of dualities. Not only do we *activate* our pieces — but also we *restrain* our opponents'. This constant struggle is an important dynamic to keep in mind.

35...Rhd8

Black had played ...Ra8-h8 to stop Qb4-h4+; now that the h4-square is blocked, Black looks for another way of utilizing his pieces. The text introduces the idea of ...Rd5-d4, to pick off the h4-pawn.

36.Re4!

White cold-bloodedly stops Black's threat and prepares Re4-f4+ to attack Black's King. Because of his material advantage, White is able to create more and more threats.

36...Nd6?

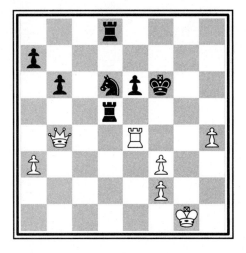

In a losing position, Black makes an error. He is tired of having a passive Knight and tries to activate it by planning for ...Nd6-f5. It would be better to play 35...Rf5, covering the King, but White would still win in the long run.

37.Qc3+!

A harsh blow — whichever way he moves, Black has to cough up material.

37...e5

Black chooses from a host of miserable options:

■ 37...Kg6 38.Rxe6+.

■ 37...Kf7 38.Qc7+ Ke8 39.Rxe6+.

■ 37...Ke7 38.Qg7+! Nf7 39.Qg6 R8d6 (39...Ne5 40.Qg5+ wins) 40.Rf4 Rf5 41.Rxf5 exf5 42.Qxf5, winning a pawn.

38.Rxe5

Une petite combinaison — White wins a pawn by force.

38...Rxe5

Black does what he has to do. Other moves such as 38...Rd1+? 39.Re1+! would allow White to win on the spot.

39.f4

White uses one of his doubled pawns to win back the Rook.

39...Nf7

Black tries to make the best of it.

After 39...Re8 40.fxe5+ Rxe5 41.f4, Black would lose his other Rook, too. Also, 39...Nf5 40.Qxe5+! Kg6 41.Qe6+ would pick up the f5-Knight. This variation shows the futility of 36...Nd6? — a misguided attempt to activate the Knight.

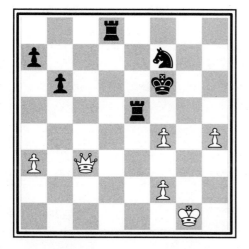

41.Qc4+

With a decisive check, Black is driven back: 41...Ke7 (41...Rd5 42.f4! with the threat Qc4-c6+ wins) 42.f4!. He cannot stop White's passed kingside pawns from a triumphant march down the board.

Black resigns.

This victory was especially invigorating, characterized by the original attacking flavor combined with the technical ease demonstrated at the end.

Like most sports, chess favors young players with intense energy. Even so, veterans can show the value of experience. As the first World Champion Wilhelm Steinitz was reputed to say in the twilight of his career, "I may be an old lion, but if someone sticks his head in my mouth, I can still bite."

40.fxe5+

White regains the Rook and undoubles the f-pawns. The e5-pawn is immune to capture because 40...Nxe5? 41.f4 would win the Knight.

40...Ke6

Other moves — 40...Kg7 41.e6+; 40...Kf5 41.Qf3+ Ke6 42.Qf6+ — would win the Knight.

▀▄▀▄▀▄▀▄▀▄▀▄▀▄▀▄▀▄▀▄▀▄▀▄▀▄▀▄▀▄▀▄▀▄▀▄

Supreme Effort

The Hoogoven tournament at Wijk aan Zee, the Netherlands, is the second-longest-running tournament in the world, currently approaching its sixth decade. Many sparkling games have been played in these tournaments. The following game was played there in 1985 between Ukrainian grandmaster Alexander Beliavsky and the Englishman Dr. John Nunn.

Both players have reputations for their fighting and calculating abilities. Another shared skill is their ability to produce the occasional masterpiece. When both players are in fighting form, their games can be explosive: this game serves as a case in point.

In annotating this game I've relied upon the remarks of Alexander Beliavsky in *Chess Informant 39,* and of John Nunn and Peter Griffiths in *Secrets of Grandmaster Play*.

■ ■ ■ ■ ■ ■ ■ ■ ■ ■ ■ ■ ■ ■ ■ ■

King's Indian Defense,
Saemisch Variation E81

GM Alexander Beliavsky
GM John Nunn
Hoogoven Tournament, Wijk aan Zee, 1985

Opening

1.d4

Like many of today's top grandmasters, Beliavsky can punch with either hand; that is, he can play both King Pawn and Queen Pawn Openings. He tends to rely upon Queen Pawn Openings when confronted by players who like to play sharply as Black.

1...Nf6

Nunn has a reputation for indulging in sharp opening play. He has played the Queen's Gambit, Tarrasch Variation, as well as the Benoni and the King's Indian. The text is the most flexible option because Black can still choose to play any of these defenses.

145

2.c4

This is the most consequent move. White is anxious to discover what defense his opponent has in mind.

2...g6

Black prepares to fianchetto the King's Bishop with the same move that we saw in Game Six. Since Nunn hasn't yet taken up the Grunfeld Defense — a defense played in combination with the move ...d7-d5 — it is safe to say he intends to play the King's Indian Defense.

3.Nc3

With the most favored move, White develops a piece to control the d5-square and the e4-square. If White can follow up with e2-e4, he will have an impressive pawn center, which will control nearly all the key squares.

3...Bg7

Completing the fianchetto, Black initiates the King's Indian Defense.

In the nineteenth century, most games featured what are called "classical openings." When White opened with either his King Pawn or his Queen Pawn, Black would try to reestablish the equilibrium by answering in kind. These classical defenses were considered to be mandatory, in line with the rule of the day: *whoever controls the center wins the game.*

By the turn of the twentieth century, as the world experienced extraordinary changes in technology, science, and philosophy, long-held precepts were questioned in every field of endeavor, including chess. The era gave rise to a group of "hypermodern" players. The two high priests of this new school of play were Aaron Nimzovich and Richard Reti. They attempted to prove that central control was overvalued. Instead they tried to strengthen their wings with fianchettos and played for a blocked center. They were so content to create their own plans, it seemed as if they would seize the initiative only after being threatened.

Naturally the classical players weren't very happy with these young hypermodern whippersnappers. They smugly termed these fianchetto plans as "Indian defenses," referring to those lacking civilization and said to be "backward." The hypermodernists were of course delighted that their new ideas had created such a stir. They immediately adopted the criticism as a badge of honor — a kingside fianchetto was dubbed the King's Indian Defense, and a queenside fianchetto the Queen's Indian Defense.

The hypermodernists aimed to build up a flank with a fianchetto and ceded control over the center to the opponent. Thereafter, they tried to blockade or close the center when play would turn to the flank, where they possessed an advantage. At least this was the theory. Sometimes the center was ripped open, and the hypermodernist was dispatched by his own petard. At other times the ideas of the hypermodernist worked beautifully, sending the classical player into fits.

Now we know the battle lines that are being drawn. Black will be happy to cede the center in order to develop wing play. White hopes to grab the center in order to effect a spatial squeeze and stop Black from getting any play with his pieces.

4.e4

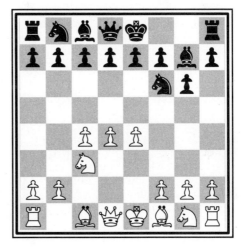

Dr. John Nunn

John Nunn was born on April 25, 1955, in London. He became an international master in 1975 and an international grandmaster in 1978. He earned a doctorate degree in mathematics, which helps explain his profoundly professional approach to the game. He is very objective when looking at the position at hand, avoiding the emotional upheavals of the moment. Keeping a cool head, he is ruthless with the initiative, and always on the lookout to exploit the tactical nature of a position.

An impressive piece of work — after only four moves, White has complete control of the center of the board. He either occupies or controls all the key squares. He also possesses the threat e4-e5, attacking the f6-Knight and forcing it to move, thereby gaining time and space. Such a deal!

Still, the hypermodernists wouldn't be easily convinced that White truly has the ascendancy. From their perspective, Black's kingside fianchetto has built a nice, safe home for his King. Once the King is tucked in, Black will turn his attention to carving out a strong position in the center. The clash will then begin in earnest.

4...d6

This is the first move to suggest that the center does count for something. Black prevents e4-e5 while preparing either ...e7-e5 or ...c7-c5, fighting to stake out some central squares.

Thus far the players are following the most standard moves of the King's Indian Defense. As the opening unfolds, the opening and defensive ideas will be further refined.

5.f3

White draws the battle lines by playing the Saemisch Defense.

This move is named for the grandmaster Friedrich Saemisch (1896–1975). Its guiding principle is quite similiar to White's attacking plans of Game Two: White readies his play with Bc1-e3 and Qd1-d2, planning Be3-h6 to exchange the fianchettoed g7-Bishop. The move prevents ...Nf6-g4, which would attack the c1-Bishop when it comes to the e3-square.

But the text isn't so single-minded in purpose. It is also directed against Black's strategic aims. If Black intends to cede the center and then close it down to play on the flank — especially the kingside — White wants to be ready for play on the kingside flank as well. The text can serve as a prelude to g2-g4-g5 or, in some cases, to pushing the h-pawn, known as the bum's rush.

Of the many ways of meeting the King's Indian Defense (5.Nf3, 5.f4, 5.Be2, 5.Bg5, 5.Nge2, 5.h3), the Saemisch is known as one of the most dangerous. Perhaps it is for this reason that King's Indian Defense players love to condemn the variation. In the words of King's Indian Defense aficionado GM Eduard Gufeld, "Please, ask the opinion of the gentleman sitting on the g1-square what he thinks of the move f2-f3."

GM Gufeld has a very good point. The move f2-f3 robs the g1-Knight of the f3-square. White also moves a pawn for the fourth time in five moves — hardly a blueprint for quick piece development.

5...O-O

Black has accomplished his goal: he has strengthened his flank by means of the fianchetto and has safely tucked away his King. He will now turn his attention to the center.

6.Be3

White develops his pieces behind the broad back of his pawn center. Having a pawn center brings this advantage: your pieces can take up active central squares, while your opponent's pieces get squeezed out of the action.

With the text, White intends to play Qd1-d2 and probably Be3-h6, seeking to trade Bishops. White embarks on this plan because the g7-Bishop will serve as an excellent defender of the Black King. The move also radiates a subtle influence queenside.

6...Nbd7!?

Though not unknown, this isn't Black's most standard move in this position.

Most common would be 6...e5, taking a stand in the center. After 7.d5 clamps down the center, Black would take up his play on the kingside with 7...Nh5 8.Qd2 f5 (8...Qh4+ is an interesting idea of GM David Bronstein) 9.O-O-O, with a difficult fight ahead. Besides 6...e5, Black's choices would include 6...a6, 6...c6, 6...c5, 6...b6, and 6...Nc6, all pointing in the direction of queenside play.

The text is intended to disguise Black's plan. He may still play for ...a7-a6, ...c7-c6, and ...b7-b5, to accomplish queenside expansion. Black could also play for ...c7-c5, aiming for a Benoni Defense style of play. At this stage of the game, the choice of opening and defensive moves is largely a matter of taste.

7.Qd2

The text offers the most standard treatment of the position. White keeps a flexible approach. He may castle queenside and go for a kingside attack, or he may castle kingside and play for a queenside attack! Once again, White's central pawn advantage gives him the choice of where to attack.

This move would not be my choice for White in this particular position. The major drawback for White when playing the Saemisch is deciding what to do with the g1-Knight. I consider Black's sixth move to be imprecise because it helps White answer this question. My choice would be 7.Nh3!, taking advantage of Black's previous move. White would now be ready for Nh3-f2 and further development of his position.

A recent game of mine, played in Moscow against Andrei Istratescu in 1994, continued with 7.Nh3 e5 8.d5 Nh5?! 9.g4 Nf4 10.Nxf4 exf4 11.Bxf4 Ne5 12.Be2 f5

13.exf5 gxf5 14.O-O fxg4 15.fxg4 h5!? 16.Bxe5 Bxe5 17.Qd3!, giving a clear advantage to White.

Another approach featuring rapid piece development would be 7.Bd3 c5 8.Nge2, developing behind the central pawn front.

7...c5

Before this game was played, the text had a poor reputation. According to the *Encyclopedia of Chess Openings* — a five-volume series cataloging the thousands of various openings — the text leads to an inferior position. But as we shall see, GM Nunn had come to the game with a special piece of preparation in mind. Black now takes an interest in fighting for central control.

8.d5

White makes the move recommended by nearly all opening books on the King's Indian Defense. He creates a powerful pawn wedge in the center to keep Black's pieces as cramped as possible. White now has a formidable spatial advantage that Black has to counter with great precision or else he will be choked.

A less impressive move would be 8.Nge2 (intending to answer 8...cxd4 9.Nxd4 to bring the g1-Knight to the powerful d4-square) 8...a6!, leaving White in a quandary. The f1-Bishop couldn't move, and White would be reluctant to castle queenside because ...b7-b5 would offer fine play for Black. After 9.Nc1 cxd4! 10.Bxd4 b6!, the players would have moved into a Hedgehog Defense, granting a favorable boost to Black. The c1-Knight would be momentarily misplaced.

8...Ne5!

This extremely combative move — GM Nunn's new idea — suddenly puts a great deal of pressure on White's position. Psychologically, White has been looking forward to nursing a nice positional advantage. Now he has to shift his thinking and decide how to develop his kingside pieces. Although the text looks very suspicious — the e5-Knight can get the boot by f3-f4 — it is by no means easy to refute.

In other grandmaster games, Black has played 8...Re8, preparing ...e7-e6 and 8...a6 and then planning a queenside break with ...b7-b5. In response to both moves, White played 9.Nh3!, solving the problem of what to do with the g1-Knight. White thus kept his spatial advantage and therefore dictated the course of play.

Middlegame

9.h3?

This serious mistake weakens White's kingside, especially the g3-square.

But I shouldn't be too critical. The text is the most direct attempt at refuting Black's scheme of development. White would dearly love to play 9.f4, but 9...Neg4! would allow Black to trade off the e3-Bishop. Other choices, such as 9.Nh3? Bxh3 or 9.Nge2? Nxc4, would both lose material. The idea 9.O-O-O? a6! would allow Black to play for ...b7-b5, keeping White's King from a comfortable future. With the text, White threatens 10.f4, forcing 10...Ned7; then 11.Nf3 would leave White with a large advantage.

White's best line of play was discovered by GM Jan Timman against Nunn in 1985: 9.Bg5! a6 10.f4 Ned7 11.Nf3 b5 12.cxb5 axb5 13.Bxb5 Qa5 14.O-O Nxe4 15.Nxe4 Qxb5 16.Bxe7 earned White an advantage. Thus Nunn's idea of a quick ...Nb8-d7-e5 was eventually shown to favor White. In any case, his preparation was hard to meet at the board because the move Be3-g5 — moving a piece that is already nicely developed — doesn't immediately spring to mind.

9...Nh5!

White has started the game with the goal of taking control of the center and pursuing the initiative. Instead, Black's Knights have charged out of their stables to harass White's position. This surprising move is thus quite logical. Black

immediately jumps at the chance to occupy the weakened g3-square, forcing White to react. In view of White's threat to play f3-f4, driving back the e5-Knight, the text could well be considered to be forced.

10.Bf2!

Both Beliavsky and Nunn now consider this to be an inferior move.

I disagree with them. Black's threat of ...Nh5-g3 is quite real. Therefore White must defend the g3-square.

This proves to be a bit more awkward than you might imagine. Here are the choices:

- 10.Ne2? Nxc4 loses the c4-pawn.

- 10.Kf2? e6 creates the threat of ...Qd8-h4+. White has managed to misplace his King.

■ In the counterattack 10.f4? Ng3 11.fxe5 (11.Rh2 Nxf1 12.Kxf1 Nxc4) 11...Nxh1 12.exd6 exd6, White's exchange sacrifice is not justified — analysis by GM Nunn.

■ According to both players, the best move would have been 10.Qf2, significantly complicating the play. White intends 11.f4 Nd7 12.g4 Nf6, driving the Knights to passive squares. Black has to react in a resolute manner: 10...e6! (a tempting but inaccurate switch would be 10...Qa5?! 11.Rc1! f5 12.exf5 Rxf5 13.g4 Nf4 14.Qd2!, treating White to a big advantage, according to GM Beliavsky) 11.g4 (11.f4 Bf6! 12.g3 [alternatives: 12.h4 Ng4 or 12.Nf3 Nxf3+ 13.Qxf3 Bh4+] 12...Nxg3! 13.fxe5 Bh4! gives Black the advantage; note how Black employs every resource he can to maintain his advanced Knights) 11...exd5 12.cxd5 (12.gxh5? d4! or 12.Nxd5 Nf6 would be good for Black) 12...Bf6! 13.h4 Bxg4! 14.fxg4 Nxg4. Black has sacrificed a piece for three pawns and an attack.

This is an excellent position to plug into your computer chess program and play against your computer. Or draft a friend or a family member to play the White pieces, and give them the business.

As you can see, the best moves after 10.Qf2 lead to Black's earning a strong,

probably winning attack. That is why I disagree with both players. In my view, the text was simply forced. Fireworks lie ahead as White gains an opportunity to improve his play.

10...f5!

A sharp, crucial move. As before, White threatened to knock Black's advanced Knights backward with g2-g4 and f3-f4. Besides facing this threat, the text is necessary because Black needs to take advantage of his better development by opening up the position. (The reader is referred to *Play Winning Chess* and *Winning Chess Strategies* for tips on how to play with an advantage in time.) Black attacks the e4-pawn, preparing to open up the f-file with ...f5xe4 and thereby developing the f8-Rook. The text also prepares for the development of the c8-Bishop.

Note that 10...e6 would be too slow since 11.g4! exd5 12.cxd5 Nf6 13.f4 now favors White, and the piece sacrifice 13...Nexg4 14.hxg4 Nxg4 15.Bh3! wouldn't offer Black sufficient compensation.

11.exf5

This capture is forced. Black has a strategic threat of ...f5-f4, which would allow him to maintain both Knights upon excellent outposts, especially the e5-Knight.

White can't expell the Black Knights by 11.g4? fxg4 12.hxg4 Nf4! — curing the weak g3-square would be worse than the disease. The f4-square and the e5-square are firmly in Black's mitt. With 13.Bg3 g5! 14.Qh2? h6!, White would be strategically lost. The line 11.f4? Bh6! 12.g3 fxe4 13.Nxe4 Bf5! would increase Black's advantage in development. White would face a harsh invasion with the continuation 14.Ng5(?!) Bxg5 15.fxg5 Be4 16.Rh2 Rf3!, which would result in a big advantage for Black.

11...Rxf5!!

This move is the heart of Nunn's new idea. He tries to stop White from playing f3-f4, driving back the e5-Knight.

Apparently, Black had to play 11...gxf5, but 12.f4 Ng6 13.g3 would give White a

big advantage, according to GM Beliavsky. White's advantage is based on the fact that Black's Knights have been rendered harmless. By continuing with Bf1-e2 and Ng1-f3, White would indeed enjoy the superior position. The other recapture, 11...Bxf5? 12.g4, would simply cost Black a piece.

12.g4

White is obliged to take up the challenge and fork Black's pieces. He has no way of developing his pieces, so he decides to grab the offered material.

Black threatens to increase the activity of his pieces by playing ...Qd8-f8 and ...Bg7-h6. White also has to take into account the possible move ...Nh5-f4, which would bring additional pressure against White's position.

12...Rxf3!

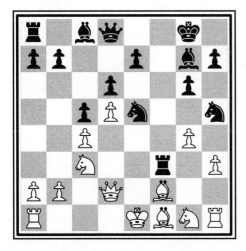

Black grabs the f3-pawn, which stabilizes the e5-Knight. He also opens the f-file. If Black can now create a battery down the f-file, White will sink into deep trouble.

13.gxh5

Naturally, White accepts the sacrifice. Other tries would lose quickly:

- 13.Nxf3? Nxf3+ forks White's King and Queen.

- 13.O-O-O (now planning to capture the f3-Rook) 13...Rf7! 14.gxh5 Qf8! 15.Rh2 Bh6! 16.Be3 Bxe3 17.Qxe3 Rxf1 allows Black to emerge a pawn ahead, with the better position.

- 13.Bg2? Nd3+ wins the f2-Bishop.

- 13.Be2 (trying to push back the f3-Rook before capturing the h5-Knight) 13...Rxf2! 14.Kxf2 Qf8+! 15.Nf3 Nf4 gives Black excellent compensation for his exchange. His grip on the dark squares offers a promising attack.

Since all these possibilities favor Black, taking the Knight immediately is the best practical decision. If White can weather Black's attack, his extra material will give him winning chances.

13...Qf8!

A beautiful follow-up. Black develops his Queen to a perfect square, producing a battery along the f-file and menaces ...Bg7-h6.

Nunn had reached this position in his preparations. It was nearly impossible for him to come to a conclusion regarding the validity of the sacrifice. He intuited that Black would get fair compensation. He based his judgment on several factors:

■ White's King is stuck in the center. He will never be able to castle queenside because ...Bg7-h6 will win.

■ White has great difficulties trying to develop his kingside pieces, especially the g1-Knight. Any move it makes will cost White the game.

■ Because of his lack of development, it is impossible for White to conduct a counterattack, which creates serious difficulties in practical play. White will spend a lot of time on his clock trying to devise a defensive plan.

With these factors in mind, Nunn prepared by acquainting himself as thoroughly as possible with the tactical and strategic themes of the position. If nothing else, he'd be far more familiar with the position than his opponent would be.

14.Ne4!!

White puts forth a superb defensive reaction. (Nunn confesses in *Secrets of Grandmaster Play* that he had overlooked it.)

White is facing two severe problems: Black's pressure along the f-file and the possibility of ...Bg7-h6, creating threats on the h6-c1 diagonal. Now White's move has made the threat of 15.Ng5 Bh6 16.h4!, blocking the diagonal and attacking the f3-Rook.

This stunning move was discovered only after rejecting several other weaker possibilities:

■ Trying to involve the Rooks in the defense would fail: 14.Rh2 Bh6! 15.Qe2 Qf4! 16.Rg2 Nd3+ 17.Qxd3 Rxd3 18.Bxd3 Qd2+ ends disastrously for White — analysis by GM Nunn.

■ With 14.Rd1 Bf5!, Black would threaten ...Bg7-h6, placing White's Queen in an awkward position. The developing move ...Bc8-f5, taking control of the d3-square, causes White to avoid the next line.

■ After 14.hxg6? Bf5! 15.gxh7+ Bxh7, White would have difficulties meeting Black's threat of ...Bg7-h6 and ...Bh7-d3, which would win. For example, 16.Rd1 Bh6 17.Qe2 Bd3 18.Rxd3 Nxd3+ 19.Qxd3 Rxd3 20.Bxd3 Qf4 gives Black a winning position.

These variations illustrate the enormous defensive difficulties that White must counter. Black's threats — which have appeared seemingly by magic — are all based on his superior development.

14...Bh6!

Black is up to the challenge as well. He had to reject two other ideas:

- Further development by 14...Bf5 would fail to crack the whip. After 15.Ng5 Nd3+ (15...Bh6 16.N1xf3! Nxf3+ 17.Nxf3 Bxd2+ 18.Nxd2 gives White a lot of material for the Queen) 16.Bxd3 Rxd3 17.Qe2, White will have traded off the powerful e5-Knight. The entrance of the c8-Bishop into the game would not make a big splash.

- Trying to get rid of the e4-Knight with 14...Rf4 15.Qe2 Bf5 16.Bg2! would be ineffective — White has managed some piece coordination.

The text is far more to the point. Black is very pleased with his e5-Knight, but as long as it remains parked there, the g7-Bishop remains largely silent. The text forces White to make an awkward decision: where will he move his Queen?

15.Qc2?

Surprisingly enough, this natural move is a critical error.

Nunn gives a superb analysis that proves that 15.Qe2 would have been White's best move. His main line runs thus: 15.Qe2! (threatening Ng1xf3, at last capturing the Rook; Black is compelled to win White's Queen) 15...Nd3+ 16.Qxd3 Rxd3 17.Bxd3 Qf4! (creating a powerful battery on the h6-c1 diagonal — when Beliavsky saw this move at the board, he gave up on his position, considering it to be hopeless) 18.Rd1! (protecting the d2-square) 18...Bf5 19.Ne2! Qf3 20.N2g3 (White is ready for Bd3-e2, kicking back the Black Queen) 20...Be3! 21.Rf1! Bxe4 22.Nxe4 Bxf2+ 23.Rxf2 Qxh5, producing a rough equality. I completely agree with this analysis, which confirms my comment about White's tenth move.

As this analysis points out, Beliavsky is facing a very unpleasant decision. The move 15.Qe2 would force him to give up his Queen, a prospect he thinks would lose the game for him. He therefore chooses the text, which leads to a labyrinth of complicated piece play, a labyrinth he has hoped would lead his opponent astray. White now threatens Ng1xf3, to pick off the invading Rook.

15...Qf4!

Ignoring the dangers to his f3-Rook, Black boldly plunges ahead. The Queen takes up a dominating influence in the center of the board. Black now threatens ...Bc8-f5 and ...Ra8-f8, involving all his pieces in the attack.

16.Ne2

White makes a heartbreaking decision.

He had desperately wanted to eliminate the f3-Rook, but after the capture, White would land in a much inferior ending: 16.Nxf3?! Nxf3+ 17.Kd1 Bf5 18.Bg3 (the alternative 18.Bd3 allows Black to clear the f3-square: 18...Nd4! 19.Bxd4 Qf3+ 20.Qe2 Qxh1+ 21.Kc2 Qxa1 — Black wins material) 18...Qe3! (drawing the g3-Bishop

back to the inferior f2-square) 19.Bf2 (forced, as the threat ...Bf5xe4 is too strong) 19...Qxe4 20.Qxe4 Bxe4 21.Bg2 Rf8. Nunn feels that this ending would favor Black. I agree. White's a1-Rook is particularly useless, and Black's minor pieces are playing dominating roles.

Although the final position in the above analysis is playable for White, GM Beliavsky himself had missed 18.Bg3, considering only 18.Bd3, which would fall victim to a clearance tactic. That said, he turned to the text, which makes a great deal of sense. White is facing the severe threat of ...Bc8-f5, which would win on the spot. He therefore develops and attacks Black's Queen. If he can force Black to move his Queen, he will have developed with tempo, turning back the attack.

16...Rxf2!

With this superb move, Black sacrifices an exchange in order to keep his attack alive.

Black would be lost after 16...Nd3+?? 17.Qxd3 Rxd3 18.Nxf4, which would stop him cold. If Black were forced to retreat with 16...Qf7 17.N2g3!, White would have stopped the fearful ...Bc8-f5 threat and developed his kingside.

Essentially the text is forced. Black is committed to go forward and cannot retreat. The f3-square is cleared, permitting ...Ne5-f3+ to harass White's King.

17.Nxf2

This is a forced recapture.

After 17.Nxf4?? Rxc2, Black would have won back his sacrificed material, investing him with active pieces and a winning position.

17...Nf3+

This is the key check that GM Nunn had in mind when he embarked on 15...Qf4 to invade White's position.

Black would lose if he had to move his Queen. For example, with 17...Qh4? 18.Qe4! or 17...Qe3 18.Bg2! Bf5 19.Qc1, White would win. Black is trying to

weave an extraordinary position that he hopes will prohibit White's Rooks from taking part in the defense.

18.Kd1

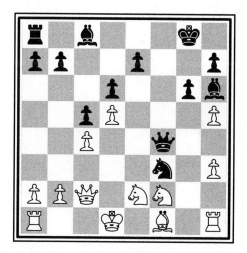

The only possible move denies the f2-Knight protection.

18...Qh4!

This fine move eyeballs the f2-Knight.

The attractive-looking 18...Qe3 would actually have been a mistake. The line 19.Ng4! Bxg4 20.hxg4 Qf2 21.Bh3! would stop the threat of ...Qf2-e1 checkmate and prepare a counterattack by h5xg6 or Rh1-f1.

White now faces a perplexing predicament. Despite being an entire Rook ahead, he has serious problems deciding what to do with his f2-Knight. If he tries to defend the Knight with 19.Rh2?? Nxh2 or 19.Nc3? Nd4! 20.Qe4 Qxf2, the result would cost him material. The f2-Knight is obliged to move.

19.Nd3

White moves the Knight while guarding the e1-square against the possible ...Qh4-e1 checkmate.

White cannot sacrifice the f2-Knight for a counterattack because his position is undeveloped. The following variation illustrates a constant truth: *don't start an attack without development.* For example, 19.hxg6? Qxf2 (threatening ...Qf2-e1 checkmate) 20.gxh7+ Kh8 21.Qg6 (threatening his own Qg6-g8 checkmate, White vacates the c2-square) 21...Qe1+ 22.Kc2 Qd2+ 23.Kb3 Qe3+! 24.Kc2 Bd7! gives Black a winning attack. Threats include ...Bd7-a4+ and ...Nf3-e5, which would enforce ...Bd7-f5+ and a mating attack.

Nunn proposes a continuation that illustrates the power of Black's attack: 25.Qd3 Qxd3+! (a stunning move — Black agrees to trade Queens despite

being a Rook behind) 26.Kxd3 Bf5+ 27.Kc3 Bg7+ 28.Kb3 Nd2+ 29.Ka3 (29.Ka4 Bc2+! wins) 29...Nxc4+ 30.Kb3 Nd2+ 31.Ka3 b5!.

This nice piece of analysis is a bit overdone. Neither grandmaster analyzed this variation to its conclusion at the board. Both players understood that the counterattack 19.hxg6? would fall flat on its face because of White's lack of development. Still, it's of great practical value to play through such variations because they will give you an appreciation of just how dangerous Black's attack has become.

19...Bf5

At last Black is able to introduce his c8-Bishop.

It is through this simple device of development (time) that Black is able to create further threats. Because of the pin that the text produces, White now faces the winning ...Nf3-e1. White also has to consider moves such as ...Nf3-e5 or ...b7-b5, taking aim at the c4-pawn. At this point, Black's concern is how to involve the a8-Rook in the attack. Thus the moves ...b7-b5 and ...Ra8-b8 become possibilities.

20.Nec1

White deals with the threat of ...Nf3-e1 by reinforcing the d3-Knight.

White has two other ways to meet Black's threat — 20.Qc3 or 20.Nc3.

GM Nunn offers long-winded but convincing refutations of these options:

■ 20.Qc3 (20.Qb3? encourages the winning 20...b5) 20...Bg7 21.Qb3 Bxd3 22.Qxd3 Qe1+ 23.Kc2 Qxa1 24.Qxf3 Qxb2+ 25.Kd1 Qa1+ 26.Nc1 Bh6! 27.Qa3 Rf8 (intending ...Rf8-f3) 28.Be2 Rf2 29.Re1 Rh2 (threatening ...Rh2xh3) 30.Kc2 Bxc1 31.Qxc1 Qxa2+ 32.Kd1 Rxh3 — Black has garnered a harvest of four pawns for his piece, with further threats like ...Rh3-b3 in sight.

■ 20.Nc3 (GM Nunn considers this move to be best, and in the following analysis concludes that White would likely win with it; he criticizes the game move because, as Black, it simplifies his task to victory) 20...Nd2! (the exclamation mark is GM Nunn's; as we shall see, I disagree with him) 21.Qxd2 (GM Nunn cites quite a bit of analysis to prove that White has to give up his Queen, and he is correct, because the threats of ...Nd2xc4-e3+ or even ...Nd2xf1 would be too powerful to meet) 21...Bxd2 22.Kxd2 Qxc4 — at this point the threat of ...Qc4-d4 and ...c5-c4 will force victory.

In my view, the defense 20.Nc3 is not better than the text. Black could move into a simple endgame win by playing

20...Nd4 21.Qf2 Qxh5+! (GM Nunn considers only 21...Qxf2 22.Nxf2 Bc2+ 23.Ke1 Nf3+ 24.Ke2 Nd4+, which forces only a perpetual check) 22.Be2 (or else 22.Ke1 Rf8! wins; with 22.Ne2?, Bxd3 wins) 22...Nxe2 23.Qxe2 Bxd3 24.Qxh5 gxh5 — a quite hopeless turn of events for White. Black's Bishops would dominate the board, locking up the a1-Rook. He already has two pawns for the exchange with another, the c4-pawn en prise.

20...Nd2!

Nunn describes this choice as "a strangely powerful move, threatening above all 21...Qe4 22.Rg1 Qe3 and if 23.Rh1 Qf3+ [winning]."

I agree with him. The move is strange because Black's Knight sidles up to White's King without threatening him

directly. It powerfully prevents White's Queen from sliding over to the kingside. The defensive move Qc2-f2 is stopped, leaving White's pieces bottled up in the center.

21.hxg6!

White resorts to tactical tricks to save his position.

Endgame

21...hxg6!

Black is up to the task.

The tempting 21...Qe4? would fall into White's trap. After 22.gxh7+ Kh8 (22...Bxh7? 23.Rg1+ would stop ...Qe4xh1 with check; 22...Kxh7? 23.Ne1! would rescue White's position) 23.Rg1 Qe3 24.Qc3+ Kxh7 25.Rg7+! Bxg7 26.Qxd2, White would be alive and kicking. By recapturing, Black keeps his winning threat of ...Qh4-e4.

22.Bg2

An unhappy decision. Although the text stops ...Qh4-e4, it does nothing to cover the c4-pawn. White's position is quickly slipping.

The alternative 22.Qxd2 Bxd2 23.Kxd2 Qxc4 24.Bg2 Qd4, intending ...c5-c4, would lead to a convincing win for Black.

22...Nxc4

The Knight emerges recharged. Besides pocketing a pawn, Black now threatens a devastating fork on the e3-square.

23.Qf2

White gets out of the fork and hopes to find his way into an ending without Queens.

A bad choice would have been 23.Re1? Qh5+ 24.Qe2 Ne3+, allowing Black to win at once.

23...Ne3+

Black could also have chosen 23...Qxf2 24.Nxf2 Ne3+ 25.Ke2 Nxg2, securing a winning ending, but Nunn has calculated that he doesn't have to cash in his chips so easily — his pieces create a beautifully coordinated attack.

24.Ke2

It's amazing that despite being a Rook ahead, White has to walk such a narrow path of moves.

The choice 24.Ke1? Nxg2+ would cost the g2-Bishop with tempo.

24...Qc4!

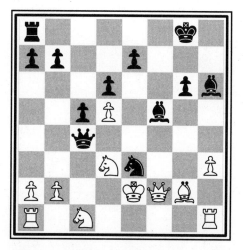

Nunn sums up the text perfectly: "There seems to be something slightly comical about this switch to the queenside, just when the White Queen has managed to crawl painfully across to the f2-square."

The Black Queen's position on the h4-square has been devastating, threatening to pop down to the e1-square with a sudden mate or to go after the h1-Rook. Now Black intends to pick on the d3-Knight.

25.Bf3

White acknowledges that he can't rescue his d3-Knight.

With 25.Rd1 Nxd1 26.Kxd1 Bxd3, Black would win back the Rook and continue his attack. The inadequate 25.Qxe3 Qc2+! 26.Kf3 Bxe3 27.Kxe3 Qxg2 would be curtains.

25...Rf8!

Black correctly chooses time over material. By introducing the a8-Rook into the attack, White's position becomes engulfed. He goes down in a blaze of glory.

Black could play 25...Bxd3+ 26.Nxd3 Qc2+ 27.Ke1 Qxd3, winning a piece. In that case, doing his best to hang on, White would play 28.Bd1, stopping ...Ne3-c2+.

26.Rg1

White has no defense. He is hopeful that after Black exchanges his f5-Bishop, the g6-pawn will be weakened. In any case, White has been up a Rook for nearly the entire game. It's about time he put it to use!

26...Nc2!

Black delivers an absolutely devastating move. Black could win a piece with 26...Bxd3+ 27.Nxd3 Qc2+ 28.Ke1 Qxd3, but the text will win two pieces!

27.Kd1

White tries to escape the threat of ...Nc2-d4+ which would fork King and Bishop. White's last hope is that Black will be lured into taking the a1-Rook as bait.

27...Bxd3

No such luck. Black accepts the harvest. He threatens ...Nc2xa1 as well as ...Nc2-d4, leaving White defenseless.

White resigns.

I feel that this game was the best one of the 1980s. A novel opening idea, followed by a series of sacrifices, kept Black's initiative alive. White's errors were subtle and were only uncovered by precise play. GM John Nunn considers this game to be the supreme effort of his illustrious career.

Moscow Miracle

I n the FIDE candidate cycle of 1984, a substantial challenge to FIDE World Champion Anatoly Karpov emerged, embodied in young Garry Kasparov. Kasparov had fought his way through the zonals, interzonals, and three elimination matches. In succession he defeated Alexander Beliavsky, Victor Korchnoi (as we saw in Game Six), and Vassily Smyslov. The FIDE championship match was staged in the prestigous Hall of Columns in Moscow from September 9, 1984, to February 15, 1985 — a grueling six-month match unprecedented in the history of chess.

The rules for the FIDE title were the same in 1984 as they had been in the 1978 and 1981 matches. The winner would be the first to win six games. Draws did not count, keeping the possibility open for an unlimited match. At first, no one worried about such a fate. On November 24, Karpov won game 27. He had won five games; the rest of the games had been draws. It seemed that the match would end at any moment.

At this, the darkest moment in his career, Kasparov changed his tactics. He started a rearguard action to avoid the sixth loss. With superhuman calm, Kasparov managed to prevent defeat. Three weeks later, on December 13, Kasparov had won his first game ever against Karpov, and the score was now 5–1. Officials of the Soviet Chess Federation and FIDE were getting restless. All state functions at the Hall of Columns had been postponed because of the match. When would it end?

Karpov himself was unable to end the match. By the sixth month, the match stood at 5–3, and Kasparov had won games 47 and 48. Having come from behind with virtually no chance at winning, Kasparov had become buoyant. He now estimated that his chances to win the match were somewhere between 25 and 33 percent. But not everyone was as enthusiastic: the organizers were exhausted, and hasty backroom deals took place when the president of FIDE stepped in to call the match to a halt. On February 15, 1985, the match was stopped without a decision. Karpov's two-point lead was negated. The new match would start from scratch.

The second match was staged in the Tchaikovsky Concert Hall in Moscow from September 3 to November 9, 1985. The match's rules stipulated the traditional 24-game conditions. The first player to reach $12^1/_2$ points would be the winner; if the match was tied 12–12, Karpov would retain his FIDE crown. After 15 games, the match was tied $7^1/_2$–$7^1/_2$. Both players had managed two victories each, with the other games drawn. The players and observers were nearly choking on the tension. It seemed that the players were equally matched, and the next victory would be sure to decide the FIDE World Championship.

In my annotations to this game, I've relied on two of Garry Kasparov's works, *Garry Kasparov: New World Chess Champion* and *Fighting Chess*.

■ ■ ■ ■ ■ ■ ■ ■ ■ ■ ■ ■ ■ ■ ■ ■

Sicilian Defense B44

GM Anatoly Karpov
GM Garry Kasparov
Moscow, 1985 (Game 16)

Opening

1.e4

Up to this match, Karpov would invariably choose to open with his King Pawn. In sharp positions his opening preparation gave him a large advantage against his rivals.

1...c5

For his part, Kasparov has nearly always chosen the Sicilian Defense. In his razor-sharp style of play, the Sicilian provides a perfect match for his arsenal. His favor-ite variations of the Sicilian include the Scheveningen and the Najdorf.

2.Nf3

Playing for an Open Sicilian with d2-d4, White is anxious to test his opponent's preparation.

2...e6

With the text, Kasparov indicates his preference for a Scheveningen Defense.

The Najdorf Sicilian would be initiated after 2...d6 3.d4 cxd4 4.Nxd4 Nf6 5.Nc3 a6, setting up a fathomless position. Many books have been written that deal exclusively with only one or two lines of the Najdorf.

3.d4

White makes this move in order to open the game for his pieces.

3...cxd4

Black trades a wing pawn for a central pawn.

4.Nxd4

White recaptures the pawn and positions the Knight in the center of the board.

4...Nc6

Here is the same position that we saw in Game Three. Black invites a Scheveningen.

By this move order, Black avoids the Keres Attack, which would occur after 4...Nf6 5.Nc3 d6 6.g4!, introducing the threat of g4-g5 with a kingside initiative.

5.Nb5

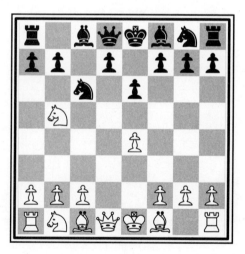

Although White moves his d4-Knight yet again, the text is considered the most challenging. Black's move 2...e6 has weakened the d6-square. White hopes to play Nb5-d6+, forcing Black to give up his f8-Bishop, which would leave the dark squares c5, c7, d6, e5, and e7 without a defender.

5...d6

Black prevents Nb5-d6+ and at the same time prepares ...a7-a6 in order to drive the b5-Knight away.

6.c4

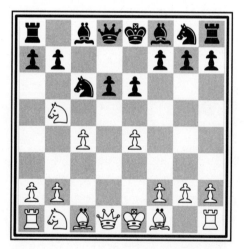

White erects the Maroczy wall (also known as the Maroczy Bind). White's idea is as simple as it is purposeful. He intends to control the d5-square with all his might.

Why is this square so important? The answer is the d6-pawn. As long as White controls the d5-square, Black's d6-pawn will be weak. As pieces are traded, the game shifts toward an endgame, and the d6-pawn will grow weaker and weaker.

The idea of the Maroczy wall is to restrain Black in the center, keeping him pinned down, and then to start to direct operations against the d6-pawn. If Black is unable to shake off the shackles (the e4-pawn and the c4-pawn) in the center, he will have a difficult struggle.

6...Nf6

Black develops his position with the intention of throwing White's development into disarray.

Black's natural inclination would be to play 6...a6, driving White's b5-Knight away. Play might develop along these lines: 6...a6 7.N5c3 Nf6 8.Be2 Be7 9.O-O O-O, which would allow White to solve the problem of his b1-Knight by playing Nb1-d2, thus keeping the Maroczy wall.

The purpose of this move is to get White first to play Nb1-c3 and then to drive the b5-Knight to the offside a3-square — an important opening nuance.

7.N1c3

White defends the e4-pawn.

After the retreat 7.N5c3 Be7 8.Be2 O-O 9.O-O b6, Black would try to do without the tempo-losing ...a7-a6. The pinning of 7.Bg5 would do no good, since 7...Qa5+ 8.Qd2 (8.Bd2 Qd8 9.Bg5 Qa5+ would only repeat the position) 8...Nxe4 9.Qxa5 Nxa5 10.Nc7+ Kd7 11.Nxa8 Nxg5 would win material in the short term. White would face the problem of how to rescue the a8-Knight. According to theory, this variation is considered to be good for Black.

7...a6

As White's threats of Bc1-f4 or Bc1-g5 grow serious, Black hastily kicks away the invader.

8.Na3

White's a3-Knight hasn't made a happy journey. But despite all his hopping, White still has the comfort of controlling the d5-square.

After 8.Nd4 d5!, Black could take advantage of the opportunity to get in the freeing break ...d6-d5, with equality.

The players have now reached a position played in hundreds of previous games.

8...d5(?)

A courageous idea. White's whole strategy was based on preventing this freeing break, which Black makes anyway!

Four games earlier, in game 12 of this match, Kasparov had played the same gambit. Taken by surprise, Karpov had played carefully, and the game was drawn after a mere 20 moves. In the intervening days between these two games, both camps had gone to work analyzing the position for the next clash. Whose preparation was superior?

The text has a certain appeal. White has worked hard to stop ...d6-d5, which Black achieves at once. If after the many captures on d5, White is unable to keep the extra pawn, Black will achieve a simple equality.

The justification for the text is based on the tempi that White has spent in playing Ng1-f3xd4-b5-a3. Black has played solid moves while White has been hopping about. Black hopes to prove that all the tempi were misspent. Unfortunately, as we shall see, the idea doesn't work. And a good thing too! If it did, the decades-old idea of the Maroczy wall would be unplayable.

9.cxd5

White has no choice. He must accept the gambit.

9...exd5

Black recaptures in order to isolate a White pawn on d5. Black will try to regain the pawn by playing ...Nc6-b4 — but that is skipping ahead!

10.exd5

This move is the only way to play for an advantage.

After 10.Nxd5 Nxd5 11.exd5 (with 11.Qxd5 Bb4+ 12.Bd2 Be6! 13.Qxd8+ Rxd8 14.Bxb4 Nxb4, Black would have excellent compensation) 11...Bb4+ 12.Bd2 Qxd5 13.Bxb4 Nxb4, the game would be equal. By avoiding a trade of Knights on d5, White prevents the possibility of ...Bf8-b4+.

10...Nb4

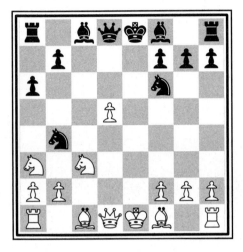

Black leaves White with a simple task: defending the d5-pawn. If Black recaptures the d5-pawn, he can expect a satisfactory position.

11.Be2!

Karpov reveals his preparation. He has discovered that with swift development, he will have the advantage of a symmetrical position.

This plan is revealed by considering 11...Nbxd5 12.0-0 Be7 (12...Bxa3 13.Qa4+ would be followed by Qa4xa3) 13.Nxd5 Nxd5 14.Bf3 Be6 15.Nc2! which offers a clear advantage because of the threat of Nc2-d4 — analysis by GM Kasparov.

In game 12, Karpov had played 11.Bc4 Bg4! 12.Be2 Bxe2 13.Qxe2+ Qe7 14.Be3

Nbxd5, and Kasparov achieved a comfortable draw.

In the stem game (the first game in which a new idea is played) between Károly Honfi (White) and Péter Dely (Black) in the 1965 Hungarian championship, White played 11.Qa4+?, developing his Queen too early. With 11...Bd7 12.Qb3 Bf5, Black enjoyed a fine game.

11...Bc5 (!)

Kasparov makes his masterstroke. He intends not to win back the d5-pawn immediately; indeed, he may play the position as a gambit altogether.

The justification for Black's sacrifice is based upon the fact that White's a3-Knight is out of play, whereas Black's pieces can be quickly developed to take up active squares. It seems that Karpov's preparation was superficial. He had mainly prepared for 11...Nbxd5, expecting to receive an advantage.

12.O-O?

White misses his chance to refute Black's gambit.

Karpov reached the same position against Dutch GM John van der Wiel in the 1987 SWIFT tournament in Brussels. Karpov played 12.Be3! Bxe3 13.Qa4+! Nd7 14.Qxb4 Bc5 15.Qe4+ Kf8 16.O-O, providing a big advantage for himself. As John van der Wiel remarked to me after this game, "If Karpov had played the way he played against me today, he might still be FIDE champion!"

The text is certainly not a bad move and perhaps doesn't deserve the question mark that I give it. It is a reasonable move in that it helps White's position, but it is a mistake in that it takes a position that offers a big advantage and turns it into one that will probably be merely balanced.

12...O-O

Black too is quick to castle, looking forward to the approaching middlegame.

In *Garry Kasparov: New World Chess Champion*, Kasparov notes:

> White is at a crossroad. If he wishes he can of course immediately simplify the position: 13.Bg5 Nbxd5 14.Nxd5 Qxd5 15.Bxf6 Qxd1 16.Rfxd1 gxf6, when Black

should be able to draw without any particular difficulty. But why should White voluntarily part with his material advantage, when Black does not appear to have any threats, nor even any serious counterplay? And although he sensed that I had made a thorough study of the resulting positions, Karpov nevertheless considered himself obliged to play for the win.

Middlegame

13.Bf3

Indeed, White can't prevent himself from playing for a win, mainly because his keen sense of danger doesn't register any problems. The text is a natural move. White reinforces his extra d5-pawn and will then consider what to do about the offside a3-Knight.

13...Bf5!

Black at once makes it clear what his source of counterplay will be: the a3-Knight. The text stops Na3-c2, and 14.Nc4? Bd3! is unplayable.

The text is the first link in a long strategic chain. Black intends to control as many squares as he can using his pieces. Simultaneously he will limit the activity of White's pieces. As you play through the next moves, keep a space count.

14.Bg5

White follows the principle that, strategically speaking, when your opponent's pieces control more space than your own, it is a good idea to trade pieces.

In this case the choice was between the text and 14.Be3, opposing the c5-Bishop. After 14.Be3 Bxe3 15.fxe3 Qb6 16.Qd2 (in 16.Nc4!? Qc5 17.Qd4 Qxd4 18.exd4 Bd3 19.Nb6 Bxf1 20.Nxa8 Bxg2!, Black would win back his pawn and achieve an unclear position) 16...Rfe8, the newly created e3-pawn would become a target. White sees no reason to be so generous.

14...Re8!

Again I stress that Rooks need open files. It is essential to control the e4-square. The text complements Black's strategy, controlling the open e-file and gaining space.

After 14...h6 15.Bxf6! Qxf6 16.Be4, White's problems would vanish. He would be able to play Na3-c2 and, with his extra pawn, have the better position.

15.Qd2

White connects the Rooks and prepares to challenge the e-file.

White avoids 15.Re1? Bxf2+! 16.Kxf2 Nd3+ because it would cost him material. White had the opportunity to return the pawn by playing 15.Nc4!? Bd3 16.a3! Bxc4 17.axb4 Bxb4 18.Re1 Rxe1+ 19.Qxe1, resulting in a roughly balanced position. As before, Karpov prefers to keep his extra pawn.

15...b5!

Black rules out Na3-c4 once and for all and his strategy begins to really take shape. His pieces are active, controlling many squares, whereas White's pieces are becoming more confined.

16.Rad1

White continues to make natural moves, ignoring his lack of piece activity.

This was the moment for active operations: 16.d6 Ra7 17.Rad1 Rd7 18.Qf4 Bg6 19.Bxf6 Qxf6 20.Qxf6 gxf6 21.Nd5! would secure an equal game. As we've seen, White has to return his pawn to get activity, and when he does, the game becomes balanced. Karpov continues to keep his extra pawn, believing it will bring him victory. After all, he will always have a chance to return the pawn . . .

16...Nd3!!

Black's Knight takes up a tremendous outpost.

In the words of GM Raymond Keene and IM David Goodman in *Manoeuvres in Moscow*, "This piece starts out as a Knight but shortly transforms into a monstrous centralized octopus, tentacles grasping out in all directions, hovering over the key squares."

This comment is right on the mark. The d3-Knight is an octopus controlling eight key squares. The text also opens the way for ...b5-b4, winning a piece. The warning lights are beginning to flash.

17.Nab1?

White continues to make natural moves. White assumes that he will be able to evict the d3-Knight by way of Bf3-e2 without giving up the d-pawn. The text sidesteps the threat ...b5-b4, which would win a piece. Presumably, it also prepares to bring the Knight into play. But where is it going? And how is it going to get there?

Kasparov recommends 17.d6! Ra7! (17...b4? 18.Bxa8 Qxa8 19.Bxf6 gxf6 20.Na4 bxa3 21.Nxc5 Nxc5 22.Qd5! Qxd5 23.Rxd5 Re5 24.Rxe5 fxe5 25.bxa3 would make a better ending for White) 18.Nd5 with an unclear position. White would lose his d6-pawn but would be able to double Black's kingside pawns.

17...h6

A useful move. Black questions the g5-Bishop, forcing it to declare its intentions. Sometimes White employs the defense Bg5-e3, and Black wants to rob White of this opportunity.

18.Bh4

White has no choice. After 18.Bxf6 Qxf6, Black would win the two Bishops and would be prepared to continue to bring his pieces to better squares. White can't continue with 19.Be2? Nxf2! because 20.Rxf2 Bxb1 would win for Black.

18...b4!

With admirable consistency, Black continues his strategy of denying White's pieces useful squares. In the short term, the c3-Knight has got to go. In the longer term, the b1-Knight has a dreary future. White's minor pieces lack coordination, whereas Black's minor pieces, particularly the d3-Knight, work wonderfully.

19.Na4

White's Knight is forced to the side of the board. With the text, White hopes for relief by threatening Na4xc5 in order to trade pieces.

After 19.Ne2 g5! 20.Bg3 (20.Bxg5 Nxf2 [threatening ...Nf2-e4+] 21.Rxf2 Bxf2+

22.Kxf2 hxg5 23.Qxg5+ Bg6 gives White inadequate compensation for the exchange, and Black threatens ...Nf6-e4+ to win White's Queen) 20...g4 21.Qxh6 gxf3 22.Qg5+ Bg6, Black would have a winning advantage.

19...Bd6!

Black preserves his Bishop while letting the a4-Knight stew on the a4-square.

Black now threatens ...Ra8-c8 and ...Bd6-f4, trapping White's Queen in the center of the board. Black's opening and middlegame preparation has worked spectacularly well. How much of this did Kasparov prepare?

In *Garry Kasparov: New World Chess Champion*, Kasparov himself gives us this answer:

A position for which I had aimed in my preparatory analysis! Black's achievements are now patently obvious. White's minor pieces are scattered about on either flank and are quite unable to coordinate, the placing of the Knights being particularly depressing. But Black's main achievement is that the wonderful duo of Bf5 and Nd3 completely paralyzes all three White major pieces — a very rare occurrence in a practical game!

20.Bg3

White stops the previously mentioned threat. He would like to exchange a few pieces to ease the pressure.

A weak choice would be 20.Qc2? Rc8 21.Qb3 Nf4 (threatening ...Bf5-c2) 22.Rc1 Rxc1 23.Rxc1 g5 24.Bg3 g4, with a big advantage for Black. Because Black's pieces control so many squares, he's able to generate numerous threats.

20...Rc8!

Black sends his Rook to the open c-file, seizing control of four White squares.

Black had to reject two other interesting moves:

■ 20...Ne4 would win the two Bishops. Play would be forced, with 21.Bxe4 Bxe4 leaving the d5-pawn ripe for plucking. White could slip out of Black's grip with 22.Qe3! if he threatened to trade Queens by Qe3-b6.

■ Black could play to win the d5-pawn: 20...Bxg3 21.hxg3 Qa5 22.b3 Rad8 23.Nb2! Nxd5! 24.Nc4! (the complications of 24.Nxd3? Nc3! 25.Qc2 Nxd1 26.Rxd1 Rxd3 27.Rxd3 Qb5! 28.Be2 Bxd3 29.Bxd3 Re1+ would lead to 30.Kh2 Qh5 mate) 24...Qc5 25.Bxd5 Rxd5 26.Ne3 Rdd8 27.Nxf5 Qxf5 would give Black a large positional advantage — analysis by GM Kasparov.

This second possibility was obviously very attractive to Kasparov — the great deal of calculation shows that he was interested in winning back the d5-pawn. What caused him to choose the text was his own preparation. He understood that Black's pieces contained so much dynamic attacking possibility, that he should be more ambitious and aim for more than just winning back the d5-pawn.

In this second possibility, the reader should note how many pieces White has been able to trade. With the text, Black tightens the screws on the position and asks White how he intends to solve his problems. In chess, there is always a fine tension between risk and reward. Black has risked a pawn and would like to win it back with interest. On the other hand, by not cashing in his chips too early, perhaps he can earn more!

21.b3!

Despite the presence of the powerful d3-Knight, White finds the best way to repair his position. The problem is the White Knights. If White is able to play Na4-b2, he will be right back in the game. It seems that White doesn't have too much to worry about — Black has maximized his pieces and failed to produce a concrete threat.

21...g5!!

Here's another move that could drive a chess teacher nuts. Under normal circumstances, it would be a big mistake to weaken the pawn shield covering your King. But in this particular position, Black needed to introduce more forces into the game. The text prepares either ...g5-g4 or ...Nd3-f4, and then ...Rc8-c2, allowing a strong attack.

Securing the f4-square is a crucial consideration. White has two ways of driving away the d3-Knight, and Black prepares its evacuation, just in case.

22.Bxd6

Black's previous move prevented 22.Nb2? Nxb2 23.Qxb2 g4 24.Be2? Rc2, which would win. The other way to kick the d3-Knight would also fail: 22.Be2? Ne4! 23.Qxd3 Nxg3 would win because of the double attack on the d3-Queen and e2-Bishop. It seems that White has to live with the d3-Knight for a moment or two longer.

Kasparov's notes state that White should have tried 22.h4!? to strike back on the kingside. He goes to great lengths to prove that 22...g4? would be a bad move because 23.Be2 Ne4 24.Qxh6 Bf8! would come out okay for White. The immediate 22...Ne4 23.Bxe4 Bxe4 24.hxg5 Bxg3 25.fxg3 Qxd5 would end up favoring Black. Although Kasparov's notes are detailed and interesting, the move 22.h4 has a simple answer.

Karpov demurred from 22.h4 because it would definitely weaken his kingside. Black would voluntarily move away from the d3-square and aim his pieces directly at White's King: 22.h4 Nf4! 23.hxg5 (it is important to weaken the g5-pawn) 23...hxg5 (Black could also consider 23...Rc2, invading with tempo) 24.Bxf4 (24.Rc1 Ne4 25.Bxe4 Bxe4 26.f3 Bxb1! would be very strong for Black) 24...Bxf4 25.Qxb4 Bd6 26.Qd2 g4 27.Be2 Nh5! — Black would gain a winning attack through the threats of ...Rc8-c2 and ...Qd8-h4, playing for mate — analysis by GM Kasparov.

I conclude that White is facing a host of unpleasant choices: 22.Be2?, 22.Nb2?, or 22.h4 would weaken his King; the text means having to trade pieces. Karpov chooses the text on principled reasons: he is happy to trade pieces, and he doesn't want to start an attack (h2-h4) from an inferior position. At this point in the game, White realizes that he should rein in his ambitions and try to equalize the game.

22...Qxd6

In recapturing the Bishop, Black's Queen is brought into the battle. Opportunities to go after the h2-pawn grow instantly enticing.

23.g3

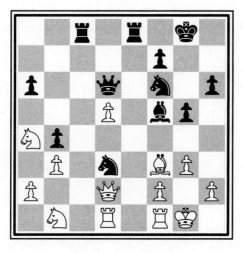

White stops the retreat ...Nd3-f4 and prepares Na4-b2, getting rid of the d3-Knight once and for all.

White's King would get scorched after 23.Be2? Nf4 24.Bc4 Ng4! (threatening ...Nf4-e2+ — as I said, attacks against the h2-pawn would be enticing) 25.g3 Rxc4! 26.bxc4 Re2! 27.c5 (with 27.Qd4 Be4! threatening ...Nf4-h3 mate, White's kingside would be overwhelmed) 27...Qg6 28.gxf4 Qh5!, and White would soon be mated — analysis by GM Kasparov.

As before, 23.Nb2? Nxb2 24.Qxb2 g4! 25.Be2 Rc2 would result in the loss of the e2-Bishop.

23...Nd7!

A brilliant move. Black declines the opportunity to win the d5-pawn: 23...Nxd5 24.Nb2! Nxb2 (24...Nc3 25.Nxd3 Nxd1 26.Nxb4 Qxd2 27.Nxd2 Nc3 28.Nc4 offers some chances to hold despite being an exchange down) 25.Qxb2 (25.Bxd5?! Qf6!) 25...Qf6 26.Qxf6 Nxf6 would force White to struggle into a difficult ending.

Black is not interested in endings. He simply wants to reinforce his d3-Knight with ...Nd7-e5 and then play for an attack on the weak light squares (h3, f3, and e2). The text prepares an absolutely insidious trap.

24.Bg2

This move causes quite a stir. For the last few moves, White has been preparing Na4-b2. Now that he has his chance to get rid of the octopus on d3, he refuses! Why? Because of a trick of profound elegance: 24.Nb2 Qf6!! 25.Nxd3 Bxd3 26.Qxd3 Ne5!.

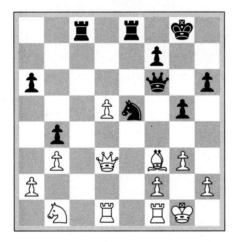

Lo and behold, with such a progression of moves, White's Queen would be trapped in the middle of the board! There would be no squares to which it could escape.

A more tenacious move would be 24.Nb2 Qf6!! 25.Nc4, but even here, Black would have a forced win: 25...N7e5 26.Nxe5 Nxe5 27.Bg2 (27.Be2 Rc2 28.Qe3 Bd3 would threaten 29...Rxe2, and 29...Nf3+ would win) 27...Bd3 28.f4 (forced because 28.Rfe1 Nf3+ would win) 28...Rc2! 29.Qe3 (29.fxe5? Qb6+ would win)

29...Bxf1 30.Rxf1 gxf4 — Black must win — analysis by GM Kasparov. In this final line, 31.gxf4 Qg6! is Black's point.

With the text, White enters a defensive shell. He retreats the f3-Bishop from possible attacks, ...Nd7-e5 in particular, and simply tries to maintain his position as best he can. Since Karpov is a superb and gifted defender, his failure to try to solve the problems of his Knights is most surprising.

I think it was strategically *required* that 24.Nb2 Qf6 25.Nc4 be played. As we saw in the previous paragraph, White would lose an exchange, but I don't think that in the final position, things are so cut and dried. After 31.Rxf4, White would still be kicking. It would be good practice to play this final position with a friend or on your computer.

24...Qf6!

Strategically, White's fate is sealed. Now that control of the b2-square has been secured, White is unable to redeploy the a4-Knight. The a4-Knight will be shut out for much of the rest of the game, and Black will be playing the position a piece or more ahead. (Besides the offside a4-Knight, what is the b1-Knight doing?)

25.a3

White gropes to find squares for the Knights.

25...a5

Black keeps control over the c3-square. White's Knights are bottled up.

The move 25...bxa3?? would be a horrible strategical blunder; 26.Nxa3 and White's Knights are ready to prance like chargers.

26.axb4

White continues to fight for squares for his Knights.

26...axb4

Black continues to deny him those same squares.

27.Qa2

This move is not much of an achievement. White can finally move his Queen and make way for Nb1-d2, where he can at last get some action going.

27...Bg6!

Beautifully done. Black continues to deny White any minor piece activity. Black's plan is to meet 28.Nd2 Re2 with a decisive pin along the second rank. The moves 29.Bf3? Qxf3! would win a piece for Black. Thus the text stops Nb1-d2, leaving White to look for something else. The text also casts desirous eyes upon the f3-square. The idea of pursuing an attack based on ...Nd7-e5-f3+ appears very promising.

28.d6

At long last, White decides to give back his extra pawn to promote piece activity. The pawn's value has gone far down. After 28...Qxd6 29.Nd2, White will get to activate only one Knight while still leaving the d3-Knight unfettered.

28...g4!

My admiration for Black's play grows with each and every move. Black sees no reason to pick up White's d-pawn. Instead he continues to pursue his gathering of squares. Virtually all of White's pieces are dominated! With the text, Black nails down the f3-square, readying his attack on the light squares.

29.Qd2

This is a sad commentary on White's position. He has nothing to do, reduced to moving to and fro.

The line 29.f3 (29.f4 Bf5!? again would give White nothing to do) 29...h5 30.fxg4 Qd4+ 31.Kh1 hxg4 would leave White worse off than before. He has weakened his King's position.

29...Kg7

Black prevents any active play that might result from 29...h5 30.Qh6 Re2 31.Rd2, which, though giving Black a much better position, would allow White to activate his Queen. The text is sweet poetry; White is being bound hand and foot.

30.f3

White has no other place to move. He has to weaken his King with the text or simply resign himself to a slow death. If nothing else, Black could play ...h6-h5-h4-h3, making strong threats.

30...Qxd6

Now that the f-file is coming open, Black removes his Queen. At long last the d6-pawn is captured, and White has no trumps to offset the d3-Knight.

Another interesting idea would be 30...h5!? 31.fxg4 Qd4+ 32.Kh1 hxg4 33.Rf4 Qa7, controlling a host of crucial squares. The text is definitely the simplest.

31.fxg4?!

White avoids the hopeless ending 31.Qb2+ Qf6 32.Qxf6+ Nxf6 33.fxg4 Nxg4, in which Black's Rooks are perched to parachute into White's position. As bad as this ending may be, the middlegame is worse for White.

31...Qd4+

Black robs White of the chance to utilize the b2-square again.

32.Kh1

There is nothing else to be done. With 32.Rf2 Nf6! 33.h3 Qxf2+ 34.Qxf2 Nxf2 35.Kxf2 Bxb1! 36.Rxb1 Rc2+ 37.Kg1 Re3, Black would win.

32...Nf6!

Black is starting to move in for the kill. The text envisages ...Nf6xg4-f2+ with a smothered mate in view.

33.Rf4

White desperately tries to retain the g4-pawn.

After 33.g5 Ng4! 34.gxh6+ Kh7, Black would win. The line 33.h3 Re3! 34.Rf3 (34.Rf4 Qe5 would threaten ...Re3-e2, to win) 34...Rxf3 35.Bxf3 Ne4 36.Bxe4 Qxe4+ 37.Kh2 Ne5 would end with a smashing victory on the light squares. Black threatens ...Ne5-f3+ and ...Rc8-c2 with a decisive attack.

33...Ne4!

This move spells doom. Black threatens to play ...Ne4-f2+ to win.

34.Qxd3

White gets rid of the horrible "Knight-mare." The moves 34.Rxe4 Rxe4 35.Qxd3 Qxd3 36.Rxd3 Re1+ would win all of White's pieces.

34...Nf2+

Black wins White's Queen, but White has one trick left.

35.Rxf2

White makes a forced move. After 35.Kg1 Qxd3 36.Rxd3 Nxd3 37.Rf1 Rc2, White would be material down and tied up once again.

35...Bxd3

Black happily nips White's Queen.

36.Rfd2

This is White's trick: he hopes to pick up a third piece for his Queen. He is one move away from Na4-b2, which would do precisely that.

36...Qe3!

Kasparov has calculated a beautiful finish that quickly ends the game. The text gets him out of the pin and threatens the winning ...Bd3xb1.

37.Rxd3

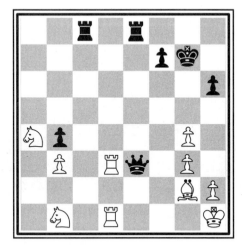

The only move — White had to grab the d3-Bishop before it grabbed him!

37...Rc1‼

With dazzling brilliance, Black offers back his Queen to get a basketful of pieces in return.

The tempting 37...Qe1+? 38.Bf1! (38.Rxe1? Rxe1+ 39.Bf1 Rxf1+ 40.Kg2 Rxb1 would win) would stymie Black momentarily.

38.Nb2

White has been trying for this move since the opening. He is still trying to coordinate his Knights.

38...Qf2!

Black continues with blow after blow. He could also win with the mundane

38...Rxd1+ 39.Rxd1 Qxb3, but the text is much prettier.

39.Nd2

The c1-Rook is poison: 39.Rxc1 Re1+ 40.Rxe1 Qxe1+ would lead to mate the next move. Meanwhile, Black's last move also threatened ...Qf2xb2, capturing White's errant Knight.

39...Rxd1+

Black uncovers the first rank. The next check will be decisive.

40.Nxd1

Making the time control, Karpov insists upon seeing the final move.

40...Re1+

Convincing. After 41.Nf1 Rxf1+ 42.Bxf1 Qxf1 mate, the game will be finished once and for all.

White resigns.

This extraordinary, simply outstanding game elated grandmasters around the world. Black's opening and middlegame preparation followed by the execution of his plan was simply stunning — it was all over before the players even moved into the endgame. Kasparov, who has won many brilliant games, considers this to be his supreme creative achievement. No one will argue. For me, it was simply a miracle in Moscow.

À la Morphy

I t is hardly a surprise to anyone who has even a passing interest in chess to be told that the sport is dominated by Soviet, or rather Russian, players. Since the end of World War II, Soviet chess players have held a complete hegemony over the World Championship title. Only Bobby Fischer broke their dominance. It has often been said that Russian players are to chess what French chefs are to cooking. Simply put, they are the best.

Although Russia continues to produce the world's finest chess players, their Western colleagues aren't ceding them the whole field. Following Bobby Fischer's victory in 1972, Western players as a group have become more challenging. This is especially true in the 1990s. Holland's finest player, Jan Timman, once rose in the world's rankings to become the second-best player in the world. In 1993 Jan Timman competed with Anatoly Karpov for the FIDE championship. Indeed, although the West has yet to produce another Bobby Fischer, as a group, Western players now compete equally with their Russian colleagues.

In 1990, the Dutch broadcast station KRO sponsored a match between Jan Timman and me in Hilversum, Holland. The match was well attended, piquing a great deal of media interest. It was seen as a duel between the best of the West. I disappointed the Dutch audience by decisively winning, 4–2 (three wins, one loss, and two draws). The following was my best win of the match. Enjoying the lead for the first time in the match, I knew that Timman would be spoiling for a fight. This suited me fine. I just wanted to be sure that this would take place on my terms, in a variation of my choosing. I consider the game to be my gem in the style of Paul Morphy. To enjoy the comparison I'd like to make, the reader must be familiar with the game played between Morphy and the Duke of Brunswick, Count Isouard, in Paris in 1858 (see *Winning Chess Tactics*, pp. 146–148).

My annotations for this game first appeared in *Inside Chess* magazine. They were written right after the match was completed and reflect the elation I felt at the time. I've modified my notes to give a deeper explanation of the ideas behind the moves.

■■■■■■■■■■■■■■■■

Nimzo-Indian E21

GM Yasser Seirawan
GM Jan Timman
KRO, Hilversum, 1990 (Game 5)

Opening

1.d4

For many years this has been my favored opening move. Today's grandmasters tend to employ Indian and modern defenses, eschewing classical defenses. I enjoy the spatial advantages that White gets playing against these modern defenses.

1...Nf6

This is Timman's favored defense, which he had employed all throughout the match.

2.c4

As we've seen, this is the standard response.

2...e6

Black chooses to play a Nimzo-Indian or a Queen's Indian Defense.

It was a bit of a relief to see Timman stick to his guns. I hadn't prepared for either a King's Indian Defense or a Grunfeld. If

Timman had chosen either of these, I would have opted for a quiet line.

3.Nf3

I develop and control the e5-square.

White has three major choices: 3.Nc3, fighting for the e4-square (this would invite 3...Bb4, transposing into the Nimzovich Defense); the text, 3.Nf3; or 3.g3, the Catalan Opening. By playing the Catalan, White would fianchetto and prevent the Queen's Indian Defense, 3...b6, in which Black fianchettos his Queen's Bishop.

Timman's favorite defense is the Queen's Indian. I have an opening weapon against the Queen's Indian Defense that I love to employ. The games in this match in which I was White featured important battles in this opening.

3...b6

Timman is faithful to his favorite Queen's Indian Defense.

Black intends either to fianchetto with ...Bc8-b7, controlling the e4-square, or to employ what I call an *extended* fianchetto with ...Bc8-a6, attacking the c4-pawn. The idea behind this defense is similar to

what I explained in Game Eight. Black takes a restrained approach to the center. He strengthens his queenside flank with a fianchetto and intends to block the center. This done, Black will enjoy an advantage on the queenside.

4.Nc3

This constitutes the most direct challenge to the Queen's Indian Defense — going after the e4-square.

If White can accomplish e2-e4, Black's position would become very difficult because Black's opening revolves around controlling the e4-square. If Black loses control, or if White gains control, of the e4-square, the fianchetto will lose its effectiveness. White will have a massive pawn center that could bury Black under an avalanche of pawns.

Because the c3-Knight is such a useful piece, Black is quick to play the move ...Bf8-b4, pinning the Knight. Therefore Tigran Petrosian's move 4.a3, preventing ...Bf8-b4 and preparing Nb1-c3, has become popular.

4...Bb4

Black develops his position and pins the c3-Knight.

In some cases it is natural for Black to follow up with ...Bb4xc3+ to double White's queenside pawns. In that case, the c4-pawn can become vulnerable to the maneuver ...Nb8-c6-a5 as well as ...Bc8-a6, attacking the c4-pawn directly.

5.Qb3

This is an opening specialty of mine. To answer Black's strategic threat of doubling the queenside pawns, White normally counters with 5.Bg5, creating a pin on the kingside. My idea is straightforward: protect the c3-Knight while simultaneously attacking the b4-Bishop. The idea hasn't gained a lot of adherents because White has to commit his Queen rather early.

5...c5

With the most consequent move, Black protects his b4-Bishop while attacking the center.

In this position, Black has also tried 5...a5 and 5...Qe7, protecting the Bishop. A mistake would be 5...Bxc3+? 6.Qxc3, allowing White to gain a tempo over classical Nimzo-Indian variations.

6.a3!

I put the question to the b4-Bishop. White's Queen is vulnerable to ...Nb8-c6-a5 with tempo. The idea of the text is to force Black either to trade pieces on c3 or to occupy the a5-square.

6...Ba5

Black sees no reason not to maintain the pin. After 6...Bxc3+ 7.Qxc3, White would earn the two Bishops and an opening advantage.

7.Bg5

It's a wonderful feeling to see your preparation on the board! I aim for rapid development, in particular the move

Jan Timman

Jan Timman was born in Amsterdam on December 14, 1951. He became an international master in 1971 and a grandmaster in 1974. In 1993 he played for the FIDE championship but lost the match to Anatoly Karpov. Jan has a very enterprising approach to the game. He often challenges his opponents directly in their areas of strength. This has caused him to lose a number of games but equally makes him a much-feared competitor. No one likes to lose from their favorite positions!

O-O-O; breaking the pin is important for White's control over the center.

7...Nc6?!

This move is excessively aggressive. Black tries to force White to make a decision in the center by attacking the d4-pawn.

Today's theoreticians consider 7...Bb7 or 7...h6 8.Bxf6 Qxf6 to be Black's safest choices.

8.O-O-O

A stunning move. White voluntarily brings his King to the queenside, where he has a poor pawn shield, the c4-pawn being far too advanced to offer protection.

After 8.e3 O-O 9.Be2 cxd4 10.exd4 d5!, Black would be allowed to achieve a fine game. With the text, White threatens d4-

d5 followed by e2-e4-e5, blowing Black off the board.

8...Bxc3!

Black parries with the best way of dealing with the threats that White's last move offered. White has broken the pin and could play Nc3-e4, leaving the a5-Bishop stranded with nothing to do. Black now lays a cunning little trap.

9.d5!

This is the only move that will maintain my advantage.

After 9. Qxc3 Ne4!, Black would break the g5-d8 pin to secure a comfortable game. The proof is that 10.Bxd8 Nxc3 11.bxc3 Kxd8 would leave White with doubled pawns on the queenside. In this ending it wouldn't be important that

Black has lost the right to castle, since White would be unable to coordinate a mating attack. The text avoids this line and offers a promising pawn sacrifice. My idea is to play in the center and to take advantage of his better development.

9...exd5?

Black makes a crucial mistake — in fact, a losing mistake! Black voluntarily trades his e6-pawn for White's c4-pawn.

Why is this so crucial? Consider White's f1-Bishop. With the c4-pawn traded, the Bishop has much greater mobility; it will be released with devastating effect. Before the game, Timman had prepared 9...Be5! 10.dxc6 Bc7! 11.cxd7+ Bxd7 12.g3 Qe7 13.Bg2 Rd8 with equality — analysis by GM Timman. Timman had an over-the-board inspiration and decided to opt for a complicated game, the type I really enjoy.

- Black avoided 9...Bxb2+? 10.Qxb2 Na5 11.e4, which would give White an awesome pawn center for his one-pawn investment.

- Black also avoided 9...Nb4?! 10.bxc3 Na6 11.e4, which is similar to the previous line and very good for White.

- Another strong position would be 9...Nd4!? 10.Qxc3 Ne4 11.Bxd8 (11.Qxd4!?) 11...Nxc3 12.bxc3 Nxf3 13.Bc7 Ng5 14.f3!, threatening to trap the g5-Knight with h2-h4. Play would remain forced: 14...f6 15.dxe6 Nxe6 16.Bd6 would allow White's d6-Bishop to take up a powerful outpost.

These variations show how tricky the nature of the position really is. That is why preparation before the game is crucial at the highest levels. Grandmasters don't have enough time on their clocks to wade through such a tangle of variations. Black would have been better off sticking to his preparation.

10.cxd5

I recapture the pawn and prepare to grab one of Black's pieces on the next move. By trading a pair of pawns, we have opened up the board. *Never forget that open positions favor the player who is better developed.* The elements of timing and space in chess were covered in depth in *Play Winning Chess.*

10...Be5

Black removes one of his pieces from capture.

The text is a forced move because other options are inferior:

- 10...Na5? 11.Qxc3 would leave the a5-Knight misplaced. White would soon take the center with e2-e4, garnering a much better position.

■ 10...Nd4? 11.Qxc3 Nxf3 12.gxf3 would be in White's favor, too. The open g-file, the two Bishops, and the large pawn center would certainly come in handy.

■ 10...Ba5 11.dxc6 would misplace the a5-Bishop. White would continue to play in the center with e2-e4 and develop the f1-Bishop. Black would have a difficult game.

■ 10...Bd4!? would be a sharp try to win the f2-pawn, but the tactics would work out badly for Black because 11.dxc6 Bxf2 12.e3! would entrap the Black Bishop. By continuing with Rd1-d2, White would enjoy a winning position.

11.dxc6

I recapture the sacrificed piece.

At this point I am very satisfied with my position and optimistic about an early knockout. First, I have a direct threat of Nf3xe5, simply winning a Bishop. My other pieces have also landed upon excellent squares. The d1-Rook, b3-Queen, and g5-Bishop all join to put pressure on Black's position. Because Black's c5-pawn is on the board and the c-file is half closed, even my c1-King isn't under any pressure. If I can quickly bring my kingside pieces into play, things will work out wonderfully.

11...Qe7!

Black also plays for development. The text gets out of the pin on the d-file, making ...d7xc6 possible. By defending the e5-Bishop, Black avoids the problems stemming from 11...Bc7? 12.e4! d6 13.e5, which would place him in a deep quagmire.

Before reading on, take a good look at White's position and consider how you would continue here. General principles tell us to pursue quick development, control of open lines, and so on, while preventing our opponent from doing the same. The most likely moves for White appear to be 12.Nxe5 and 12.e4, playing in the center. We would reject 12.dxc7 on principle: why help the opponent develop? Armed with my two candidate moves, my thought process unfolded as follows:

■ 12.Nxe5 Qxe5 13.f4 would look nice, especially after 13...Qf5?? 14.e4 Nxe4 15.Bd3 d5 16.Bxe4 dxe4 17.Rd8 checkmate! How sweet! After enjoying a few more crunching lines, my enthusiasm soured: 13...Qe6! 14.Qxe6+ fxe6 15.Bxf6 gxf6 16.cxd7+ Bxd7 would amount to nothing. So much for grabbing the two Bishops.

■ Therefore, 12.e4 had to be right. Certainly 12...Bc7? 13.e5! Bxe5 14.cxd7+ Bxd7 15.Rxd7 Kxd7 16.Bb5+ Kc7 17.Re1 would convince one and all that I was on the right track. Also, 12...h6 13.Bxf6 Bxf6 (13...Qxf6 14.cxd7+ Bxd7 15.Nxe5 Qxe5 16.Rxd7 Kxd7 [16...c4 17.Qd1] 17.Qxf7+ Kc6 18.Ba6 would be the end of the game for Black) 14.Qd5 d6 15.c7 would pocket the a8-Rook in the corner. All my instincts told me that 12.e4 *must* be right.

Still, I had some nagging doubts. Wilhelm Steinitz once said, "The best way to refute a gambit is to accept it!" I couldn't see how White would proceed after 12.e4 dxc6! 13.Nxe5 Qxe5 14.f4 Qc7! when not a single convincing blow was in sight — only feeble moves such as 15.Bc4, 15.Qg3!?, and 15.f5, playing for a positional advantage. So my mind drifted back to the position at hand. After visualizing a lot of cxd7+ variations, it

became clear that I needed to play Bg5-f4. This led me to the right idea.

Middlegame

12.cxd7+!

This move is absolutely contrary to my approach. I've been seeking a way to develop my pieces, and here I'm developing my opponent's. What gives? The point will be obvious within the next two moves. Essentially, the move doesn't develop my opponent's pieces so much as it clarifies the position and lures Black's pieces to vulnerable squares.

12...Bxd7

Naturally Black is happy to capture the pawn that has managed to zigzag all the way down the board (c2-c4xd5xc6xd7).

13.e3!

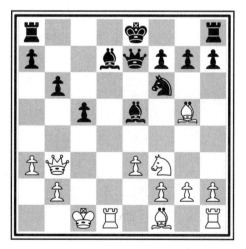

As Victor Korchnoi would say, "Really! *Sooo* simple." White prepares to develop the f1-Bishop and leaves it up to Black to find a decent reaction.

13...Rd8

With the text, Black at last plans to bring his King to the kingside and to safety. It's clear Black's King can't go to the queenside or remain in the center.

Black faces an amazing shortage of moves:

- 13...O-O-O is out of the question: 14.Ba6+ Kb8 15.Nxe5 Qxe5 16.Bf4 wins. This is the essence of the move e2-e3: White protects the f4-square, making Nf3xe5 and Bg5-f4 possible.

- 13...Bc6, getting out of harm's way along the d-file, would result in 14.Bb5 Rc8 15.Bxc6+ Rxc6 16.Qa4; White wins material.

- 13...O-O? 14.Nxe5 Qxe5 15.Bxf6 Qxf6 16.Rxd7 grabs a piece, which illustrates the point behind 12.cxd7+ — to lure the c8-Bishop to the d-file.

- 13...h6 14.Rxd7! Kxd7 15.Nxe5+ Qxe5 16.Qxf7+ Kc6 17.Bf4 features the same points. White's Bishops and Queen would combine for a winning attack.

- Finally, 13...Bd6 would be a mistake because the d-file is crowded with Black Bishops: 14.Bc4! (threatening the f7-pawn, 14.Bxf6 Qxf6 15.Qd5 Ke7! would allow Black to defend) 14...Be6 (14...O-O 15.Qd3 would win a Bishop along the d-file) 15. Qa4+ Bd7 16.Bb5 O-O-O 17.Qa6+ followed by Rd1xd6 would be curtains.

All these variations left the Dutch commentators wondering how Timman would resolve his tactical malaise.

14.Rxd7!

Morphy would be proud. White doesn't waste a tempo in attacking.

After 14.Bb5? Bd6!, Black would still be kicking. Now my fantasy is 14...Kxd7 15.Qa4+! Ke6 (as we've seen, when Black's King steps on the h2-b8 diagonal, White wins material by 15...Kc8 16.Ba6+ Kb8 17.Nxe5 Qxe5 18.Bf4, winning the Black Queen) 16.Bc4+ Kf5 17.Qc2+ Kg4 18.h3+ Kh5 19.g4+ to win. No kamikaze

King today! These lines show how terribly Black is being punished for trading my c4-pawn on move 9.

14...Rxd7

Shucks! My fantasy will have to remain just that. In the other possible recapture, 14...Qxd7? 15.Bb5 would win Black's Queen.

15.Bb5

The Bishop enters the game with devastating effect, threatening to capture the d7-Rook, . . . and then the e5-Bishop, . . . and then the f7-pawn. More important, with each developing move, White's attack is picking up speed.

15...Bd6

Black desperately tries to block the d-file.

Black has no time for 15...O-O? 16.Bxd7 Qxd7 17.Nxe5, which would win a piece. And 15...Kd8 16.Bxd7 Kxd7 17.Nxe5+ Qxe5 18.Qxf7+ would allow White to implement his threat.

16.Rd1!

I develop and pile up the threats.

16...O-O

The Black King gets to safety at last. Black was facing far too many threats to keep his King in the center.

17.Bxd7!

This move recaptures the sacrificed exchange. Black's Queen is forced into an unpleasant pin on the d-file.

17...Qxd7

Black has no choice but to recapture the piece.

18.Bf4!

This is the clearest move. The tempting 18.Bxf6 gxf6 19.Qd5 Rd8 20.Nh4 Qe8 21.Nf5 Bc7! wouldn't produce an immediate win. The text poses a painful question to Black: how will he handle the d-file pin?

18...c4

The only chance.

The option 18...Ne8? 19.Qd5 would win for White. The series 18...Ne4 19.Qd5! Qa4

(19...Nxf2 20.Bxd6 [20.Qxd6 is also strong] 20...Nxd1 21.Ne5 Qd8 22.Kxd1 would be over soon after e3-e4) 20.Bxd6 Rd8 21.Ne5 Nxd6 22.Nc4! would exploit the d-file pin once again. The back-rank mate after 22...Nb7 23.Qxd8+ Nxd8 24.Rxd8+ Qe8 25.Rxe8 checkmate would be a nice touch. The purpose of the text is to prevent either Qb3-d5 or Qb3-d3, which would create a battery on the d-file.

19.Qc2!

I prevent the defense ...Nf6-e4 by controlling the e4-square.

After 19.Qc3? Ne4 20.Qd4 Qe6 21.Bxd6 Rd8, Black would be able to turn the tables with his own pin along the d-file. He would then be forced to address the question of how he's going to defend the d6-Bishop. A horrible mistake would be 19.Qxc4?? Rc8!, allowing all of White's hard work to go up in smoke. Black would win because of his pin on the c-file.

19...Ne8

Black makes the only possible move. After 19...c3? 20.Rxd6 cxb2+ 21.Kb1!, he would have insufficient play for the sacrificed piece. In this case, White's King could use Black's b2-pawn as a shield.

20.Ng5!

This beautiful move forces Black to create new weaknesses. White has two threats, Qc2xh7 mate and Ng5-e4, piling up the pressure on the d6-Bishop. At first, creating the battery by 20.Qd2 looks quite strong, but 20...c3! 21.Qxc3 (21.bxc3? Bxa3+ would allow Black to save his skin) 21...Qe6 would break the pin on the d-file with the minimum loss of a pawn. I was greedy and wanted to win more than a pawn.

20...f5

This is the only move that can stop both of White's threats.

21.Qxc4+

I give Black no reprieve. After 21.Qd2 h6 22.Nf3 Rf6, Black would still cling to a bit of hope. Now I could calculate the sequence of moves that would bring a won position.

21...Kh8

Black is forced to move his King into the corner, setting himself up for various kinds of mates, including a Philidor and back-rank mate.

22.Bxd6

I put forth the best move, again nudging Black.

22...Nxd6

Black is forced to bring his Knight to the vulnerable d6-square.

Endgame

23.Qd5!

This is the key move. From the exalted outpost of the d5-square, White's Queen lords it over the position. Black is given one tempo to deal with the pin on the d-file, but that will not be the end of his problems.

23...Rd8

The text is quite sensible. Black protects the d6-Knight and prepares to move his Queen, getting out of the pin along the d-file.

Still, there is no defense. Black has a lot of choices, but, for one reason or another, they all lose:

- With 23...Rf6 24.Qa8+ Qe8 25.Qxe8+ Nxe8 26.Rd8 Rf8 27.Ra8, the game would be over. White has an extra pawn and would win another one on the queenside. He would then be two pawns ahead with good positions for his pieces, locking up a technical win.

- With 23...Rc8+ 24.Kb1 Rc6 (protecting the d6-Knight) 25.Nf7+ Qxf7 26.Qxc6, White would win an exchange with a continued attack.

- Black could try to evacuate his Queen from the d-file with either 23...Qc7+ or 23...Qc8+ 24.Kb1, lines that either way transpose into the same outcome that actually occurred in the game.

24.Ne6!

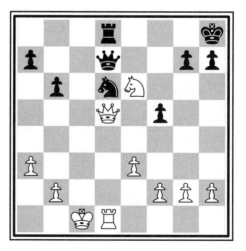

I sidestep Timman's last trap. The text is cold-blooded. Black's Rook protects the d6-Knight. I'm just trying to drive the defender away.

My original intention was 24.Qxd6 Qc8+ 25.Kb1 Rxd6 26.Rxd6; I thought that the threat of 27.Rd8+ Qxd8 28.Nf7+ to fork Black's King and Queen would win. I stopped myself when I realized Black could play 26...Kg8! with the better game.

24...Qc8+

Black desperately tries to clear the d-file. After 24...Rc8+ 25.Kb1 Rc6 26.Nd8!, the Rook would be forced to abandon the d6-Knight.

25.Kb1

White's King skips out of danger. Black is left dealing with the threat to his Rook.

25...Rd7

Black finds the only way to protect the d6-Knight as well as avoid having the Rook captured.

26.Qxd6!

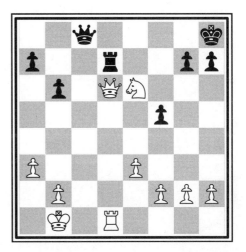

In this simple and shocking finale, White invites 26...Rxd6 27.Rxd6, and Black can't prevent Rd6-d8 from winning back the Queen.

Black resigns.

Jan Timman was the first to congratulate me on winning the match. For just a moment, I felt as if I was the best of the West. More than anything, I was very happy with my victory in this game. With sharp development play, I felt a momentary kinship with Paul Morphy, one of history's greatest players.

▀▄

Lightning and Thunder

The 1990 FIDE World Championship match was again a duel between Garry Kasparov and Anatoly Karpov. The match had two sites and two sponsors. The first half of the 24-game match was played in New York City and sponsored by Ted Field of the Interscope group. The second half of the match was played in and sponsored by the city of Lyons, France.

The players were playing for three million dollars and the diamond-studded Korloff trophy, valued at over half a million dollars. Big stakes for a chess match? You bet. But a mere two years later, Bobby Fischer and Boris Spassky would be playing a match for over five million dollars!

The following is game 20 from the series in the 1990 match. More than any other, it features the attacking skills that make Kasparov such a dangerous player. Dutch grandmaster Jan Timman joked with me that for this game, Karpov wanted to test Kasparov's attacking skills and that "Kasparov passed the test!" I added, "Yes, with flying colors."

The 1990 match featured a healthy debate concerning the classical King Pawn Opening known as the Ruy López. Karpov chose a modern defensive line of the Ruy López discovered by his trainer, the grandmaster Igor Zaitsev. The Zaitsev Variation has been Karpov's first line of defense for nearly a decade. For this game, Karpov came prepared with an improvement: 18...Nf6. But Kasparov was ready. He quickly responded, causing Karpov to freeze on his very next move. To no avail, Karpov tried to sidestep Kasparov's attack. Soon Kasparov had both Bishops, both Knights, both Rooks, and the Queen lined up against Karpov's King. The only thing missing was the kitchen sink.

The tension did not last long. Kasparov unleashed lightning bolts, first with a Knight sacrifice, then a Bishop sacrifice, and finally a Queen sacrifice. Thunder followed 15 moves later in this vintage Kasparov game, combining naked aggression, attack at all costs, and chaos in harmony. The notes from this game include comments from my book *Five Crowns*, about the fifth FIDE championship match played between these two players.

■ ■ ■ ■ ■ ■ ■ ■ ■ ■ ■ ■ ■ ■ ■ ■

Ruy López Zaitsev C92

GM Garry Kasparov
GM Anatoly Karpov

FIDE championship, Lyons, 1990 (Game 20)

Opening

1.e4

Using a King Pawn opening in his first 11 games as White during this 1990 FIDE championship, Kasparov would win 4 of those games. He would eventually also win the championship itself that year.

1...e5

Karpov in turn always answers with this classical King Pawn Defense.

This defensive reaction is the oldest way of countering White's opening move. Before the start of battle, both armies are in perfect equilibrium. White's opening joust breaks the equilibrium and gives him an advantage by letting him mobilize the first unit. Black matches White's opening move, thereby returning the game to its equilib-

rium. This duel of thrust and parry is what makes the opening battle such a fiercely fought one. Whoever emerges from the opening with an advantage will have the right to be on the attack!

Just as White's e2-e4 move grabs a piece of the center, Black's ...e7-e5 responds in kind. It also allows for the fluid development of the King's Bishop and Queen if needed.

2.Nf3

Naturally enough, White has many choices on his second move: 2.f4 would introduce the King's Gambit, 2.d4 the Center Game, 2.Nc3 the Vienna Game, and so on. The text is the oldest and most frequently chosen move. White develops and attacks the e5-pawn.

When playing as Black, beginning players are forever falling into the trap known as the "Scholar's Mate." It begins with 2.Qh5? — a bad move that develops the Queen too early. Black then plays 2...Nc6, defending the e5-pawn. White plays 3.Bc4, developing his Bishop and threatening mate in one. Black fails to play 3...g6, which would utterly refute White's play. Instead, Black plays 3...Nf6?? and after 4.Qxf7 suffers a checkmate, like countless others.

2...Nc6

With attack and parry, Black develops and defends the e5-pawn.

Another one of Karpov's favorite defenses is 2...Nf6, with a counterattack against White's e4-pawn. In the West, this reaction is known as the Petroff Defense, whereas players in the East call it the Russian Defense in honor of Alexander Dimitrievich Petroff (1794–1867) who favored it.

3.Bb5

With this natural move, White develops and puts pressure upon the c6-Knight

that holds up the e5-pawn. If White can successfully remove the c6-Knight and pick up the e5-pawn, he will pocket an extra pawn for his trouble.

The text bears the name of Ruy López (c. 1530–1580), a priest from Estremadura, Spain. Therefore, this opening move is also known as the Spanish Game; the long-term pressure that White gains from the Spanish inspired its nickname, the Spanish Torture. Other well-documented openings include 3.d4 (the Scotch Game) and 3.Bc4 (the Italian Game). The text is a favorite of America's Robert James Fischer; he has wielded it as a sword against the world's best grandmasters.

3...a6!

Black makes the move of choice of nearly all the world's grandmasters.

This move was discovered by Paul Morphy (1837–1884) and is therefore called Morphy's Defense. As usual, after more moves are played, the opening will become further refined or, we might say, defined.

Morphy's Defense has had an enthusiastic following for well over a century. Before Morphy's discovery, Black players were quick to defend their e5-pawn with either 3...d6 or 3...Nge7 to protect the c6-Knight. Others tried 3...Nf6, with a counterattack on the e4-pawn. Morphy had a nice tactical justification for the text. He reasoned that if he could force 4.Bxc6 dxc6, he would earn the two Bishops, an advantage for later in the game. If White tried 5.Nxe5, Qd4! would allow Black to win back his pawn with advantage. On the other hand, if after the text White didn't trade his Bishop, Black would have the possibility of playing ...b7-b5, further driving away White's Bishop.

4.Ba4

Kasparov keeps his Bishop.

A considerable number of books have been devoted to the variation 4.Bxc6 dxc6, known as Exchange Spanish, or the Ruy López, Exchange Variation. A lot of controversy still exists among theorists as to whether or not White can earn an advantage with it. White gives up having both Bishops, but Black has doubled queenside pawns. The variations tend to be rather dry and technical in nature, so most players prefer to keep their Bishop. However, the debate is not trivial and goes right to the center of the game: if White can earn a clear advantage against a classical defense, does it mean that White might win from the start?

4...Nf6

Taking advantage of the lull in the action, Black counterattacks the e4-pawn.

5.O-O

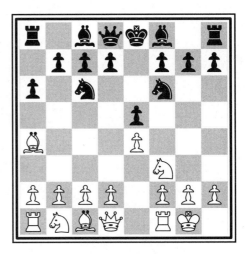

Perhaps the most well-known position in chess opening manuals. White ignores the threat to his e4-pawn, preferring to castle instead. He reasons that if Black tries to capture his e4-pawn, he will then have an opportunity to play Rf1-e1, thereby utilizing the e-file.

White could also choose 5.d3, which is a bit passive, or 5.Qe2, which involves an early commitment of his Queen.

5...Be7

Black declines the opportunity to munch White's e4-pawn.

After 5...Nxe4 6.d4 (6.Re1 Nf6 7.Nxe5 Nxe5 8.Rxe5+ Be7 would offer a symmetrical pawn position with only a small edge for White) 6...b5 7.Bb3 d5 8.dxe5 Be6, the players would have landed in the Open Spanish, or the Open Ruy López. The open variation is marked by sharp piece play. Black usually has to defend his b5-pawn and d5-pawn weaknesses. If he manages to do so, he will secure equality. Karpov has always preferred the text. Now Black *is* threatening to grab the e4-pawn.

6.Re1

Although moving the same piece twice in the opening is usually a no-no, here the text is the best move. White defends his e4-pawn and at the same time rekindles his old threat of eliminating the c6-Knight and winning the e5-pawn.

It would make sense to play 6.Nc3, developing a piece and defending the e4-pawn. White, however, has a deeper idea. He intends to build a broad front of center pawns by c2-c3 and d2-d4, earning the classical center pawn duo. The text gives him flexibility to develop this plan.

6...b5

Black stops White's threat of winning the e5-pawn. The text is a double-edged sword. On the one hand, Black gains a tempo by attacking the a4-Bishop. On the other hand, he severely weakens his queenside flank, thereby making it susceptible to attack. Still, theoreticians consider the text to be Black's most stable choice.

7.Bb3

The Bishop redirects its energies to another diagonal.

Although White has wasted some tempi maneuvering his Bishop around the board, he's not completely unhappy. His King is safe, and his pieces are directing their energies to the center of the board. If he can establish a pawn duo, life will be good.

7...d6

Black fortifies the e5-pawn. As in most classical defenses, Black's goal is to maintain his central pawn, whether it is the e5-pawn or the d5-pawn. Now Black can also consider developing ...Bc8-g4, creating his own pin.

8.c3

The text is the prelude to playing d2-d4 and earning an advantage by control of so many central squares.

It has taken countless thousands of master games to definitively confirm that White's best strategy is to establish a pawn duo. Generations of players have tried a number of defensive setups for Black from this point onward. We are just beginning to scratch the surface of the theory for this opening.

8...O-O

Holding to established opening principles, Black has determined that the kingside is the safest place for his King and acts accordingly.

It would be a bit early for 8...Bg4?! 9.h3! Bh5 10.d3 O-O 11.Nbd2; White could play the maneuver Nd2-f1-g3, earning an advantage. White is usually able to force the trade of a Knight for Black's light-squared Bishop.

9.h3

White is anxious to play d2-d4 but doesn't rush this decision.

After 9.d4 Bg4! 10.d5 Na5 11.Bc2 c6 12.h3 Bxf3! 13.Qxf3 cxd5 14.exd5 Nc4!,

Black would have managed to achieve a dynamic equality. The text prevents the pinning move ...Bc8-g4 and prepares d2-d4 at last.

9...Bb7

The text is a defining moment. Black had a wide variety of choices, including Chigorin's move 9...Na5 10.Bc2 c5; the Breyer Defense, 9...Nb8 10.d4 Nbd7, rerouting the c6-Knight in order to make the queenside fianchetto more effective; and one of the many no-name defenses, 9...Be6, offering a trade of Bishops in order to neutralize the a2-g8 diagonal. Having made the necessary repairs, however, Karpov selects the Zaitsev Variation even though he had lost an earlier Zaitsev game in this match.

The move fulfills the not-so-secret hope of the pressroom; the Keres Variation,

9...Nd7 10.d4 Bf6, which Karpov had used in the previous games, is dull. The Zaitsev has a reputation for fireworks, and everyone was ready for action.

In the Zaitsev, Black will give up the center and aim for reckless play on the queenside, a risky strategy to be sure. On the other hand, if White misplays the attack that he has been *forced* to assume, Black will gain a queenside advantage. Black then completes his fianchetto and prepares for further play on the queenside.

10.d4

All the necessary preparations have been made, and White seizes the center. The amount of space that White's d4-pawn and e4-pawn control is what makes the classical center pawn duo so powerful. Our chess ancestors understood that if White can maintain these pawns, he'll have a tremendous, perhaps winning, advantage. For Black to have any kind of counterplay, he will have to destroy White's central control. At last, the battle is being joined.

10...Re8

Black repositions his pieces in the center. The f8-Rook is deployed to the e-file, where it will put pressure upon White's e4-pawn. The e7-Bishop, which is currently in the way, will drop back to the f8-square, thereby reassuring the Black King that he hasn't been forgotten.

These redeployments are designed to keep an eye in the center and to shore up the kingside. That done, Black will then play for sharp queenside action.

Middlegame

11.Nbd2

At last, White develops his queenside pieces. White defends the e4-pawn and intends to deploy Nd2-f1-g3, migrating toward Black's King.

Dutch broadcaster and international chess master Hans Bohm asked me, "With a lead, why doesn't Kasparov just play 11.Ng5 and offer a draw?" The move 11.Ng5 would force 11...Rf8, defending the f7-pawn (11...d5? 12.exd5 Nxd5 13.Nxf7 Kxf7 14.Qf3+ would be too dangerous for Black), and 12.Nf3 Re8 would result in a repetition and a draw. Still, repeating moves and making an early draw, though it would annoy the audience, would perhaps be the professional approach. (A comparison could be made with boxing. One fighter realizes that he is ahead on points going into the last round. Rather than take any risks, he begins to run around the ring, avoiding the risk of being knocked out.) But Kasparov is Kasparov, and one of his strengths is that he believes in himself. Rather than duck a good fight, Kasparov revels in one.

White avoids 11.Bg5 Nd7! which wouldn't net him any particular advantage. Black would be happy to trade his inactive e7-Bishop.

11...Bf8

In this important move, Black freezes the d2-Knight to the defense of the e4-pawn. Thus 12.Nf1? exd4 13.cxd4 Nxe4 (13...Na5 is also good) 14.Bxf7+ Kxf7 15.Rxe4 Rxe4 16.Ng5+ Kg8 will ruin White's center and cost him his b3-Bishop.

If Black can keep White's d2-Knight glued to its current square, White will have a development problem. What will he do with his c1-Bishop?

12.a4!

An excellent move. If the c1-Bishop can't move, by extension the a1-Rook remains bottled up in the corner. The text is an alternative way of developing the position. White can now play a4xb5 ...a6xb5, followed by trading Rooks on the a-file, thereby solving his development problem. Or he can try a Rook lift on the a-file. The move has another ulterior motive, which is to weaken the b5-pawn.

12...h6

Black makes luft. He also indicates that he is happy with his current piece deployment and isn't trying to reshuffle any of it. He stops the possibility of Nf3-g5 and asks White what he intends to do.

13.Bc2

The move is not an ideal response. White's b3-Bishop had been quite happy with the diagonal it was sitting upon. The text draws a frown because the Bishop will be less active on the c2-square.

Currently, White is facing a problem with completing his development. He'd love to play Nd2-f1-g3, but his e4-pawn lacks protection; therefore he makes this retreat. By protecting the e4-pawn, White plans to redeploy the d2-Knight.

13...exd4!

This move ignites tactical fireworks. Black gives up the center, trading his valued e5-pawn for the lowly c3-pawn. In return, Black aims for rapid play on the queenside, hoping to earn an advantage there.

White's only response will be to prosecute the advantage of his majority in the center and on the kingside.

A safer move would be 13...g6, preparing to fianchetto and build a house. Karpov has employed the text to his advantage on many occasions, however.

14.cxd4

Naturally, White is happy to take control of the center and to utilize his c3-pawn.

14...Nb4

This move hatches Black's big idea. The pawn trade in the center has given him control over the b4-square, which he immediately jumps upon. Because White controls more space, Black would like to make a few minor piece trades.

15.Bb1

White keeps the c2-Bishop and protects the e4-pawn.

White's pawn duo makes a very pleasing impression. Black will have to put more pressure on the center or face the prospect of getting throttled. White's pieces are still bottled up, and his plan of Nd2-f1-g3 still remains on hold because the e4-pawn requires more protection. One plan for White could be Ra1-a3-e3, making a nice Rook lift to guard the e4-pawn.

Note in the diagram how White's pieces are focusing toward the kingside and how Black will start his play on the queenside.

15...c5

In game 2 of this match, Karpov tried 15...bxa4!? 16.Rxa4 a5 17.Ra3 Ra6; then Kasparov played 18.Nh2 and f2-f3, cementing the e4-pawn. Team Karpov still hadn't found an acceptable antidote to Kasparov's plan. The text takes a different approach altogether. Black immediately attacks the pawn duo in order to force White to make his center less fluid. He will then try to attack White's center from another direction.

16.d5

White is eager to keep his central grip. He doesn't want to allow ...c5xd4 and a possible ...d6-d5, disrupting the entire center structure and leaving White with no advantage. By blocking the b7-Bishop, White tries to stifle Black's piece activity while looking toward improving his own piece play.

16...Nd7

With this far-reaching and consequent move, Black seeks to reinforce his play on the queenside and center. He can then employ the plan of ...f7-f5, attacking White's center, or play for ...c5-c4 and ...Nd7-c5, aiming to invade the d3-square. Noble ambitions — but another of the King's defenders has moved away.

17.Ra3

If White must defer trading Rooks along the a-file, what should he do with his a1-Rook? The text is the answer. White intends to swing his Rook across the third rank in order to launch an attack against Black's King. The players are warming to the battle.

Previous games have shown that White cannot hope to get an advantage by 17.axb5? axb5 18.Rxa8 Qxa8 because Black can utilize the open lines on the queenside.

17...f5

The older move 17...c4 has been replaced by the text in Karpov's repertoire. The purpose of the move is straightforward. If Black can trade his f-pawn for White's e4-pawn, the d5-pawn would be left unprotected. Both players would then enjoy large majorities on the flanks. A razor-sharp game would result. The first error would cost either player the game. The move ...f7-f5 has its own drawbacks, which I mention in *Five Crowns*:

> A move such as this is a red flag to Kasparov, who has far more in his arsenal than a bull's horns.

> Black seeks to undermine White's center but has compromised his own kingside.

> Previously, Karpov tried the positional 17...c4, planning ...Nd7-c5-d3. Kasparov himself discredited that idea with 18.Nd4!, planning Ra3-g3 with a terrific kingside attack. My approach to the position would be 17...g6, intending ...Bf8-g7 with

Benoni type of play. Thus 17...g6 18.Nh2 Bg7 19.Ndf3 Qe7!? seems most natural with unclear play.

My basic point is that ...f7-f5 is a very dangerous move!

18.Rae3

Completing the Rook lift, White now brings his cannons (Rooks) to the e-file, where he hopes to cause Black a lot of distress.

In the New York City half of the match, I was convinced that 18.exf5, as played in game 4 of this match, was a mistake. The newly born f5-pawn interferes with White's kingside attack by closing the b1-h7 diagonal. Kasparov agrees with my analysis and chooses the text. Another controversial move — 18.e5!? — was suggested by Kasparov.

18...Nf6

This move is probably the best.

In the 1989 FIDE candidates finals in Kuala Lumpur, Malaysia, Karpov played 18...f4!? against Jan Timman. In training games, GM John Fedorowicz demonstrated to me that Black's position would be rickety: 19.Rc3! g5!? 20.Nf1! Bg7 21.N1h2, with the idea of h3-h4 to let White's pieces flood the kingside. It seems that the moves ...f7-f5 and ...f5-f4 contain a logical glitch and are not recommended.

Also dangerous for Black would be 18...fxe4 19.Nxe4 Nxd5 (19...Bxd5 20.Bd2 would be good for White) 20.R3e2 N5f6 21.Nxf6+ Nxf6 22.Rxe8 Nxe8 23.Qc2!? Nf6 24.Nh2!?. The resulting position is shown in the analysis diagram below.

The position is typical of the Zaitsev Variation. White has given up a pawn for open lines and an attack on Black's King.

Karpov chooses to reinforce his kingside and to win the d5-pawn. But his King will be subject to a scorching attack, not too different from that of the analysis diagram.

19.Nh2!

White plays quickly. Team Karpov loses the opening preparation duel today, and Karpov sinks into a 23-minute think.

I was surprised that 19.Nh2 had not been foreseen by Karpov and his deep team of trainers. The move accomplishes a lot: it prepares Re3-g3 and also Nh2-g4, potentially attacking the f6-Knight. This softens up Black's defense on h7, making the battery of White Qc2-h7 mate a real threat. Moreover, the move deserves consideration because White has no better move!

After 19.exf5, White would be forced to do what he doesn't want to do: block the diagonal of the b1-Bishop. Playing 19...Rxe3 20.Rxe3 (20.fxe3!?) 20...Nbxd5 21.Re1 Nc7 gave me good positions in the training games with Fedorowicz. I then took to pushing forward the center c5-pawn and d6-pawn, which Fedorowicz dubbed "the Wall." Both White's and

Black's pawn structures limit the scope of White's Bishops.

19...Kh8!?

Karpov already feels queasy about his King.

A gruesome justification of 19.Nh2 would rise from the crypt after 19...fxe4 20.Nxe4 Nbxd5 21.Nxf6+ Nxf6 22.Rxe8 Nxe8 23.Qc2 Nf6 24.Ng4! Qd7 25.Bxh6! — Black's King would be hacked to pieces.

Black's other possible capture, 19...fxe4 20.Nxe4 Nfxd5, would fail because 21.Rg3 threatens Bc1xh6, allowing a devastating kingside attack. Karpov prepares for such a position by breaking the potential pin on his g7-pawn. It seems that neither player wants to resolve the e4-f5 pawn tension.

20.b3!

Simply an excellent move. Black's last move reduced the effectiveness of the c1-Bishop. By fianchettoing it, White makes every one of his pieces bear down upon Black's King. In the meantime, Black's a8-Rook, b4-Knight, and b7-Bishop fail to guard their monarch.

The ultimate objective of chess is to checkmate the enemy King. If you count attackers and defenders around Black's King, you'll see that Karpov is on the ropes.

20...bxa4

Black plans to utilize his queenside pieces. He begins his plan with a pawn trade.

21.bxa4

There is no reason not to recapture the pawn. Admittedly, 21.Bb2 axb3 22.exf5 would be tempting, but why sacrifice unnecessarily?

21...c4?

In Black's precarious position, the text is fatal. His idea is reasonable, however: to mess up White's attack by throwing in ...Nb4-d3, trying to cause a little confusion. The trouble is, it doesn't work.

Isn't hindsight wonderful? For better or worse, Black had to risk 21...fxe4 22.Nxe4 Nfxd5 (with 22...Nbxd5 23.Nxf6, White would line up the Queen and Bishop battery against the h7-square again) 23.Rg3 Nf6 24.Nxf6!? (the natural line, but now 24...Qxf6 25.Bd2 Nd5 [stopping Bd2-c3] 26.Qc2 would be killing; Black, therefore, has to toss in a trade of Rooks on the e1-square) 24...Rxe1+ 25.Qxe1 Qxf6 26.Bd2. The analysis diagram shows the resulting position.

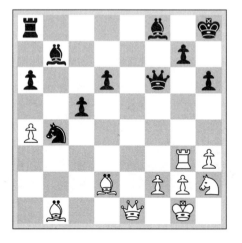

White threatens Bd2-c3, Nh2-g4, or Rg3-g6, giving White superb compensation for his pawn. But in comparing this analysis and the game, Black has better chances to defend. It seems that White can improve his position while avoiding e4xf5, whereas Black can't improve his position without playing ...f5xe4, opening up the b1-h7 diagonal.

22.Bb2

White's Bishop finds an ideal diagonal. Look at the treasure at the end!

White had to avoid the mistaken 22.Nxc4? fxe4, which would only help Black isolate the d5-pawn. Now at last White can play e4xf5 and Nh2-g4 because his b2-Bishop will help generate a number of threats. It seems that Black must win the d5-pawn that White has been offering as bait and hope for the best.

22...fxe4

Biting the bullet, Black decides it is time to win the d5-pawn. The delay, however, has allowed White to play Bc1-b2, improving his attacking chances.

Now the audience and the commentators are getting excited. Kasparov is beginning to lean hard into the board with flickering eyes. One can sense that he likes his position very much.

23.Nxe4

White brings the most passive piece into play. The number of White pieces aimed at Black's King has become alarming.

23...Nfxd5

Capturing with the other Knight would let White line up his pieces: with 23...Nbxd5? 24.Nxf6 Rxe3 25.Rxe3! Nxe3 26.fxe3 gxf6 27.Qc2 Qe7 28.Qg6, Black would be helpless to prevent the winning Bb2xf6. Note that in this final position Black could find no solace in 28...c3 29.Bxc3 Qxe3+ 30.Kf1 Qc1+ 31.Kf2 because of multiple threats of checkmate.

24.Rg3!

Kasparov must be in heaven. He attacks his archrival with every piece. The queenside is largely irrelevant because Black has no targets to attack. White has a free hand to sacrifice against Black's King.

24...Re6!

Black reinforces the g6-square and the h6-square, proving Karpov's reputation as a fierce defender.

White had threatened an invasion by way of Qd1-h5, planning to whomp the h6-pawn. Now, however, Black has the sly defense ...Qd8-e8, which covers all the weak spots.

This is an excellent moment to stop and reflect. With the FIDE championship and three million dollars on the line, what would *you* play as White?

25.Ng4!

With this natural move, White brings the final unit into play. The text softens up the h6-pawn and prepares Qd1-d2, going after Black's kingside.

At first, the move 25.Qd4 looks very strong, creating a battery on the long diagonal. But Black would have a saving grace with 25...c3!, which would encourage favorable trades. Never forget the importance of *inviting all your pieces to the party.*

25...Qe8?

Karpov spends 17 precious minutes on this mistake. He now has 19 minutes to make the time control of move 40. Black wants to pin the e4-Knight and control the g6-square and h5-square. But in this laudable plan, Black's Queen is left resting on the e8-square, becoming a tactical target.

Black has *two* other plausible defenses: 25...Qd7, covering the g7-pawn, or 25...Nd3, breaking the b1-h7 diagonal.

British grandmaster Tony Miles and I jointly tackled the first line with an analysis that provides insight into White's possibilities. After 25...Qd7 26.Nef6!? (quite spectacular — White could make the mundane play 26.Qd2!? Rae8 27.Re2!? just asking Black how he will defend the h6-pawn) 26...Rxf6 (otherwise, 26...gxf6? 27.Rxe6 Qxe6 28.Nxh6 Bxh6 29.Qh5 Qe1+ 30.Kh2 Qd2 31.Rg6 Qf4+ 32.Kg1 would let White win — analysis by Tony Miles) 27.Bxf6 Nxf6 28.Nxf6 gxf6 29.Qd4 Bg7 30.Qxc4 a5 31.Bf5! Qxf5 32.Qf7 Qh7? 33.Qxb7 Rg8 would lead to the position illustrated on the following analysis diagram:

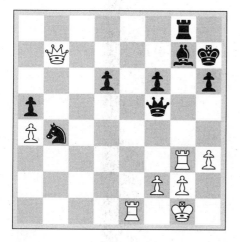

GM Miles concludes that Black is not dead. But after 34.Re7, *nobody* would want to play Black's position. Coincidentally, this analysis diagram has a strong resemblance to game 2 of this 1990 match. In that game, White's Rooks also did nasty things to Black's minor pieces.

Please don't conclude that the foregoing was a forced line and that White was ready to unleash all these sacrifices if given a chance. Rather, this line is one of the many ways in which White could combat 25...Qd7 by breaking down the h6-pawn while utilizing the e-file and the g-file.

In view of the previous variation, it makes a lot of sense for Black to use his unemployed b4-Knight. He should try to trade pieces before White decides to embark on a long-winded combination. Thus Black's best chance would be 25...Nd3! 26.Bxd3 cxd3 27.Qxd3!? Qe7, with Black still hanging in there. It is conceivable that Karpov didn't like the exchange sacrifice 26.Rxd3!? cxd3 27.Qxd3, but as before, Black has managed to trade in his b4-Knight for a scary-looking g3-Rook.

26.Nxh6!

This beautiful tactical shot rips away the pawn shield. Besides winning a pawn, White levels the threats of Nh6-f5, Qd1-g4, and a host of other harsh ideas.

26...c3

Black tries to stem the tidal wave. He can win a Knight or a Bishop, and he chooses the Bishop.

What would happen if he were to grab the h6-Knight? The resulting moves would be 26...Rxh6 27.Nxd6! and would allow Black four defenses:

■ 27...Rxd6 is the least difficult because 28.Rxe8 Rxe8 29.Qh5+ would win right away.

■ 27...Qd7 28.Nf5 (piling up on the g7-pawn — the combination would be forced) 28...Rh7 29.Re7! (using the pin on the d-file) 29...Bxe7 30.Rxg7 Rxg7 31.Qh5+ Kg8 32.Nh6+ Kf8 33.Bxg7+ Kxg7 would lead to the position below on the analysis diagram:

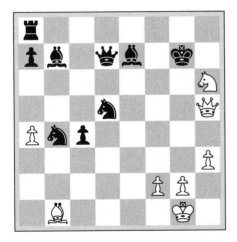

White would conclude with the brutal 34.Qf7+ Kxh6 35.Qg6 checkmate. Ouch!

■ 27...Qh5 loses in a pretty way: 28.Rg5!! Qxd1 29.Nf7+ Kg8 30.Nxh6+ Kh8 31.Rxd1 c3 32.Nf7+ Kg8 33.Bg6! cxb2

34.Rh5 — the Rh5-h8 mate would be unpreventable.

■ 27...Qxe1+ tries to grab all of White's pieces but would fail: 28.Qxe1 Rxd6 29.Qe4! Nd3 (29...Rh6 30.Bc1 would win) 30.Qh4+! Kg8 31.Bxg7 Bxg7 32.Qg4!. Black's armada would be strangely impotent to block White's threat of Qg4xg7 checkmate.

Given all the preceding scenarios and Karpov's growing time trouble, his choice is his best practical chance. He blocks the long diagonal, leaving White with two pieces en prise.

27.Nf5!

White continues to pressure the g7-pawn. With Black's h6-pawn missing, White's Queen has an open invitation to visit Black's King down the h-file.

27...cxb2

At least Black has won the b2-Bishop, saving himself from that powerful piece.

28.Qg4!

White delivers a devastating blow. The threats include Nf5xg7 and Qg4-h4+ and the *slow* variation Kg1-h2, with Ne4-g5 to follow. The slow variation is calculated to prevent giving up the e1-Rook with check. In view of all of White's threats, not even Karpov can save the position.

28...Bc8

With this desperate trick, Black stops 29.Nxg7? Rxe4! with a tricky double attack. Such variations would allow Black to trade Queens, helping him save his King.

Black didn't have better options. He would also lie helpless after 28...g6 29.Kh2! Be7 (29...Qd7 30.Nh4 would win) 30.Ng5 Bxg5 31.Qxg5, with a simple win for White.

29.Qh4+

White nails down the most forcing move. Dutch international master Hans Bohm suggests 29.Kh2!, intending Ne4-g5, which would win rather convincingly. Yet, though 29.Kh2 might win more quickly, it is impossible to criticize the text. Kasparov is now able to calculate a *forced* win, and one win per game is all you'll ever need.

29...Rh6

Black avoids 29...Kg8 30.Nh6+ Rxh6 (30...Kh8 31.Nf7++ Kg8 32.Neg5 Rxe1+ 33.Kh2 would create two checkmates on the h-file) 31.Qxh6 (White threatens Ne4-f6+ to win Black's Queen) 31...Qf7 32.Nxd6 Bxd6 33.Re8+, which would allow White to finish with checkmate on his next move. The text allows Black to hold on a moment or two longer. Where there's life, there's hope.

30.Nxh6

Although Black's h6-Rook was a stubborn defender, White's Knight returns with relish. This Rook's removal renders the Black King that much more vulnerable.

30...gxh6

Black's only chance is to recapture and to pray.

31.Kh2!

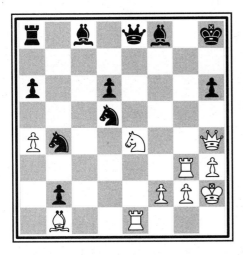

Everyone in the press gallery has been waiting for this excellent move. White prepares the simple Ne4-f6 and Rg3-g8 mate, which could prevent Black from taking the e1-Rook with check. Black has to stop Ne4-f6 at all costs.

31...Qe5

Black covers the f6-square.

He can't play 31...Bg7? because 32.Nxd6 Qf8 (32...Qxe1 33.Qd8+ would be mate in two moves) 33.Re8 would win Black's Queen.

32.Ng5

With this devastating blow, White threatens Ng5-f7 checkmate because Black's monarch has no palace guards.

32...Qf6

The beleaguered Queen must move again. With 32...Qxe1 33.Nf7, checkmate would abruptly end the agony.

Endgame

33.Re8!

Now White's attack has gotten completely out of hand. His pieces are charging the position with a multiplicity of threats. Two include Ng5-f7+, followed by Qh4xh6+ and Ng5-h7, followed by Re8xf8+ and probable mate.

33...Bf5

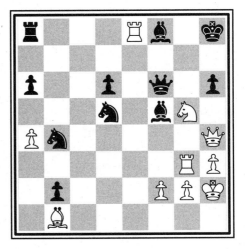

Karpov can barely dash this move off with the time remaining on his clock. It is the only possible move, but it allows White to win half of Black's army.

34.Qxh6+!

This wicked shot wins the house. We now expect Karpov to resign, but he doesn't have enough time on the clock to think about it.

34...Qxh6

Black has to accept White's offer, but he should beware of Greeks bearing gifts.

35.Nf7+

This move forces Black's King onto a nasty square.

35...Kh7

The only possible move. Black's King is definitely not a happy camper.

36.Bxf5+

White picks up on his investment with interest. He starts capturing booty with check.

36...Qg6

The only way to stop the check is to give away the Queen for free.

37.Bxg6+

Black's pieces are disappearing from the board at an alarming rate.

37...Kg7

Black's King is forced to walk the plank. At this moment it is easy to imagine Black's King scolding the b4-Knight: "What are you doing on b4?"

38.Rxa8

The harvest is complete. White is an exchange and a Rook ahead. Again, resignation would be the best response from Black, but the players are in time pressure and don't have the time for cool, objective thought.

38...Be7

Black plays on in hope of a miracle. Perhaps the b2-pawn will Queen, or better yet, White's flag might fall.

39.Rb8

White keeps the b2-pawn under scrutiny.

39...a5

Black is still hoping for a rescue.

40.Be4+

Kasparov makes the time control. Although the text gives away a piece, he can afford to be generous.

Another convincing sequence would be 40.Nh6 Kxh6 41.Be4 Bf6 42.Rg6+ Kh5 43.Rbg8; there would be no stopping Be4-f3+, followed by g2-g3 mate.

40...Kxf7

Black accepts his fate. The move 40...Kf6 would be a little trickier, but now that White has made the time control, resignation becomes imminent.

41.Bxd5+

Black resigns.

Karpov didn't have enough time on his clock to think about giving up, so the game went on longer than it might have. *Everyone* in the audience, however, knew the result when Karpov held out his hand in resignation. The audience applauded thunderously. FIDE champion Garry Kasparov garnered an absolutely devastating win and retained his title.

A Rapid Coup

T he following game occurred under extraordinary circumstances. It was the 1991 FIDE semifinals candidate match played in Brussels between Artur Yusupov of Russia and Vassily Ivanchuk of Ukraine. The players are two of the best of modern times. Ivanchuk is the younger of the two and was tapped by Garry Kasparov as a likely successor to his FIDE crown. After a hard-fought, eventful match, Yusupov staged a dramatic comeback and was able to force the match into overtime.

At the time this match squared up, a political coup to oust Mikhail Gorbachev was taking place in Moscow. Both players admitted to being glued to the CNN channel on the TV sets in their hotel rooms. They worried about their families back home; no one was certain what the coup meant for the country. With the match on the line and with the world seemingly turned upside down, the one retreat the players had was the chessboard.

I was an eyewitness to this game and wrote the following introduction to it for *Inside Chess* magazine:

"An extraordinarily exciting game. Both players were extremely nervous at the start. They raced through their opening moves and the game started to resemble a blitz match. When Ivanchuk blundered with the known mistake f2-f4, instead of f2-f3, he opened the gates to his King, and Yusupov's pieces flooded in. Yusupov's attack was overwhelming, but he mistakenly sacrificed a Knight on h4. Suddenly, Ivanchuk was winning, but he immediately blundered by checking with the wrong Knight. Ivanchuk stopped the piece in midair, but to his horror the damage was done. He had touched the wrong Knight. Yusupov shed a Bishop and a Rook to mate

Ivanchuk's King. The packed audience burst into applause as Yusupov took a one-point lead with one game to go! A modern brilliancy."

Sometimes a chess game is played at such a deep level that months, years, or even decades go by before it is fully understood. Witnessing such a game can be, on the one hand, exhilarating, hair-raising, and marvelously uplifting. It can also be a very unpleasant experience. Sometimes during the Ivanchuk–Yusupov game I felt like a puzzled spectator at the *Immortal Game* between Adolf Anderssen and Lionel Kieseritzky.

This game was the first of a two-game tiebreaker that was to decide the candidates' semifinalist, the chess world's version of college basketball's Final Four. As a tiebreaker, the game was played within the odd time limit of 60 moves in 45 minutes, vastly reduced from the standard 40 moves in 2 hours. Under such pressure, it's impossible to imagine what the players were sensing in this, the most controversial game of 1991.

The annotations for this game are based upon my own reports filed in *Inside Chess* magazine as well as the notes of Artur Yusupov from *Chess Informant* 53.

■ ■ ■ ■ ■ ■ ■ ■ ■ ■ ■ ■ ■ ■ ■

King's Indian Fianchetto E67

GM Vassily Ivanchuk
GM Artur Yusupov
Brussels, 1991
FIDE Semi-Finals Match (Game 9)

Opening

1.c4

As one of the world's premier players, Ivanchuk has a mastery of both King and Queen Pawn openings. He chooses the English move order to try to bring about the opening variation that he wants. Yusupov has a reputation for using classical Queen Pawn Defenses, and Ivanchuk is aiming for a particular line.

1...e5

Ivanchuk doesn't get the line that he wants.

This reaction is the drawback of the English Opening. With the text, Black gets a toehold in the center with fair chances of seizing the initiative. Still, these early initiatives don't usually concern White because the English Opening can provide him with a powerful counterattacking position.

2.g3

White's move is very much in the style of the hypermodern school of chess. He prepares a kingside fianchetto, taking a restrained view of the center at this early stage.

2...d6

I'm not a fan of this move. Black intends to transpose back into normal lines of the King's Indian Defense. There's nothing wrong with that approach except that Black gives up the opportunity to take advantage of the English move order set in motion by White.

The positions after 2...Nc6! 3.Bg2 g6! 4.Nc3 Bg7, controlling the d4-square and fighting for space, would be easier positions for Black to play than the King's Indian variation that Yusupov has in mind.

3.Bg2

White completes his fianchetto.

The move 3.d4 would be more effective, grabbing the center. At this point the players' tastes in opening variations rule the day. It is too early to say, "This is an inferior move." Nonetheless, for *my* taste, the text is a mistake.

3...g6

Black sets about with a fianchetto of his own. Again, Yusupov has a variation of the King's Indian Defense in mind to the exclusion of other opening opportunities.

Black could also consider 3...c5!?, opting for a Botvinnik Pawn Triangle in the center. Or 3...Nc6 could lead back into classical English Opening patterns.

4.d4!

White correctly grabs the center. Now he will have an easier game because of his space advantage, which will give his pieces greater mobility.

4...Nd7

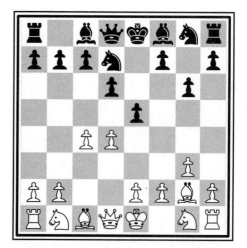

Black is concerned about 5.dxe5 dxe5 6.Qxd8+ Kxd8, which would lose him his castling privileges. The text, although a standard feature in the King's Indian Defense, boxes in the c8-Bishop.

It would be a mistake to play 4...exd4? 5.Qxd4 Nf6 6.Bg5, which would allow

White to develop his pieces quickly and generate threats. This move also exemplifies a fundamental mistake that beginning players tend to make in the opening; that is, they see an opportunity to make "an even trade" and go for it, believing themselves to be very clever. But after 5.Qxd4, all they have accomplished is developing the opponent's pieces, thereby losing a tempo. When getting ready to trade, it would be wise to ask yourself this question before making the move: "Who benefits more from this trade?"

5.Nc3

White develops his forces and gains control of the d5-square. Thus far, White's pieces enjoy greater harmony from the opening scheme.

5...Bg7

Black completes the fianchetto and pressures the d4-pawn.

Black would like to force White to resolve the central tension. If White would now play 6.dxe5?, Black would benefit nicely with ...dxe5. Why? The answer again is space. Currently, Black's d6-pawn controls none of White's squares. On the other hand, White's d4-pawn controls two of Black's squares. After 6.dxe5? dxe5, a transformation will have taken place: Black's d6-pawn will

have become an e5-pawn watchdog growling at the d4-square and the f4-square.

A contrary voice may argue that 6.dxe5? dxe5 would *gain* space for White because his d1-Queen suddenly would control squares d5, d6, and d7. Indeed, this point would be a valid one. Unfortunately for White, this would be but a *temporary* spatial advantage. The open d-file would attract the Rooks like bees to honey. White's Queen would be driven off the d-file while the e5-pawn would remain on the board! In the long term, the trade d4xe5 and ...d6xe5 would very much favor Black.

6.Nf3

White protects the d4-pawn.

As I've mentioned, White isn't eager to play 6.dxe5; neither is 6.d5 very attractive.

Why? The problem with 6.d5 is that although gaining space is important in the opening, the priority is to *develop pieces*. The move 6.d5 would cost White a tempo. It would be much better to develop a piece instead. Other reasons cause White to avoid d4-d5: the move blocks the long diagonal of the g2-Bishop, and it takes the pressure off in the center, encouraging Black to play 6.d5? f5!. Because of the moves ...Ng8-f6 and ...Nd7-c5, the e4-square might fall into Black's control.

6...Ngf6

Black develops a piece and prepares to castle. He then will work on finding an active plan for his pieces.

Yusupov had an unpleasant experience with 6...Nh6 in game 5 of this match. He therefore understandably sidesteps that move and plays into an ancient line of the King's Indian.

7.O-O

White happily brings the King to safety.

7...O-O

Black does the same.

8.Qc2?!

Because this game is being played at a faster time control than a normal tournament game, Ivanchuk tries to catch his opponent off guard by making a little twist in the opening. This is a dubious deviation from the well-trodden path of 8.e4, grabbing more of the center, which gives White some pull.

8...Re8?

White's opening gamble pays off. Yusupov answers quickly, indicating that he isn't familiar with the nuances of the opening.

Black misses his chance to achieve quick equality: 8...exd4! 9.Nxd4 Nb6! (going after the c4-pawn, White would have an awkward task) 10.Rd1 (10.b3 c5! 11.Ndb5 a6 12.Na3 Bf5! would be good for Black; also, 10.Qb3 Nfd7! menacing ...Nd7-c5 would force White to further misplace his Queen) 10...Nxc4 11.Ncb5 a6 12.Qxc4 axb5 13.Nxb5 Ne8 would set up a fine game for Black.

The problem with the text is that it allows White an even more favorable position versus the normal 8.e4 opening lines. The move Qd1-c2 is quite useful; White vacates the d1-square, allowing him to quickly bring a Rook to the d-file. And lo and behold . . . .

9.Rd1!

This is the immediate benefit of White's opening gamble. The Rook is indeed ideally stationed on the d-file. Because of the tension between the center pawns, the d-file may at any moment be ripped open by d4xe5 or ...e5xd4, thrusting the d1-Rook immediately into play.

9...c6!

This good move, although it weakens the d6-pawn, lends Black a measure of control over the d5-square. The long diagonal h1-a8 is also closed, making the g2-Bishop a little less effective.

10.b3!

White makes a solid move.

Although the last two moves of both players are "standard" theory, in my view they merit exclamation marks. Many times beginners memorize opening moves without understanding the ideas behind them, but grandmasters know when to use them to their advantage. At the moment, White has a problem concerning what to do with his c1-Bishop. Playing 10.Bg5? h6! would put the question to the Bishop. White might not want to trade his Bishop, believing that in the long run it would be better to keep it. A weak move would be 10.Be3; it is vulnerable to ...Nf6-g4, forcing it to move again.

The text, on the other hand, is the perfect solution. White protects the c4-pawn while preparing a fianchetto, which would neutralize the strength of the g7-Bishop. In comparison, Black doesn't have the same possible solution to the problem of his c8-Bishop.

10...Qe7

In this variation of the King's Indian Defense, it is known that the e7-square is not an advantageous placement of the Queen. Since White has forgone the standard e2-e4, Yusupov feels compelled

224

to induce that move. Black is a little uncomfortable about keeping his Queen opposed to the Rook on the d-file. He is cramped and doesn't have a clear idea of how to further develop his game. He thus tries this developing move with the strategic threat of ...e5-e4, which gains space.

If Black had been forced to resolve the central tension by playing 10...exd4? 11.Nxd4, White would gain everything he wants. The e2-pawn is not so much a target as it is when the pawn is moved to the e4-square. The fianchettoed g2-Bishop eyes an open diagonal because the e2-pawn is not in the way. For these reasons, Black is trying to force White to play e2-e4.

Middlegame

11.Ba3?!

Ivanchuk is seduced by this attractive-looking move. He knows that Black is trying to provoke him to play e2-e4, and he refuses to go along. However, this move is asking for trouble. He should have accepted his central gains by playing 11.e4! exd4 12.Nxd4 Nc5 13.f3 a5 14.a3 to keep White at a consistent spatial advantage.

White is attracted to the text because the d6-pawn is weakened. Now the d1-Rook and the a3-Bishop combine to put a lot of pressure upon this pawn. White anticipates that Black will be forced to play ...e5-e4, in order to keep the d-file closed. His strategy holds that the advancing e-pawn will be a fatal weakness for Black. Because the follow-up ...d6-d5 is prevented, Black's advanced e-pawn will lack protection. White intends to lure the e-pawn to its death.

This nice strategy is also double-edged. Inviting the tiger into your home in order to make a quick meal will save you the time spent hunting for it. It does, however, have a few more risks. What if you fail to tame the tiger?

11...e4!

A good and forced move. Black cannot tolerate the threat of 12.dxe5, making the d6-pawn ripe for plucking. Also, at this time control it's nice to have the initiative.

Black gains space and advances his plan. He knows that he will have to throw all his forces to the kingside because the queenside offers him no possibilities.

12.Ng5

White continues to lure Black's e-pawn forward to its death. Other moves would be bad for White:

■ 12.Nd2? e3! would let Black happily trade his e-pawn, making his major pieces on the e-file perfectly placed.

■ The move 12.Ne1? would fail to pressure the e4-pawn. With 12...Nf8! followed by ...Bc8-f5 supporting the e4-pawn, Black would savor a good position. He could employ the well-known maneuvers ...h7-h5 and ...Nf8-h7-g5-h3, attacking White's King.

12...e3

Black has no choice. If he allows Ng5xe4, he will lose his e-pawn for nothing and face a hopeless challenge.

13.f4?

This natural-looking move is actually a careless blunder.

It's easy to see that Black is overextended in the center. His future therefore depends upon a do-or-die attack on White's King. The text makes White's kingside structure quite brittle. Black

can now concentrate on conceptions such as ...h7-h5-h4xg3 and ...Nf6-h5, pulling apart White's kingside.

The correct alternative would be 13.f3!. It would retain greater kingside flexibility. The move would protect the e4-square and lead to a long, forced sequence of moves: 13.f3! Nf8 14.Nge4 Bf5 15.Qc1 Bxe4 16.Nxe4 Nxe4 17.fxe4 c5! (17...Bh6 18.e5 would help White) 18.e5! Ne6 19.exd6 Qxd6 20.Bxb7 Nxd4, resulting in an unclear position — analysis by GM Artur Yusupov.

Yusupov believes that this variation, although White's best, leads to a position of equal chances in which either side might have an advantage. This analysis demonstrates that 11.Ba3 is a faulty move and that White's provocative strategy fails to pay off. The text will earn White a disadvantage, as we shall see.

13...Nf8

Suddenly Black's attack is looking very ominous. The e3-pawn isn't so overextended after all, since attacking it isn't easy. Ways of advancing the kingside pawns such as the bum's rush ...h7-h5-h4 or ...h7-h6 and ...g6-g5 are easy to find. It will be a simple matter to pry open lines on the kingside.

At this point, Ivanchuk slows down his pace of play in order to give his King a measure of comfort. Convinced that he can't capture the e3-pawn, he has reason to worry about his King. He decides that the best defense would be a quick offense on the queenside. He therefore plans to press matters there as quickly as possible.

14.b4

A sign that something has gone wrong is that White is no longer trying to capture the snarling tiger on e3. The attempts to win the pawn with 14.Nge4 or 14.Rd3 and Nc3-d1 would meet with 14...Bf5!, offering a clear advantage to Black. White therefore decides to "live with" the e3-pawn.

Of course this is good news for Black. The e3-pawn could serve as a base to support the launching of a kingside attack.

The attacked f2-square acts as a magnet, inviting Black's pieces to converge on it.

White fully appreciates these dangers to his King and therefore quickly puts together an attack of his own. The text envisages b4-b5 or d4-d5, trying to pry open the queenside, and aims to distract Black from his own attack.

14...Bf5

In pursuing the attack, Black does not overlook the opportunity to develop with tempo.

It is crucial for the student to learn the value of developing with tempo. You can mobilize your pieces and force your opponent to move a previously developed piece again. A marvelous opportunity is seized.

If, as Black, you would prefer to play 14...h6, pat yourself on the back. That move would also develop with tempo because White's g5-Knight would be forced to skip a retreat.

15.Qb3

Since White's Queen is forced to move, he places it where it can remain as active as possible. White envisions playing b4-b5xc6, opening up the b-file. An open b-file would allow White's Queen to become quite frisky.

15...h6

This is the prelude to an energetic clash.

There is little that Black can do to stop White from opening up the queenside. With 15...a6 16.d5!, White will be able to open lines. Thus, Black has to retaliate by cracking things on the kingside. Indeed, Black's pieces are tightly coiled and ready to spring. Black has to open the kingside, but the question remains: should he play the bum's rush ...h7-h5-h4, or should he try ...h7-h6 and ...g6-g5? Although both plans have their justification, expediency rules the day. The text comes with tempo. Any dillydallying would leave Black engulfed on the queenside.

16.Nf3

White chooses a solid move. Retreating with 16.Nh3? Qd7! would be a prescription for disaster.

16...Ng4!

Black launches his attack. As mentioned, the f2-square is like a siren calling upon Black's pieces to invade. The text also readies ...g6-g5, opening up lines on the kingside. As well, this possibility exposes why 13.f4 was a mistake: it weakened the g4-square while making the f4-pawn itself an ideal target.

Another attractive move would be 16...g5!? 17.fxg5 hxg5 18.Nxg5 Ng4 19.Nf3, in which Black sacrifices a pawn for some open lines and a few tempi. The move ...Nf6-g4 will play an integral part in most attacking plans, so the text is quite sensible.

17.b5!

The approaching storm on the kingside is quite discernible. White wastes no time in initiating his own attack.

17...g5!

Now the battle lines have been clearly drawn. Whoever gets in his attack first will win.

Note that Black has no choice but to go on the offensive. If he played 17...c5?, trying to keep the queenside closed, 18.dxc5 dxc5 19.Nd5 would be excellent for White. Also, 17...cxb5? 18.Nd5! Qd7 19.Qxb5! would be good for White. By trading Queens, Black's kingside attack would be robbed of an excellent attacker. White's center and queenside initiative would be more important than Black's attack.

18.bxc6

White completes his goal of opening up the queenside.

18...bxc6

Opening up the queenside was necessary; allowing c6xb7 or Nc3-d5 would be the kiss of death.

19.Ne5!?

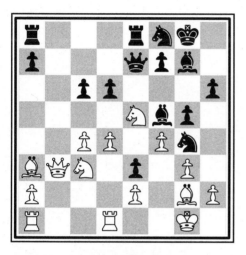

It takes nerves of steel to play a move like this one. Black's pieces are flooding the kingside, and White moves away a key defender! Ivanchuk is playing with fire.

But what else is he to do? After 19.fxg5 hxg5, it would be difficult to infuse enthusiasm into White's attack. Black could cover the weak spots in his position by playing ...Ra8-c8-c7. Black's attack is still picking up steam; he's ready to bring his f8-Knight into play. Of course the d6-pawn can't capture the intruder on e5 because it is pinned by the a3-Bishop.

When 19.Ne5 was played, an audience of several hundred people fled from the playing hall to listen to the grandmaster explanation in the commentary room. No one knew who was winning. Would White crash through on the queenside, or would Black apply a chokehold on White's King? The trainers were equally nervous. My own view is that Black should be happy. The f3-Knight is needed for the defense. Black will have to sacrifice some material to rip open the cover of White's King. But, in return, he'll have chances to nab the monarch.

19...gxf4

Black cracks open the kingside. The c6-pawn has to be jettisoned because after 19...Nxe5?? 20.fxe5!, Black's g5-pawn would no longer serve as a battering ram. The game is getting incredibly sharp, with each move partly determining the overall outcome.

20.Nxc6

White collects the harvest.

■ A serious strategic mistake would be 20.gxf4??, which would unnecessarily weaken White's kingside, especially the h4-square. After 20...Bxe5! 21.fxe5 Qh4, Black would have a decisive attack.

It would also be far too greedy to play 20.Bxc6??, forking Black's Rooks. The g2-Bishop is the King's lone defender. Trading it for one of Black's Rooks would be the last thing that White should consider. After 20...fxg3 21.Bxa8 Bxe5 22.dxe5 Qh4, White would lose not in a blaze of glory but rather in a muffled whimper.

20....Qg5

Black cozies up to the kingside. Black's prey — the White King — is in sight. He is prepared to deal blows such as ...Ng4xh2 and ...f4xg3, mauling the King. But it is White's turn to play!

21.Bxd6!

A most annoying move from Black's standpoint. On the a3-square, the Bishop was doing nothing to help White's King. Now the Bishop hopes it can serve a defensive role on the d6-h2 diagonal. If White can bring the d6-Bishop to the defense of his King, Black's attack could become stalled.

The faces of both players are showing grimaces. The audience is beginning to sense that Ivanchuk is in deep trouble.

21...Ng6!

Black pops out with impeccable timing. By defending the f4-pawn, White's d6-

Bishop is prevented from dashing over to the defense of the kingside.

Even so, Black had to reject two other promising alternatives:

- The move 21...Nxh2 looks attractive. After 22.Kxh2 Qxg3+ 23.Kh1 Ng6, the attack would be overwhelming. The problem is that White should not accept the Knight sacrifice. Instead, 21...Nxh2 22.Bxf4! Qh5 23.Nd5! would produce a sharp position favorable to White. His threats include Nd5xe3 and Nc6-e7+xf5, trading pieces. The h2-Knight isn't producing tangible results — analysis by GM Yusupov.

- The preceding variation shows why it is important to prevent Bd6xf4 but that crashing the party with ...Ng4xh2 would not be the way to do it. This led me to think that Yusupov had missed something a bit more direct. Black would have a brutal attack with 21...Qh5, involving the direct threat of ...Qh5xh2+. White cannot allow the capture 22.Bxf4 Qxh2+ 23.Kf1 Ng6, resulting in a winning attack. He must play 22.h4! (not 22.h3 Nf2 23.g4 Nxh3+ 24.Bxh3 Qxh3 25.gxf5 Qxf5, menacing ...Re8-e6 — this variation demonstrates the danger to White's King) 22...Ng6 23.Nd5, which transposes directly back into the game.

With the text, Black brings a piece into play while simultaneously preventing the opponent from bringing a piece to the defense. A very good idea!

22.Nd5

White is trying to rush his pieces back to the kingside. He is praying for the opportunity to play Bd6xf4 to bring some pieces to his defense.

22...Qh5?

This natural move is, unfortunately, a misguided one. Black wants to induce further kingside weaknesses, but it is precisely here that Black could force a win because he has ample firepower on the kingside to whomp White's King. He didn't want to allow the d6-Bishop to return to the kingside, but even if the Bishop did return, Black's pieces would overwhelm White's position.

■ The best move would be 22...fxg3!, allowing White's Bishop to return to the defense. After 23.Bxg3 h5! (23...Be4 immediately would also be very strong), White would face insurmountable problems. If White's g3-Bishop is forced to move, the King would become a sitting duck on the g-file. Moving off the g-file by playing 24.Kh1 h4 25.Be1 (else ...Ng4-f2+) 25...Nf4! would result in a rout. The only chance to meet Black's threat of ...h5-h4 would be 24.Rf1 h4 25.Bf4 (25.Bd6 Nf2 or 25.Be1 Be4 would open up the g-file)

25...Nxf4 26.Rxf4 (26.Nxf4 Nf2) 26...Bd7! — White could not handle the Black threats. A sample variation convinces: 27.Nce7+ Kh8 28.Rxf7 Nf2! would be followed by ...h4-h3. The denuded White King would get scorched. It seems subtlety wasn't needed.

■ Instead of playing 22...fxg3!, Yusupov got bogged down in analyzing 22...Nxh2, which fails him. After 22...Nxh2? 23.Nxf4! (23.Kxh2? Qxg3+ would win) 23...Nxf4 (not 23...Qxg3? 24.Nxg6 Qxd6 25.Nge7+ because it is good for White) 24.Bxf4 Qh5, White would face an unclear position since once again the Knight would be terribly misplaced on the h2-square — analysis by GM Yusupov.

Yusupov's fascination with the sacrifice ...Ng4xh2 made him miss the strength of opening up the position with ...f4xg3.

23.h4!

The game now transposes into the scenario of my note for Black's move 21.

Black had clearly underestimated the defensive value of the text. After 23.h3? Nf2!, Black would win, as we have seen. Yusupov was certain that his army, amassed on the kingside, would wipe out the defense.

23...Nxh4?

Black is quicksilver-ready for this sacrifice and whips it out at once.

Now the fun really begins. Black would have a clear advantage without the sacrifice by playing 23...fxg3 24.Bxg3 Nxh4 25.Nf4 Qg5 26.Nh3 Qf6. Black was determined to avoid ...f4xg3 and to stop White's pieces from getting back to the kingside.

24.gxh4!

Ivanchuk demonstrates nerves of steel.

Although this move seems to lead to unavoidable checkmate, in actuality it is the *only* defense! White couldn't play 24.Bxf4? Nxg2 25.Kxg2 Be4+ because mate would follow, whereas 24.Nxf4 Nf3+! 25.exf3 Qh2+ 26.Kf1 e2+! 27.Nxe2 Ne3+ would produce a winning attack.

24...Qxh4

A crucial moment. Ivanchuk thinks for several minutes, hesitates, reaches out his hand ... and grabs the wrong Knight!

Holding the wrong Knight, Ivanchuk looked grieved but continued as if nothing was wrong. The spectators were in a tizzy. What had just happened? How could the world's number two player grab the wrong piece? My guess is that Ivanchuk was calculating so far in advance that when he got "back to the position on the board," he momentarily forgot what he had in mind and touched the wrong Knight.

As a spectator, I had dismissed Black's line of play because I was convinced that he could have attained simple wins earlier. I thought that Black's attack could now be repulsed by 25.Nce7+!, followed by grabbing the f5-Bishop.

25.Nde7+??

White slips and makes a gross error. The d5-Knight was fulfilling a brilliant function. It could attack the f4-pawn and the e3-pawn, making it just one hop from the kingside. Conversely, the c6-Knight is a nearly useless piece.

I was certain that 25.Nce7+ would win for White. When I analyzed the position with grandmaster trio Larry Christiansen, John Nunn, and Willy Watson, we were astounded by the potential tactics

the position held. Instantly we became mired in the following analysis: 25.Nce7+ Kh8 26.Nxf5 Qh2+ 27.Kf1 Be5!! (with the earthquake threat of ...f4-f3) 28.Bxe5+ Rxe5 29.dxe5 Rg8, leading to an amazing position:

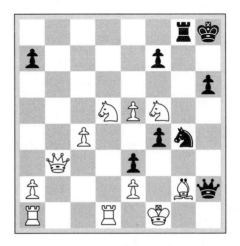

Despite being a Rook, a Knight, and a Bishop behind, Black would be ready to deliver the knockout blow 30...Qh1+ 31.Bxh1 Nh2+ 32.Ke1 Rg1 checkmate! In order to stave off defeat, it would be White's turn to sacrifice everything back. He could try 30.Ndxe3 fxe3 31.Nxe3 Qf4+ 32.Ke1! Nxe3; White would shed two pieces, and that would be just the beginning.

Larry Christiansen pointed out that after normal moves like 33.Bd5 Rg1+ 34.Kd2 Nxd1+ 35.Kc2 Ne3+ 36.Kb2 Qxe5+, White would also toss a pair of Rooks into the pot! After the laughter subsided, we tried to find something better for White.

Go back to the previous analysis diagram, and set up that position on your chess set at home.

Christiansen continued to impress us all: he uncorked 30.Ng7!!, blocking the g-file, thereby preventing Black's main threat of ...Qh2-h1+ followed by mate. This stunning move could easily confuse Black.

A sample ensuing line would be 30...Rxg7 31.Qb8+ Rg8 32.Qxg8+ Kxg8 33.Nf6+ Nxf6 34.exf6, letting White narrowly save his skin by capturing nearly the entire Black army. Black could compound his mistakes by continuing with 34...Qh4?? 35.Rd8+ Kh7 36.Be4, which would result in checkmate for White!

After these variations, the merry flock of grandmasters was really on a roll. After the preceding analysis, however, we were still no closer to determining which side was winning:

- With 30.Ng7!! Qg3 31.Kg1 Qh2+, Black could resolve the game by a repetition.

- It seemed that after winning several pieces, the best White could offer would be 30.Ng7, with a miracle draw.

I wasn't convinced. Despite the attractive nature of these variations, something was wrong. I was certain that Black had misplayed and spoiled his attack. White should be refuting Black's sacrifices, yet the best that had been found was a miracle draw for White. I returned to my apartment and devoted some serious study to the position. You might also want to break off from your reading and see if you can find where White went wrong.

I decided to go back to the position shown above in the analysis diagram just after move 24 for Black. From there, I again set off down 25.Nce7+ Kh8 26.Nxf5 Qh2+ 27.Kf1 Be5 but then stopped. Could White do better at this moment? Let's substitute 28.Qb7 (indirectly protecting the g2-Bishop) for 28.Bxe5+ and see how we do.

- Now 28...Rg8? meets the simple defense 29.Bxe5+ Nxe5 30.Ndxe3, and White is a couple of pieces ahead.

- Black shouldn't be so generous: 28...Bxd6 29.Nxd6 Qh4 30.Nxf7+ Kg8 31.Kg1 would compel Black's play 31...Qf2+ 32.Kh1 Qh4+ leading to perpetual check.

- Another try for White could be 28...Bxd6 29.Nf6!? Nxf6 30.Nxd6 Qh4 31.Nxf7+

(31.Qf3 Ng4) 31...Kg8 32.Nxh6+ Qxh6, which doesn't achieve White's desire because it gives Black nothing to fear.

How frustrating! I couldn't believe that White wasn't winning. Again I subjected the position to some rigorous analysis and gave it my final try: 25.Nce7+ (by this time, the only thing I was certain of was that this had to be the right move) 25...Kh8 26.Nxf5 Qh2+ 27.Kf1 Be5 28.dxe5!

At last, the right idea! When under attack, the first instinct of the defender is to trade off the attacking forces. The move Bd6xe5+ had seemed mandatory. However, the d6-Bishop can offer some defensive protection, as we shall see. Black has two tries in the position:

- With 28...f3 29.exf3 e2+ 30.Kxe2 Qxg2+ 31.Kd3, White's King can dance to safety.

- Black's last attacking chance is to bring a Rook to the g-file. Now 28...Rg8 runs into 29.Ndxe3! (stopping the critical threat of ...Qh2-h1 checkmate) 29...fxe3 (29...Nxe3+ 30.Nxe3 fxe3 31.Qb7 wins) 30.e6!

Now that the d6-Bishop covers the h2-square, 30...Qh1+ is no longer a game-

ending threat. My instincts were right after all!

Well, that detailed analysis was reassuring. Of course, it's possible to pick apart a great number of combinations from the comfort of an armchair in your study; under the pressure of a ticking clock in competition, however, it's a different story. Embarking on a combination is a risky business. After all, you offer a sacrifice to start things off, hoping the problems that you create for your opponent will lead him astray. Sometimes you get carried away and sacrifice more pieces than you intended, only to run out of ammunition.

To sum up this analysis, White made a horrible error on move 25. By using his c6-Knight to check, followed by a series of problematic but not impossible moves, he would have won. Meanwhile, back in the game, the fun still continues!

25...Kh8

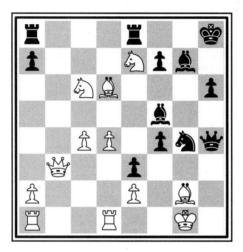

Black selects the best move.

Black poking his nose into the air by playing 25...Kh7? would only allow White a future check along the b1-h7 diagonal. Now Black can hope to use the g-file, as we've seen.

26.Nxf5

White grabs material while it is still possible. Black had threatened 26...Qf2+ 27.Kh1 Be4, with inevitable mate to follow.

This move again shows what an unfortunate mistake White made at move 25. The c6-Knight is ineffective currently standing two moves away from the kingside. Put the c6-Knight on the d5-square, and it would be playing a crucial role in the game.

26...Qh2+

Black does not benefit by going after the e2-pawn. With 26...Qf2+? 27.Kh1 Qxe2? 28.Bxf4, White emerges with excellent defensive opportunities. Black's only chance to win the game will be to mate White's King — going after a lesser gain will mean failure.

27.Kf1

White's King moves to the only safe square. The tiger on e3 is still snarling.

The last few moves have all been forced and therefore have been played quickly. Yusupov now went into a deep think of more than ten minutes. The longer he thought, the more I realized that Yusupov would have to come up with a great move. After all, White has a few extra pieces; in one or two moves (Qb3-b7xf7), he would have the initiative as well. Black's kingside attack had better come through, or else things will look bleak for him.

27...Re6!!

A fantastic Rook lift. The brilliant point of the text is getting in front of the g7-Bishop, not behind it.

After the expected move to the g-file, 27...Rg8, White could play 28.Nxe3! Bxd4 (28...Nxe3+ 29.Qxe3 fxe3 30.Bxh2 would win for White) 29.Rxd4 Nxe3+ 30.Ke1! Rxg2 31.Be5+ Kg8 32.Qd3!, and he would win. This variation seemed like the key game continuation; after seeing this line, I had given Black up for lost.

28.Qb7

Stunned by Black's last move, Ivanchuk has to take stock of the new position. Black's Rook is coming to the g-file with dreadful effect. Ivanchuk takes a deep breath and decides to counter with an attack of his own.

Amazingly enough, Black's projected Rook move to the g-file is unpreventable.

■ With 28.Nce7 Rg8!! (not 28...Rxd6? 29.Nxd6 Qg3? since 30.Nxf7+ would hurt) 29.Nxg8, Black's next move, Rg6, would accomplish the goal. Then his threat of ...Qh2-h1 would win.

■ Another try, 28.Ne5 Bxe5 29.Bxe5+ Nxe5 (29...Rxe5 30.dxe5 Rg8 31.Rd8 Rxd8 would also be good for Black) 30.dxe5 Rg8 31.Qb7 Reg6, again would make ...Qh2-h1+ a winning threat.

Since the text loses brilliantly, does White have a defense? I can't find one. I concentrated on 28.Nce7, trying to stop Black from bringing a Rook to the g-file by covering both the g8-square and the g6-square. Unimpressed, Black should continue 28...Rg8! anyway. In his notes, Yusupov considers only 28...Rxe7, which he analyzes at great length and comes to a draw. As we shall see, 28...Rg8 would be Black's best move. I now stopped myself from grabbing the g8-Rook. The moment Black achieves ...Re6-g6, the game will be curtains.

For example, 29.Nxg8? Rg6! 30.Nxe3 Nxe3+ 31.Qxe3 Qxg2+ 32.Ke1 fxe3 would win for Black. White needs a better move 29. What is Black's threat? As soon as the g7-Bishop moves, ...Qh2-h1+ will be mate.

Let's try to limit the g7-Bishop's movements. The first possibility is 29.Qd3, preventing 29...Bxd4 because 30.Qxd4+ would pick up the Bishop's movement with check. After 29.Qd3, Black needs a better move. With 29...Bf6, 30.Nxg8 works, since ...Re6-g6 will be blocked. What about 29...Bf8, with the old ...Qh2-h1+ threat? This seems to be the Bishop's only possible square. Now 30.Nxg8 Rg6 leads us to the following analysis diagram:

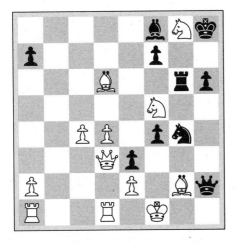

White's up by half an army or so, but he is lost! He can't prevent his King from getting mated.

Okay, 28.Nce7 Rg8 29.Qd3 isn't cutting the mustard. Let's try 29.Qb2, asking Black where he's going with his g7-Bishop. Now 29...Bf8 30.d5+ Kh7 31.Nxg8 Rg6 32.Nf6+ Nxf6 33.Nxe3 Bxd6 seems like a way to put up some resistance, but it's not enough. All of Black's pieces are taking part in the attack, and he will win. It seems that White's alternatives all lose — so let's get back to the game.

28...Rg6!!

With this fabulous move, Black pitches a Rook — with check! — in order to bring the other Rook to the g-file. Now ...Qh2-h1+ is a King Kong-size threat.

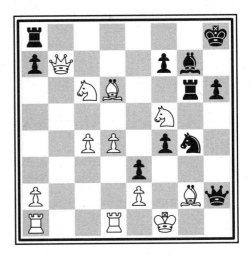

The audience was palpably gasping at this point. They realized that they were watching an extraordinary coup. White will soon have to return his horde of pieces to save his King.

Endgame

29.Qxa8+!

I like this move very much! If you're going to go down, go down in flames, taking as much with you as you can!

29...Kh7

Now the fun for White has definitely stopped. White has grabbed half the Black army, only to find himself facing the dire ...Qh2-h1+ threat. White has to return some of his loot.

30.Qg8+

White kisses his Queen goodbye.

The move 30.Nxe3 wouldn't help. After 30..Nxe3+ 31.Ke1 Rxg2 32.Kd2 Rxe2+ 33.Kc3 (not 33.Kd3? Nxd1, which threatens ...Re2-e3 mate) 33...Rb2! (stopping the King from escaping up the board) 34.Rac1 Nxd1+, White will be mated on the next move. Another failed defense would be 30.Bxf4? Qxf4+ 31.Bf3 (31.Kg1 Qh2+ 32.Kf1 Qh1+ wins) 31...Nh2+ 32.Ke1 Rg1 checkmate.

30...Kxg8

It's not every day that you get to pick up a Queen for free!

31.Nce7+

White makes his point. At least he gets to fork Black's King and Rook, thereby eliminating the g6-Rook and the ...Qh2-h1+ threat.

31...Kh7

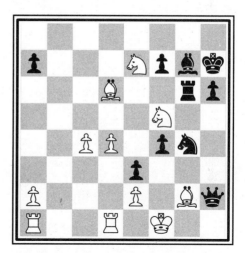

Although Black has regained some of his sacrificed material, he cannot relax. Ivanchuk isn't about to quit. Black will have to achieve victory by maintaining his compelling attack.

32.Nxg6

White eliminates the troubling Rook.

32...fxg6

With this nice recapture, Black's King is a wee bit safer, and the f5-Knight comes under attack.

33.Nxg7

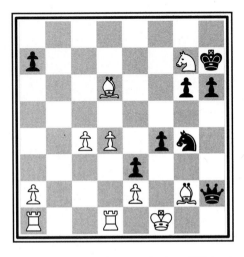

From a material point of view, White is doing great: two Bishops and two Rooks for the Queen! But, as my first chess teacher, Jeffrey Parsons, used to say, "Concentrate on what stays on the board, not on what comes off!"

33...Nf2!!

This stunning blow causes instant death. Black threatens ...Nf2-h3 and ...Qh2-g1 mate.

34.Bxf4

The only way to stave off the threat is to give back more material. White's Queen wasn't enough.

34...Qxf4

A fine capture. Black threatens ...Nf2xd1 discovered check, as well as ...Kh7xg7, picking off the errant Knight.

35.Ne6

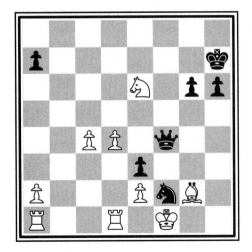

White slips out of being en prise with tempo.

35...Qh2!

The menacing ...Nf2-h3 worked once before — perhaps it will work again.

36.Rdb1

White pulls the d1-Rook out of capture. He pitches a desperate counterattack against Black's King and in fact has no other way to deal with Black's threat.

36...Nh3!

Black threatens the brutal ...Qh2-g1 checkmate.

It still wasn't too late to ruin the game by playing 36...h5?? 37.Ng5+ Kh6 38.Nf3, allowing White to defend the homestead.

37.Rb7+

This is the only move White can make (37.Bxh3 Qf2 checkmate). However, Ivanchuk can still inject a few spite checks into the position.

37...Kh8

This move leaves White with only one possibility.

38.Rb8+

In order to stave off checkmate, White must toss his Rook away as well.

38...Qxb8

At last the audience understands what is going on. Black's powerful Queen is mopping up the White army. Now the White King is a sitting duck, and White's pieces can't save their monarch.

39.Bxh3

White takes what he can.

39...Qg3

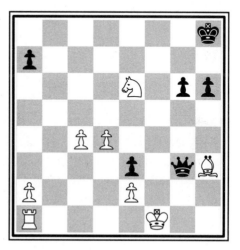

White resigns.

Facing inevitable mate on the f2-square, Ivanchuk gave up, and the Belgian audience burst into thunderous applause. They had witnessed a modern chess brilliancy and were delighted with the efforts of both players. The players quietly retreated to their rooms to follow the military coup that was taking place in Moscow.

The moral of the story is this: *the next time you invite your opponent to push his pawn to e3, be sure you can take it!*

Postscript

Unfortunately, dear readers, this book must now come to a close. Simply put, I've run out of space. When I started the *Winning Chess* series for Microsoft Press, I had planned that this, the final book, would discuss 18 modern brilliancies. I thoroughly researched and commented upon all of them, but without the space, the six others will have to wait.

You'll have to prevail upon Microsoft Press to get me to write another book through your letters and purchases of the series. I've had fun writing the four books and hope that you've enjoyed them too. The world of chess is endlessly fascinating, and I encourage you: if you want to use your brains, play chess. Perhaps some day I'll comment on one of your brilliancies.

Index

About the Author

International Grandmaster Yasser Seirawan is considered one of the top U.S. contenders for the world champion title. He was the first American contender for the world title since Bobby Fischer retired in 1975. Seirawan twice qualified for the world championships in 1985 and 1987, and he has earned numerous titles, including 1979 World Junior Champion, three-time U.S. Champion, 1989 Western Hemisphere Champion, and six-time member of the U.S. Olympic chess teams. In the 1994 Chess Olympics he earned an individual gold medal for best score. In tournament play, he has defeated both Garry Kasparov and Anatoly Karpov, the two top-ranking players in the world. He is the only American to have played in the World Cup cycle.

Born in Damascus, Syria, in 1960, Seirawan moved to Seattle with his family at the age of 7. His chess career was launched at the age of 12 when he began to play in (and win) local and regional tournaments. Seirawan lives in Seattle, Washington, where he is the editor of *Inside Chess* magazine. Readers are invited to write to *Inside Chess*, P.O. Box 19457, Seattle, WA 98109, for a complimentary copy.

The manuscript for this book was prepared and submitted to Microsoft Press in electronic form. Text files were processed and formatted using Microsoft Word. The chessboard graphics were created with the Arts & Letters Editor from Computer Support Corporation, Dallas, Texas. Pages were composed by Editorial Services of New England, Inc., with text in Century Old Style and display text in Optima Bold, using Ventura Publisher 4.2 for Windows.

Principal word processor: Carrie Cummings
Principal proofreaders: Phyllis Coyrie et al., Bettina Burch
Principal typographers: Michael Dempsey, Peter Whitmer
Interior text designer: Kim Eggleston
Principal illustrator: Jeanne Reinelt
Cover designer: Gregory E. Hickman
Cover graphics: Randy Lim
Cover color separator: Color Control

Printed on recycled paper stock.

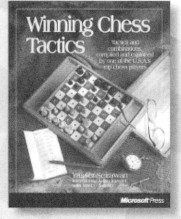
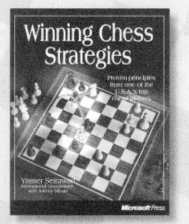